W9-DAM-806

hypnosis

Blackwell Brief Histories of Psychology

The *Blackwell Brief Histories of Psychology* offer concise, accessible, and lively accounts of key topics within psychology, such as emotion, intelligence, and stress, that have had a profound effect on psychological and cultural life. The books in this series provide a rich sense of historical context while remaining grounded in contemporary issues and research that will be of interest to both academic and general readers.

Stress: A Brief History
Cary L. Cooper and Philip Dewe

Evolutionary Thought in Psychology: A Brief History
Henry Plotkin

Emotions: A Brief History
Keith Oatley

Intelligence: A Brief History
Anna T. Cianciolo and Robert J. Sternberg

A Brief History of Modern Psychology
Ludy T. Benjamin, Jr.

Hypnosis: A Brief History
Judith Pintar and Steven Jay Lynn

hypnosis
A Brief History

JUDITH PINTAR AND STEVEN JAY LYNN

WILEY-BLACKWELL
A John Wiley & Sons, Ltd., Publication

This edition first published 2008

Blackwell Publishing was acquired by John Wiley & Sons in February 2007. Blackwell's publishing program has been merged with Wiley's global Scientific, Technical, and Medical business to form Wiley-Blackwell.

Registered Office
John Wiley & Sons Ltd, The Atrium, Southern Gate, Chichester, West Sussex, PO19 8SQ, United Kingdom

Editorial Offices
350 Main Street, Malden, MA 02148-5020, USA
9600 Garsington Road, Oxford, OX4 2DQ, UK
The Atrium, Southern Gate, Chichester, West Sussex, PO19 8SQ, UK

For details of our global editorial offices, for customer services, and for information about how to apply for permission to reuse the copyright material in this book please see our website at www.wiley.com/wiley-blackwell.

Library of Congress Cataloging-in-Publication Data is available for this title.

A catalogue record for this book is available from the British Library.

ISBN: 9781405134514 (hardback)
ISBN: 9781405134521 (paperback)

Set in 10/12 pt Book Antiqua by SPi Publisher Services, Pondicherry, India
Printed in Singapore by Fabulous Printers Pte Ltd

1 2008

In Memory of John F. Chaves (1941–2008)

Contents

Illustrations

Preface

Throughout its long history, hypnosis has been employed not only as a medical and psychotherapeutic tool, but also as a spiritual practice, an enduring form of entertainment, and a springboard for inquiry into the study of human consciousness. Theories about hypnosis, as well as popular ideas about its nature, have been repeatedly championed, rejected, and revived - and in the process have continuously contradicted, influenced, and fed back into one another. Acknowledging this complex relationship, we will be following common themes that appear throughout the history of hypnosis in both its psychotherapeutic and more popular forms.

The first thread that we will be tracing through this volume has to do with the hypnotic relation, particularly the assumptions made about the personal character of the hypnotic subject on one hand, and the skill of the hypnotist on the other. The second thread traces shifting beliefs about the nature of hypnosis; more specifically, which phenomena that occur as part of a hypnotic induction are essential, and which are epiphenomenal products of suggestion. Finally, we will examine references to the apparent power of hypnosis over memory and personal identity. At the end of the twentieth century, this aspect of hypnosis provided flint and tinder for a range of controversies, from professional and legal battles over the role of hypnosis in the creation of false memories, to the validity of the diagnosis of multiple personality disorder. The association of hypnosis with disruptions in identity, which seems so contemporary, had in fact already begun more than a century before.

In Chapter One we employ the popular late nineteenth century novel, *Trilby,* to illustrate key issues that will be explored historically through the rest of the book. The story of hypnosis proper begins in Chapter Two with the Viennese physician, Anton Mesmer, who discovered the healing properties of an invisible force he first termed "animal gravity." Mesmer's therapeutic techniques, which soon came to be known synonymously as "animal magnetism" or "mesmerism," are commonly understood to be the direct antecedents of hypnosis. We discuss mesmerism's influence on medicine during the late eighteenth and early nineteenth centuries, and the controversies that surrounded the practice. We then tell the story of one of Mesmer's followers, the Marquis de Puységur, and his transformations of Mesmer's techniques.

In Chapter Three we consider the nineteenth century manifestations of mesmerism in Britain and the beginnings of what is considered to be modern hypnosis. The work of the students of Mesmer and Puységur in the early nineteenth century helped to bring about a surge of interest in mesmerism in mid-century Europe, in both its medical and popular forms. Key elements of mesmerism were reframed in England in the nineteenth century by James Braid, the Scottish doctor who is responsible for placing the word "hypnosis" into the medical vocabulary. Chapter Four explores the social and cultural impacts of the popular manifestations of mesmerism in the United States during the same period, as well as its relationship to intellectual and spiritual movements taking place there throughout the nineteenth century.

The work of Jean-Martin Charcot in France is taken up in Chapter Five as we detail some of the most famous episodes in the history of hypnosis. The experiments taking place at the research hospital, the Salpêtrière, at the end of the nineteenth century involved hysteria, hypnosis, somnambulism, and dissociation. They inspired an intellectual battle that raged between the Salpêtrière and the researchers at the Nancy School, whose views on hypnosis can be said eventually to have "won." Hypnosis disappeared as a favored clinical technique after Charcot's death and Pierre Janet's lessening influence on the field, a trend that coincided with the rise of Sigmund Freud and psychoanalytic theory. Hypnosis continued to thrive outside the mainstream, however, in alternative and popular psychological practices.

We look at hypnosis in theory and research during the first half of the twentieth century in Chapter Six. The research contributions of Clark Hull and the therapeutic innovations of Milton Erickson are generally credited with inspiring the mainstream scientific and clinical revivals of hypnosis that were to follow, but they were not the only players in the field. In Chapter Seven we highlight the polarization of "state" and "non-state" positions among theoreticians during the later twentieth century, tracing the changing terms of the debate, as well as other key points of theoretical disagreement that drove hypnosis research during this period.

We arrive at the controversies of the late twentieth century in Chapter Eight. Hypnosis received tremendous attention as it found itself embroiled at the center of the false memory debates, and the question of whether psychotherapists using hypnosis were creating dissociative symptoms in their clients. We assess the significance of these controversies for their place in the larger story of the development of hypnosis in theory and practice. We conclude this brief history of hypnosis in Chapter Nine by noting the widespread and mainstream applications of hypnosis that came to be employed as treatment for a variety of psychological and medical conditions by the end of the twentieth century, and by speculating on the theoretical issues that will continue to be investigated into the twenty-first.

We were fortunate in the preparation of this book that there exists such a rich body of scholarship relating to the histories of mesmerism and hypnosis. Among the many works that have made substantive contributions to the field, we would like to acknowledge six in particular that we found to be indispensable resources, and that we recommend to readers who wish to undertake a deeper exploration of particular historical periods surveyed in this volume. Frank Pattie's *Mesmer and Animal Magnetism* offers a thorough and insightful history of the life and works of Mesmer. In *From Mesmer to Freud: Magnetic sleep and the roots of psychological healing*, Adam Crabtree traces the connections between mesmerism and later developments in psychology. Alison Winter offers a critical analysis of the social and cultural context within which mesmerism thrived in Victorian England in *Mesmerized: Powers of mind in Victorian Britain*, and Robert C. Fuller, in *Mesmerism and the American Cure of Souls*, analyzes the relationship of the nineteenth century magnetizers to spiritual seekers and religious movements in the United States. Touching on many aspects of mesmerism and hypnosis, Henri Ellenberger's highly acclaimed history, *The Discovery of the Unconscious*, presents a particularly detailed picture of hypnosis in late nineteenth century France and Germany. Finally, Alan Gauld's encyclopedic work, *A History of Hypnotism*, remains the most comprehensive and significant secondary source for the first two hundred years of history for both mesmerism and hypnosis.

We would like to acknowledge Irving Kirsch, John Kihlstrom, and John Chaves, as well as our anonymous readers, for their careful assessment of the book at its different stages, and their constructive suggestions for its improvement. J.P. would like to express her gratitude to David Hopping for his inexhaustible intellectual and personal support. S.J.L. would like to acknowledge Sean Barnes for his help with the final preparation of the manuscript, and to express his appreciation of Fern Pritikin Lynn's love, support, and understanding during the writing of the book.

CHAPTER ONE

Trilby and Svengali

I will tell you a secret. There were two Trilbys. There was the Trilby you knew, who could not sing one single note in tune. She was an angel of paradise. She is now! But she had no more idea of singing than I have of winning a steeplechase at the Croix de Berny. She could no more sing than a fiddle can play itself! She could never tell one tune from another–one note from the next … But all at once–pr-r-r-out! presto! Augenblick! … with one wave of his hand over her–with one look of his eye–with a word–Svengali could turn her into the other Trilby, his Trilby – and make her do whatever he liked … you might have run a red-hot needle into her and she would not have felt it. He had but to say 'Dors!' and she suddenly became an unconscious Trilby of marble, who could produce wonderful sounds–just the sounds he wanted, and nothing else–and think his thoughts and wish his wishes–and love him at his bidding with a strange, unreal factitious love … just his own love for himself turned inside out–a l'envers–and reflected back on him, as from a mirror … un echo, un simulacre, quoi! pas autre chose! … Ah monsieur, that Trilby of Svengali's! I have heard her sing to kings and queens in royal palaces! as no woman ever sung before or since.[1]

First serialized in *Harper's Magazine* in 1894, George du Maurier's novel of hypnosis, *Trilby*, was a phenomenal bestseller. Its publication set off a marketing frenzy during which the heroine's name was bestowed upon a hat, several shoes designs, candy, toothpaste, soap, a brand of sausage, and even a town in Florida. Trilby's face appeared on dolls, fans, writing paper, puzzles, and there were ice cream bars made in the shape of her feet. Trilby clubs were formed and parties held where guests would perform dramatic readings from the novel, or dress up in *tableaux vivants*, to match the story's illustrations.[2]

Given the character's enormous appeal, it is surprising that while Trilby hats by the hundreds are listed for sale on eBay, the name of Trilby as a mesmerized young woman has all but disappeared from popular awareness. The bestseller's villain, on the other hand, has held on to his infamous cultural identity for more than a century. Who doesn't recognize Svengali, the shadowy hypnotist who displays unseemly power over women?[3] It may be that Trilby has been less well remembered because she was crafted by du Maurier to end up as nothing but a simulacrum, a reflection of Svengali himself. Everything that makes Trilby an unusual and memorable character is systematically taken away from her, so that by the end of the story she is less of a protagonist than she is a clockwork doll.

The relationship between Svengali and Trilby illustrates assumptions about the nature of hypnosis and the relationship between the hypnotist and the hypnotized subject that were common at the time the novel was written, but many of them persist into the present day. Svengali's psychological and physical control of Trilby manifests in the novel in an array of phenomena that are miraculous, psychopathological, sexual, and occult. The idea that a hypnotist has the power to "create" multiple personalities in an unwitting subject seems to be an artifact of the late twentieth century, but it was dramatically represented in *Trilby* more than a century ago.

Centuries-old assumptions about the hypnotic relation and the nature of hypnosis survive today to varying degrees in popular belief and practice, despite being widely discredited by researchers who reject them as myths. They are important in this history of hypnosis not because they are damaging misconceptions that need to be once and for all unmasked as false–but because they have become *mythical*, meaning that they are cultural images that have the power to defy empirical science. As novelists, lawyers, mystics, and some practitioners champion beliefs about hypnotism that others endlessly strive to lay to rest, a cycle continues that has been going on for more than two hundred years.[4]

The Hypnotic Relation

The story of Trilby assumes that a wide gulf of character exists between hypnotists and their subjects. Those who are easily hypnotized, the novel tells us, are gullible and weak. Whatever marvels they produce during hypnosis are due entirely to the skill of

Figure 1 *Svengali mesmerizing Trilby. Illustration from George du Maurier's 1894 novel,* Trilby.

a talented hypnotist. Early in the novel Svengali hypnotizes Trilby to relieve her headaches. She is grateful but is also disturbed by the strange power the man has over her and tries to avoid him as much as she can. When a series of personal misfortunes strike her, Svengali comes to her aid, taking advantage of her vulnerability. At that point the story of Trilby becomes a drama of psychological victimization.

Du Maurier makes his villain a Jewish musician and the portrait he draws of the unsavory and morally dubious hypnotist is a study in anti-Semitic stereotypes.[5] Du Maurier describes Svengali as "a tall bony individual of any age between thirty and forty-five, of Jewish aspect, well-featured but sinister." The description continues:

> He was very shabby and dirty and wore a red beret and a large velveteen cloak, with a big metal clasp at the collar. His thick, heavy, languid, lusterless black hair fell down behind his ears on

> to his shoulders, in that musician-like way that is so offensive to the normal Englishman. He had bold, brilliant black eyes, with long heavy lids, a thin, sallow face, and a beard of burnt-up black, which grew almost from his under eyelids ... He went by the name of Svengali, and spoke fluent French with a German accent and humorous German twists and idioms, and his voice was very thin and mean and harsh, and often broke into a disagreeable falsetto.[6]

Svengali is presented as vain, egocentric, bullying, and cruel. His "love" for Trilby is, in no small measure, self-love. He possesses her parasitically, using her against her will and without her knowledge. He plays her, quite literally as his instrument, until the end of her life, which follows soon after his. The musical brilliance that Trilby demonstrates while under hypnosis is a result of Svengali's will and talent moving through her: " 'When you heard her sing the "Nussbaum," the "Impromptu," you heard Svengali singing with her voice, just as you heard Joachim play a chaconne of Bach with his fiddle! Herr Joachim's fiddle ... what does it know of Sebastian Bach?' "[7]

Although Trilby is blessed with the physiological hardware to be a great singer, she is by herself talentless. In a humorous passage early in the novel she delivers a tortured rendition of the popular tune "Ben Bolt," to the stunned silence of those around her: "It was as though she could never once have deviated into tune, never once have hit upon a true note, even by a fluke–in fact, as though she were absolutely tone-deaf, and without ear, although she stuck to the time correctly enough."[8] Trilby loses her amazing singing abilities at Svengali's demise, with one exception–the painted image of Svengali's eyes can still induce Trilby into a trance state, and allow her to sing. We are to believe that Svengali's musical talent is so powerful that it even survives his death.

Although Svengali is presented as a genius, he is an evil genius, motivated by a desire for power in general, and sexual power in particular. Du Maurier implies the existence of an intimate relationship between Svengali and Trilby while she is in trance that is completely absent in her waking life. Awake, Trilby speaks of Svengali's love for her with pity, and even disgust:

> "He always made out he was so fond of me that he couldn't even look at another woman. Poor Svengali!" (Here her eyes filled with tears again.) "He was always very kind! But I never could be fond

> of him in the way he wished–never! It made me sick even to think of! Once I used to hate him–in Paris–in the studio; don't you remember?"[9]

In this passage, the sinister undertones of the hypnotic relation come fully to the surface. Hypnosis is revealed in the novel to be a dangerous process that could have devastating consequences for a hypnotic subject, victimized by an unscrupulous practitioner.

Du Maurier's Trilby, in contrast to the nefarious Svengali, is an uneducated but sunny-dispositioned young woman of partial Irish descent, working in the Latin Quarter of Paris as an artist's model. Though Trilby is not chaste, she is innocent and trusting, sinning from weakness rather than wickedness. He had this to say about her character:

> My poor heroine … had all the virtues but one; but the virtue she lacked (the very one of all that plays the title-role, and gives its generic name to all the rest of that goodly company) was of such a kind that I have found it impossible so to tell her history as to make it quite fit and proper reading for the ubiquitous young person so dear to us all.… Whether it be an aggravation of her misdeeds or an extenuating circumstance, no pressure of want, no temptations of greed or vanity, had ever been factors in urging Trilby on her downward career after her first false step in that direction–the result of ignorance, bad advice (from her mother, of all people in the world), and base betrayal.[10]

Trilby falls under Svengali's power in the latter part of the novel because she accepts friendship from him at a vulnerable moment. Earlier in the novel when Svengali entrances Trilby to relieve her headache, a witness to the affair warns her about what has taken place:

> "He mesmerized you; that's what it is–mesmerism! I've often heard of it, but never seen it done before. They get you into their power, and just make you do any blessed thing they please–lie, murder, steal–anything! and kill yourself into the bargain when they've done with you! It's just too terrible to think of!" … Cold shivers went down Trilby's back as she listened. She had a singularly impressionable nature, as was shown by her quick and ready susceptibility to Svengali's hypnotic influence.[11]

By presenting the hypnotic subject as innocent and impressionable, Du Maurier is casting doubt on the motives of Svengali–and by association those of any hypnotist. If the subject is gullible, it follows that the hypnotist could manipulate her; if the subject is weak, the hypnotist is free to exploit her. Du Maurier represents the hypnotic relation in its essential form as a perilous encounter between a powerful actor and a passive subject.

The differences between Trilby and Svengali only thinly disguise deeper cultural messages about race, gender, social class, and mobility. These are obscured in the novel because the relationship between the characters seems to arise as a result of the personal character traits of Svengali and Trilby themselves. This pattern will appear recurrently in the history of hypnotic theory and practice: personal traits (particularly the subject's psychopathology and the hypnotist's skill and techniques) are assumed to be essential to the success or failure of a hypnotic venture, rather than the social or cultural context surrounding the event, which give it particular meanings and shape the expectations of both hypnotist and subject.

The Nature of Hypnosis

The images of hypnosis employed by Du Maurier project not only a particular view of the hypnotic relation, but also of the dynamics of hypnosis itself. If the hypnotist can impose his will upon a hypnotized subject, this implies that some aspect of the experience for the subject is involuntary–not under conscious control. In fact, the novel *Trilby* perpetuated this very particular and still widespread view of the nature of hypnosis. Most significantly, it presented hypnosis as physiologically related to sleep, and defined it as a state of consciousness characterized by enhanced and involuntary suggestibility. Du Maurier describes Trilby's experience of waking from hypnotic trance as similar to what she feels when she wakes from sleep:

> 'As soon as I felt uneasy about things, or had any pain, he would say, "Dors, ma mignonne!" and I would sleep at once–for hours, I think–and wake up oh, so tired! and find him kneeling by me, always so anxious and kind.'[12]

The idea that being hypnotized is related to being asleep is based on the related assumption that most hypnotic subjects are unaware of their surroundings while they are "under" hypnosis. A hypnotized individual, in this view, has dissociated from ordinary consciousness and is experiencing some sort of altered state.

Most people can be said to experience a more-or-less completely discrete separation between waking and sleeping selves, and experience spontaneous amnesia for their dreams, usually forgetting them shortly after waking. Du Maurier suggests in his novel that something like this is also happening to a hypnotized subject. Trilby's waking state and her hypnotized state are so discrete from one another that there is no overlap in her memory at all:

> While hypnotized she sang before the crown heads of Europe, passed by her dearest friends on the street; while "awake" she could not sing a note, and had no memory of the rehearsal process or her performances. After Svengali's death, her prior life as a singer was completely gone, simply erased: It was impossible to realize that her brain was affected in the slightest degree, except when some reference was made to her singing, and this seemed to annoy and irritate her, as though she was being made fun of. The whole of her marvelous musical career, and everything connected with it, had been clean wiped out of her recollection.[13]

Du Maurier clearly connects hypnosis with issues of memory and identity. At the moment of Svengali's death Trilby is on stage in front of a London audience. When pressed to sing, Trilby comes out with the same tuneless rendition of "Ben Bolt" that she delivered at the beginning of the novel–and this after what has amounted to years and years of training by a master. In other words, the suggestions that made Trilby a singer while under hypnosis had no effect on her un-hypnotized self. Hypnosis, it appears, has power to divide the self:

> 'When Svengali's Trilby was being taught to sing … when Svengali's Trilby was singing–or seemed to you as if she were singing–our Trilby had ceased to exist … our Trilby was fast asleep … in fact, our Trilby was dead.'[14]

The presumption that hypnosis can create two Trilbys, separate and unaware of one another, implies that hypnotists have power over the processes of remembering and forgetting and that they can create profound dissociations of identity in their hypnotic subjects.

Assessing the Myths of Hypnosis

The story of Trilby presents very strong images of the hypnotic relation, the nature of hypnosis, and, particularly, the power of hypnosis over memory. How can we evaluate these ideas: that there are some gullible people who are more hypnotizable than others, that hypnosis is a state of consciousness related to sleep, or that hypnotists have the power to alter a subject's identity?

To begin, a preview of the main theoretical positions on "hypnotizability" as they are currently understood by hypnosis researchers will help in assessing Du Maurier's version of the hypnotic relation. The most recent research findings will be surveyed in Chapter Seven; here we note only that whereas some believe *anyone* can be hypnotized given the proper procedures, others maintain that only a small number of people will spontaneously score high on clinical measures of suggestibility and other measures of hypnotic ability. A third position is that although most people can be taught to respond to hypnotic suggestion, certain phenomena associated with extremely high hypnotizability (posthypnotic amnesia, for instance) cannot be taught, and do seem to be an aptitude. Regardless of which of these three views is held, there is widespread consensus among theoreticians as well as researchers that the most "hypnotizable" people are neither more gullible, nor weaker by objective standards, than those who, within the context of a hypnotic induction, respond less dramatically to suggestion.[15]

There is much less consensus on the question of whether or not hypnosis is (or necessarily produces) a special or unique state of consciousness. Prior to the 1960s it was generally accepted by clinicians and researchers that hypnosis is itself a special state of consciousness, essentially different from non-hypnotic consciousness. But from that point on, "non-state theorists" began to challenge state theorists, maintaining that all of the phenomena associated with hypnosis could be explained by normal behavioral processes, attitudes, beliefs, and expectations.

Although during the 1960s and 1970s hypnosis research polarized into "state" and "non-state" camps, by the 1980s the two theories were no longer diametrically opposed, and now can be placed along a continuum of beliefs and theoretical positions.

At one extreme are theorists who champion the hypnotic trance as an example of a discrete altered state of consciousness that is qualitatively and objectively (biologically) different from waking states. At the other extreme are the theorists who use the term *state* in a purely descriptive, metaphorical way or who reject it altogether. At the center of the continuum is the theoretical position that hypnosis is not a special altered state, but one that is common in everyday life, the same experience we have when we are on a long car drive, or when we are particularly absorbed in a task.[16] Generally speaking, the state versus non-state issue boils down to the need to explain (or explain away) the apparent phenomenon, illustrated entertainingly by Du Maurier, that hypnotized subjects are profoundly *different* while they are undergoing a hypnotic induction, from when they are not.

Finally, despite the widespread belief that hypnotic subjects will remember nothing about what occurred while they were in trance, just as Trilby forgot about her concerts during her waking, non-hypnotized state, empirical evidence suggests that spontaneous posthypnotic amnesia is actually an unusual phenomenon. The persistence of the belief in hypnotic amnesia is not based on any particularly influential evidence, but seems to arise from a traditional connection of hypnosis with dramatic alterations of memory and identity. Among the assumptions that arise from this connection are also the beliefs that hypnosis increases the accuracy of memory, and that it can foster literal reexperiencing of past events. Although the belief that hypnosis has these effects is widespread, as no few reruns of *The X-files* reflect, it is not borne out by research which suggests that childhood episodes remembered during hypnotic sessions may be less accurate than memories that spring to mind in states of ordinary waking consciousness.[17]

From Trilby to Svengali

One reason for *Trilby*'s phenomenal success may be that Du Maurier was able to crystallize a central mythology that had developed over a century, despite medical and scientific arguments that directly contradicted its central assertions. Du Maurier conflated mesmerism with hypnosis, so that the cultural assumptions that were tied up with the earlier technique and practice were transferred to the hypnotic relation as well, regardless of the fact that practitioners of hypnosis who were working at the time the novel was written took particular pains to distinguish their practices from those associated with mesmerism.

Everyone was familiar with the characters and the plot that he presented: a personally powerful and ethically dubious (male) practitioner of the hypnotic arts takes emotional and sexual advantage of a gullible and passive (female) subject. The nature of the danger has to do with the profound personal transformation a hypnotist is supposed to be able to force upon an unwitting subject. The last decade of the twentieth century was notable for the spate of malpractice lawsuits alleging that irresponsible hypnotherapeutic clinicians were responsible for implanting false memories or constructing multiple personalities in their clients. The presentation of hypnosis as dangerous is based on the belief, matter-of-fact for Du Maurier, that because what occurs to hypnotic subjects while they are hypnotized is involuntary, their experience is controlled by the hypnotist. Regardless of the exact biological and psychological processes underlying the subjective *experience* of involuntariness for hypnotic subjects, research does not support the idea that skillful hypnotists can make subjects perform against their will.[18]

Researchers may argue that psychotherapists are not nefarious Svengalis with the power to make their gullible Trilby-like clients remember things that never happened. They may repeatedly demonstrate through empirical research that hypnosis does not deprive individuals of their agency or volition. Still, popular culture clings to the idea of the Trilby–Svengali dyad, in which the hypnotist has all the power, and the subject is always, potentially, a victim. *Fin de siècle* legal battles between hypnotists and their subjects over the "implantation" of false memories and the "creation" of multiple personalities indicate that the boundary between fact and fiction may be transgressed more often than is generally acknowledged. The history of scientific discovery is often narrated as an orderly progression of ideas, as though knowledge evolves in a linear way, truth replacing error through systematic experimentation, leading to broad consensus. The story of hypnosis suggests that the process is infinitely messier, and more interesting, than that.

Notes

1 George Du Maurier, *Trilby* (New York: J. M. Dent, 1992): 352.
2 Emily Jenkins, "Trilby: Fads, Photographers, and 'Over-Perfect Feet'," *Book History* 1 (1998): 221–267; See also Edward L. Purcell, "Trilby and Trilby-mania: The Beginning of the Bestseller System," *Journal of Popular Culture, 11* (1977): 62–76.
3 For a consideration of possible real-life inspirations for Du Maurier's Svengali, see the introduction to George du Maurier, *Svengali: George du Maurier's Trilby*, ed. Peter Alexander (London: W. H. Allen, 1982): 5–34.
4 The "myths" of hypnosis as they are presented here are based on an analysis found in Irving Kirsch and Steven Jay Lynn, "The Altered State of Hypnosis: Changes in the Theoretical Landscape," *American Psychologist* 50 (1995): 846–858. For another approach to the myths of hypnosis, see John F. Kihlstrom, "The Two Svengalis: Making the Myth of Hypnosis," *Australian Journal of Clinical & Experimental Hypnosis* 15, no. 2 (1987): 69–81.
5 For a critical analysis of race and anti-Semitism in *Trilby* in its nineteenth century cultural context, see Daniel Pick, *Svengali's Web: The Alien Enchanter in Modern Culture* (New Haven, CT: Yale University Press, 2000).
6 Du Maurier, *Trilby*, 13.
7 Ibid., 352.
8 Ibid., 21.
9 Ibid., 300.
10 Ibid., 41.
11 Ibid., 61.
12 Ibid., 300.
13 Ibid., 307.
14 Ibid., 353.
15 Steven J. Lynn, Victor Neufeld, and Cornelia Maré, "Direct versus Indirect Suggestions: A Conceptual and Methodological Review," *International Journal of Clinical and Experimental Hypnosis* 41, no. 2 (1993): 124–152.
16 Irving Kirsch and Steven Jay Lynn, "Hypnotic Involuntariness and the Automaticity of Everyday Life," *American Journal of Clinical Hypnosis* 40 (1997): 329–348.
17 See Helen M. Pettinati, ed., *Hypnosis and Memory* (New York: Guilford, 1988).
18 Steven Jay Lynn, Judith Rhue, and John R. Weekes, "Hypnotic Involuntariness: A Social Cognitive Analysis," *Psychological Review* 97, no. 22 (1990): 169–184.

CHAPTER TWO

Animal Magnetism and Magnetic Sleep

It is possible to find historical antecedents of practices resembling hypnosis going back far into prehistory. The ritual induction of trance states for spiritual and physical healing remains a central feature in Western and non-Western religious practices as well.[1] The hypnotic induction as we understand it today, however, has a mythical as well as a historical lineage that can be traced to a specific image: a charismatic and powerful figure who seems to have amazing influence over his subjects' health, minds, and memories. The man who first inspired the myth was Franz Anton Mesmer (1734–1815).

The son of a forester employed by the Prince Bishop of Constance, Mesmer was the third child of nine in a provincial Catholic family.[2] As a young man he had studied theology, and then passed through law on his way to medicine. His doctoral dissertation, completed at the University of Vienna in 1766, analyzed the gravitational influence of planets on the human body and upon illness. Mesmer's theoretical proposition was that "tidal" influences upon the human body act through a universal force that he termed "animal gravity."[3]

This thesis was not arcane astrology so much as an extrapolation of Newtonian physics. In fact, Mesmer lifted much of it intact from a work by Richard Mead, a student of Isaac Newton.[4] Mesmer's mostly plagiarized work stirred up no particular controversy or interest within the scientific or medical community, but it did qualify him at the age of 33 to be a doctor of medicine. Mesmer set up a conventional medical practice in Vienna the following year, employing the common healing techniques of the time. He bled his patients, blistered them, and prescribed them liberal dosages of opiates. The only surprise he presented to Viennese society during his early career was to arrange a socially advantageous marriage with a widow 10 years his senior.

The Archbishop of Vienna presided over the union of Maria Anna von Posch and Doctor Franz Mesmer in St Stephen's Cathedral in 1768, a spectacular and probably welcome social event in a community still mourning recent bouts of the plague.[5] The prosperous and popular couple established their household in a palatial estate near the Danube River, complete with statues, gardens, and a theater where Wolfgang Mozart (1756–1791) premiered his first opera, *Bastien und Bastinne*.[6] Mesmer was a patron of Mozart during these years, and was himself a competent musician on the violoncello and clavichord. He was best known for his mastery of the "glass harmonica," an instrument invented by Benjamin Franklin (1706–1790) that mechanized the sound a finger makes going around the rim of a crystal glass.[7] Both the harmonica and Franklin are to have significant reappearances later in his story.

Origins of Animal Magnetism

For the first few years of his marriage Mesmer's medical practice resembled that of any other Viennese physician of the time, but he found himself increasingly dissatisfied with the painful physical interventions that seemed to terrify and terrorize patients more than to cure them. One of his medical school teachers was employing the new technology of electroshock therapy to treat a wide variety of ills, but this was not a direction Mesmer felt moved to follow. He began to experiment with substantially gentler techniques of healing that involved intimacy, rapport, and touch. He would retain his distaste for pharmacological remedies until the end of his working career: "Already well advanced in age, I wish to devote what remains of my existence 'to the sole practice' of a method which I recognize as being eminently beneficial, of being able to preserve my fellow-man so that he no longer need be exposed to the incalculable hazards of drugs and their application."[8]

Mesmer's ideas began to crystallize in 1774 when he began his prolonged treatment of Franzl Oesterline, a 27-year-old woman who was suffering from a complicated set of symptoms.

As Mesmer describes the case, she "had been subject to a convulsive malady, the most troublesome symptoms of which was that the blood rushed to her head and there set up the most cruel toothaches and earaches, followed by delirium, rage, vomiting and swooning."[9] Oesterline's symptoms so incapacitated her that she lived in Mesmer's house in order to receive round-the-clock care. Mesmer was able to observe in the ebb and flow of Oesterline's symptoms a relationship to astronomical conditions, just as he had expected that he would.

After experiencing frustrating failure with ordinary medical techniques, Mesmer attempted to interfere with these apparent gravitational effects. He hoped to create an "artificial tide" through the use of magnets he had obtained from Maximilian Hell (1720–1792), an astronomer and Jesuit priest who had been experimenting with their medical use. After having Oesterline swallow a solution containing lead, Mesmer attached magnets to her body and was able in this way to produce in her, on his command, the symptoms he was trying to cure. After a number of encouraging treatments, on July 28, 1774, he finally induced in her the vivid sensation that a fluid was rushing downward out of her body, carrying her illness away. Her improvement after this was rapid and complete. She would eventually marry Mesmer's stepson. As Mozart reported in a letter to his father in 1780, "Franzl is now Frau von Posch and is here. I hardly recognized her, she has grown so plump and fat. She has three children."[10]

Mesmer was 40 years old when the dramatic healing of Franzl Oesterline allowed him to make the intellectual breakthrough that shaped the rest of his life. He had understood that the medium of healing was not the magnet, but the flow of an invisible fluid that could pass in "magnetic streams" from a healer who possessed it in abundance to a patient whose own streams were damaged in some way. His discovery of the movements of the invisible fluid that he named "animal magnetism," and its use in the healing of both physiological and "nervous" conditions, led to great celebrity, both at home in Vienna and abroad.

Mesmer was inducted with pomp into the Bavarian Academy of Science and in 1775 took a tour that included the Slovakian castle of a Hungarian baron, Horeczky de Horka. While performing numerous dramatic demonstrations of his power—he induced convulsions, sleepiness, muteness, with a touch or even a gesture—he successfully predicted that the baron himself would experience a "crisis," the moment in the healing process when symptoms would return in exaggerated and even violent fashion. Although the baron was too disturbed by the prospect of a crisis to allow Mesmer to continue, the visit was considered to be a success because of the positive publicity it engendered.[11]

Magnetism and Exorcism

Mesmer was not without competition in the art of healing beyond the pale. While he was in Bavaria in 1755, the same year that his first pamphlet outlining his theory and techniques of animal magnetism was released,[12] he was asked to evaluate the work of a country priest and exorcist, Father Johann Joseph Gassner (1727–1779). As a young man, Gassner had suffered from headaches and dizziness, symptoms that worsened when he was saying Mass. Suspecting something supernatural at work behind his physical symptoms, he had himself exorcized, which cured him of his troubles. Moved to become an exorcist himself, Gassner first distinguished illnesses that had physical causes from those illnesses whose physical symptoms had evil origin. As one witness recorded it, he would declare to his patient in Latin, "If there be anything preternatural about this disease, I order in the name of Jesus that it manifest itself immediately."[13] If the patient's symptoms did not display themselves in response to this command, Gassner sent them to an ordinary doctor. If the exorcism invoked symptoms, particularly convulsions, Gassner believed a demon was at work, and would strive to control it through words and touch.

Gassner left a trail of successful healings wherever he traveled, and his success set off a popular fad. His detractors pointed out that exorcism seemed to be particularly popular among peasants and children, who experienced epidemics of possession in advance of his arrival, and among innkeepers and carriage drivers, who profited from his popularity in casting out demons far and wide across the countryside.[14] The problem facing Gassner, much greater than the cynicism of his critics, was the growing power of the Enlightenment, which rejected supernatural interpretations of phenomena that reason and science could otherwise explain.[15] Even the Catholic Church was increasingly careful during this period, putting an end to witch hunts and practices deemed to be based on superstition rather than faith. Commissions created to inquire into his activities produced mixed reports: Gassner's technique worked, but the apparent reason why it worked was increasingly problematic for both government and church.

Now Mesmer, who had begun to achieve great success healing with the use of touch, literally following Gassner's footsteps on the European "healing circuit," stepped into the fray. At the invitation of a commission that had been appointed by Prince-Elector Max Joseph of Bavaria to investigate Gassner's work, Mesmer traveled to Munich and demonstrated his own techniques to the Academy of Science on a parade of patients, even healing successfully of convulsions the Secretary of the Academy. Mesmer's cures resembled Gassner's in many ways–they both produced symptoms on command, a "crisis," which they were able to resolve with a touch, leaving patients with the conviction of health and wellbeing. The crucial difference was that Mesmer's cure, which involved nothing supernatural, was consistent with Enlightenment values.[16]

Mesmer's symbolic triumph over Gassner was brutal and complete, though Mesmer himself was graceful in victory, declaring Gassner to be a powerful healer, possessing animal magnetism in great measure, greater even than Mesmer himself.[17] In one rhetorical swoop, Mesmer co-opted Gassner's fame and authority, encompassing his religious work within his own scientific paradigm. The end of the matter was that Gassner was dismissed from the Imperial Court and sent to a provincial Catholic community where he was not allowed to practice exorcism unless the request came officially from the church.[18]

Mesmer, riding high on his victory over Gassner, was not in the mood to share credit for his discovery with Maximilian Hell either.[19] The astronomer who had provided Mesmer with his magnets was now making moves to claim the credit for the healing of Franzl Oesterline. The conflict between the two men was short-lived, since Mesmer soon dispensed with the magnets altogether, arguing that they were simply conductors, not generators of the healing force that he now termed "animal magnetism." Mesmer claimed that any objects, inanimate or animate, could be magnetized to conduct the universal fluid. Reaching even further, Mesmer theorized that magnetism was not the only force that traveled through the fluid, but that electricity, light, and heat also traveled between physical objects and people by means of this connecting fluid.

Returning to Vienna after his tour, Mesmer expected that his popular fame would translate into acceptance by the mainstream scientific and medical community, and that he would receive the professional respect due him as the discoverer of animal magnetism. To his surprise and frustration, he was faced with the skepticism of his medical colleagues; he was even rejected by his old teachers and mentors. The disconnection between his spectacular success as a healer and his equally stunning failure to achieve recognition by his peers was to culminate in a dramatic episode worthy of a Du Maurier novel. It would lead to his professional disgrace, his departure from Vienna, and the effective end of his marriage.

Practicing Magnetism

Maria-Theresa Paradis was a brilliant young pianist who had been blind since the age of 3½, without clear physiological cause. Now 18 years old, her eye-sockets were swollen and disfigured from a variety of horrific medical interventions, including the application of thousands of electric shocks. Mesmer believed that Paradis might be helped through animal magnetism. When his early therapies proved encouraging, Paradis moved into Mesmer's home, as Oesterline had done, so that she too could receive constant care and attention. What happened next is difficult to determine, since the story is told one way by Mesmer and another by his detractors.

According to Mesmer, the eyesight of Paradis did begin to improve, but it was a mixed blessing. The images visible before her eyes were chaotic and inexplicable, and her musical ability was adversely affected. Although her family was at first overjoyed that she had regained some sight, they eventually demanded that she be returned to them. Perhaps they were influenced by the doctors who believed the healing was a hoax, or perhaps they suspected something inappropriate going on in the necessarily intimate relationship that existed between Herr Mesmer and their talented young daughter. Mesmer believed that they were motivated by greed, worrying that her status as a famous "blind" musician (and her annual government pension from the Empress Maria Theresa) was threatened if she were to be healed.

Mesmer describes the parents of Paradis storming his home, her father brandishing a sword while her mother smashed her daughter "headfirst against the wall" when she refused to leave. The effect on Paradis was dramatic, as Mesmer recalls it: "Immediately all the troubles of that unfortunate girl recommenced."[20] One gains insight, if this episode is accurate, into possible explanations for the young woman's psychological and psychosomatic difficulties.[21] Mesmer's critics were gleeful in response to his failure with Paradis, maintaining he had never actually improved her sight at all.[22]

Whatever the truth of it all, the outcome of the affair was straightforward. Maria-Theresa Paradis was again blind, and Mesmer was incontrovertibly denied entry into the scientific and medical establishment in Vienna. His own records from this time tell us that he fell into a deep depression, spending days in silence, walking and communing only with trees. He finally chose to leave Vienna altogether, abandoning his medical practice, his palatial estate, and his wife. He would not return to Vienna until after her death.

Mesmer wandered through Europe during the year of 1778 before landing in Paris. He was 43 years old. Once there, he hit the ground running, magnetizing patients in his home in Créteil and then in his mansion on the Place Vendôme. His clientele was wealthy, and subsidized a lifestyle much in the manner to which he had been accustomed in Vienna. It was in France that Mesmer would finally distill his theory of animal magnetism into the form that he would champion unwaveringly for the rest of his professional life.

In 1779, the year that the exorcist Gassner passed away, Mesmer published his treatise on animal magnetism, setting out 27 points of argument.[23] There was nothing surprising in the document to those who had been familiar with his work in Vienna. He asserted the existence of a universal fluid, invisible but physical in nature like magnetism, or electricity, which joined everything and everyone to one another. He defined disease as the manifestation of irregular or unbalanced distribution of this fluid within a human body. Correspondingly, good health was the reflection of its equilibrium. His techniques followed from the premise that it was possible for healthy people, properly trained, to channel this fluid

Figure 2 *Anton Mesmer giving a demonstration of animal magnetism at Place Vendôme. Etching reproduced in Louis Figuier, 1887,* Les Mystères de la Science. *Mary Evans Picture Library (maryevans.com).*

into a sick body, restoring it to health by restoring its "magnetic" equilibrium. The actual healing process required the patient to achieve a "crisis" in which their symptoms were produced, before being banished by the magnetizer.

Mesmer's theory of disease and healing was meant to be a universal one, encompassing and explaining any other apparent medical approaches. If they seemingly "worked" to bring about a cure, what was really happening was that the doctor, like Gassner the exorcist, was unknowingly channeling animal magnetism to the patient. Mesmer's motto was a confident, if not arrogant, one: "There is only one illness and one healing."[24]

By 1780, Mesmer was approached by more patients than he could handle. On a typical day he might be presented with 200 people who begged for his care. He made use of his odd but practical invention, the *baquet,* to treat greater numbers of people simultaneously, without his direct attention. The baquet consisted of a large covered tub filled with water that he had magnetized. People stood around the tub, placing the affected areas of their bodies against iron rods which protruded at different heights. They might also hold on to a rope that joined them together, while Mesmer, wearing a velvet cape, played ethereal music on his glass harmonica. When participants fell into a crisis, they were helped into the *chambre des crises*, a special room where they could safely endure their convulsions or whatever other symptoms overtook them at this stage in the healing.

Magnetism Assailed

As had occurred previously in Vienna, Mesmer's popular success did not translate into professional respect. He was dumbfounded by his failure to gain acceptance by the French Academy of Science, but this did not prevent him from training the men who would be his most important students. Most of these would in time disappoint and betray him, although their perspectives on the events are different. Almost as soon as Mesmer began to teach students, there was trouble. Animal magnetism was his discovery, and it is clear that he wanted to control every aspect of his technique. His first and most important student, Charles D'Eslon (1750–1786), was an established and respected doctor whose commitment to Mesmer and magnetism would cause him to be expelled from the French Academy of Medicine, and to have his medical practice several times condemned. D'Eslon set up his own clinic in 1782, and began taking patients or, in Mesmer's view, taking away Mesmer's patients. D'Eslon charged substantially less than Mesmer did for a magnetic treatment.[25]

Mesmer responded to the threat posed by D'Eslon by carrying out the suggestion of another friend and protégé, lawyer Nicholas Bergasse (1750–1832), to create a "secret" society that would provide Mesmer with control over the training of mesmerists. It would also provide him with a secure income. The idea was simple: students who paid the generous subscription, and signed agreements of confidentiality, would be taught the "secrets" of magnetism. The "Society of Harmony" was formed in 1783, and branches sprang up in cities and towns across France. It seems to have functioned as part Masonic lodge, part a private fundraiser for Mesmer.[26] Although Mesmer fell out with Bergasse during this period, fighting over control of the organization, particularly over the question of who was in control of the practices of magnetism and had the right to teach and write about them, the Society thrived and Mesmer prospered. In 1784, however, a series of public blows were struck against animal magnetism.

The American ambassador to France, Benjamin Franklin, along with prestigious members of the Academies of Science and the Faculty of Medicine, were appointed to inquire into the practice of mesmerism in France. The purpose of the commission was not to determine whether or not animal magnetism worked, but whether or not the practice of animal magnetism proved the existence of a universal fluid, as Mesmer claimed. Using the practice of D'Eslon for their inquiry, the commission observed and experimented and even allowed themselves to be magnetized. The report concluded that magnetic fluid did not exist, and that insofar as the techniques of magnetism effected cures, these were due to a combination of touch, imitation, and imagination. As a result of this report, the Public Ministry moved to make the practice of magnetism illegal in France.[27] Bergasse successfully appealed to Parliament, arguing that it had been the practice of D'Eslon rather than Mesmer that the commission had studied. Ironically, while Mesmer had been furious at the commission's preference for the medical practice of D'Eslon, this fact saved him in the end.[28]

Still, the commission's report opened up a floodgate of criticism and ridicule for Mesmer. There were songs and plays about him, and more serious books written by philosophers and scientists discounting the originality of his discovery on one hand, and its validity on the other. At the same time, Mesmer's conflicts with Bergasse erupted after his student published material Mesmer considered to be secret knowledge, and it ended with Bergasse being expelled from the Society of Harmony. Mesmer felt assailed from all sides. It is at this point in a tragic tale that the romantic heroine should return and perform the *coup de grâce*. Indeed in 1784, on Good Friday, Mesmer was reported to have attended a concert in Paris performed by none other than Maria-Theresa Paradis. As the story goes, all eyes were on him, rather than on the stage. It was a moment of supreme humiliation; as everyone could clearly witness, the beautiful young pianist was still blind.[29]

Whether or not this event actually occurred, less than a year later Mesmer would leave Paris, without telling even his disciples where he was going. Historical records do not reveal where he wandered during the period of the French Revolution and over the next 20 years, though traces of him turn up here and there across Europe. He returned to Vienna in 1793, three years after his wife's death, but stayed only long enough to become involved in a political controversy and to be thrown out. Eventually he found his way to the homes of his sisters, reestablishing warm relations with the nieces and nephews who would be his heirs. He had enough wealth remaining to retire in some comfort, far from the scientific and social spotlight he had previously coveted.

After fighting through the latter decades of the eighteenth century to have his theories accepted by the scientific and medical establishments in Vienna and Paris, and then wandering across Europe in search of an intellectual home, Mesmer at the end of his life chose to withdraw himself from the controversies that still raged around his ideas and his techniques. He continued to practice healing through animal magnetism privately and locally, but never took up his fight again. So secluded was he that many practitioners of mesmerism were unaware, during the first decade of the nineteenth century, that its creator and namesake was still alive. Other men had already taken his place on the public stage where Mesmer had first placed himself half a century before.

Mesmer died in 1815 on the shores of Lake Constance, very near to the village of Iznang, Germany where, 80 years before, he had been born. The local people remembered him not for his infamous theory of animal magnetism nor for the still burgeoning array of spiritual and healing techniques and practices that had come to be referred to as "mesmerism," but because he had been their local wizard, with powers beyond those of ordinary men. According to one tale, when Mesmer visited the island of Mainau, flocks of birds followed him, drawn to him as all creatures were. One canary alighted on his arm and would not leave him, so that he had to bring the bird home with him. Mesmer kept the bird in a cage with an open door. He could put it to sleep with the touch of a finger. It flew to wake its master with a song each morning until the day that Mesmer died. That morning it remained in its cage, refusing to sing or to eat. It soon died of grief.[30]

Mesmerism Transformed

Through the last years of Mesmer's life and beyond, mesmerism was transforming in ways he never imagined, and couldn't approve. Bergasse imagined a kind of "political mesmerism" that contributed to the philosophical underpinnings of the French Revolution.[31] Supernaturalists ignored Mesmer's insistence on the physical reality of magnetic fluid, and understood mesmerism to be an expression of occult knowledge. More disturbingly for Mesmer, the process that bore his name was changing at its center, not only at its fringes, a transformation brought about by the work of one of his students, Amand-Marie-Jacques de Chastenet, the Marquis de Puységur (1751–1825).

The Marquis de Puységur was the eldest of three aristocratic French brothers who were trained in the arts of mesmerism. Jacque Maxime de Chastenet, the Viscount de Puységur (1755–1848), the youngest brother, was a military officer, who used magnetism to treat his soldiers. Antoine Hyacinthe, the Count de Chastenet (1752–1809), the middle brother, was a naval officer who brought mesmerism to the French colony of Saint Domingue, later called Haiti.[32] There it became popular among slaveholders, as well as the enslaved, each having their own *baquets*. Laws were passed outlawing its use among slaves when it appeared to be stirring their discontent. Mesmerism supposedly fueled the mix of voodoo and other African spiritual practices that agitated the slave population into rebellion. It was because of this that Mesmer claimed some responsibility for the Haitian revolution.[33]

As the eldest of the brothers, the Marquis de Puységur inherited the family's ancestral castle and lands. He was also a military officer, but his interest in mesmerism was soon to outweigh every other consideration in his life. After receiving his training from Mesmer, Puységur began in 1780 practicing mesmerism on those who lived and worked on his estate. Just as Mesmer's healing of Oesterline was the key event in his understanding of the processes of mesmerism, Puységur also made his crucial breakthrough because of a particular subject. This was Victor Race, a 23-year-old peasant who in 1784 was suffering from congestion and fever. Puységur mesmerized him but the young man did not experience a traditional "crisis." Instead he seemed to fall asleep—except that he continued to speak. At first Race was agitated in this state until

Puységur suggested that he concern himself with more pleasant images, to hear a song in his head, and then to dance to the tune in his chair. The exertion caused him to sweat profusely, the closest that he came to a traditional crisis. That evening he was able to eat and drink, as he had not done for several days. He slept the night through, and the next day was much improved. He remembered nothing that had occurred the night before.[34]

Puységur called the sleep-waking state of consciousness that Race had experienced "magnetic somnambulism" or "magnetic sleep" and it was this experienced phenomenon, along with enhanced suggestibility and amnesia, that would come to replace the crisis as the definitive test of the success of a mesmeric induction. Mesmer had taught his students that the crisis was so crucial a part of the process that its presence was the method of validating whether or not someone was mesmerized at all. Puységur's subjects no longer had violent episodes of their presenting symptoms while mesmerized, but instead entered into an apparently unique state of consciousness, neither sleeping nor waking. This dramatic turn of events was to split the world of mesmerism into two. Mesmer's loyal followers practiced the art much as Mesmer had done, invoking crises, without producing altered states. But many more were drawn to Puységur's style of mesmerism, which eschewed the disturbing and sometimes violent crises, replacing them with the much gentler and often more wondrous spectacle of magnetic sleep.

It is clear that the changes that Puységur made to Mesmer's creation were profound, and shaped not only the direction that hypnosis would take as a psychotherapeutic tool, but also the way that popular ideas about mesmerism would influence spiritual movements on one hand, and entertainment on the other. Many of the beliefs about hypnosis that we noted in Du Maurier's story of Trilby and Svengali can be seen to have their source not in Mesmer's style of mesmerism, but in the mesmerism practiced by Puységur.

From Animal Magnetism to Magnetic Sleep

Between what Mesmer created and Puységur transmitted to future generations of mesmerizers, there had taken place a transformation in the relationship between the mesmerizer and the subject. There was also a dramatic shift in basic assumptions about the nature of mesmerism itself and in the significance of memory and identity to the process. Mesmer's flamboyant performance, his purple velvet cape, the ethereal tones of the glass harmonica, his apparent ability to mesmerize with a touch or even the point of a finger, these details make him seem to be the inspiration for Svengali. On closer examination, however, Mesmer's interactions with his subjects were actually quite narrow, having to do with producing and relieving their physiological and psychological symptoms. Although his critics accused Mesmer's subjects of extreme gullibility, Mesmer himself refused that reading of the hypnotic relation. If he had power, it was a physical power that came from the accumulation of animal magnetism in his person, an accumulation that varied, and that he feared to lose. If he was skillful as a magnetizer, this was because he was familiar with the techniques, which anyone could learn. If someone was healed, this was a physical event that did not require the belief of the subject, nor any particular psychological characteristic.

When the French investigating commission dismissed the reality of animal magnetism as the mere production of imagination, Mesmer was deeply offended and insisted until the end of his life on the physical tangible reality of magnetic fluid and its significance in disease and health. In sharp contrast, Puységur did not at all disdain the power of imagination in his practice of mesmerism. He did not reject outright the reality of animal magnetism, but its existence was irrelevant to his own practice. He knew that there was a connection between himself and his subjects that gave him the power to heal them. It bothered him not at all that the source of this power was due to a psychological bond, rather than a tangible fluid that passed between them. He attributed this power, both his and that of his subjects, to "an active will to do good; a firm belief in our power; and an entire confidence in employing it."[35] The rapport that he believed existed between mesmerist and subject required the suggestibility of the subject and a conscious sacrifice of their will to his. These were psychological, not physiological, conditions.

Secondly, Puységur radically transformed understandings of what constituted the experience of being mesmerized. Just as Mesmer had made irrelevant the essential parts of Gassner's exorcism–the verbal confrontation with demons–so did Puységur make the mesmeric crisis obsolete. In its place, the trance state of magnetic sleep came to be seen as essential, and the earlier dramatic manifestations of crisis produced in different ways by Gassner and Mesmer were judged to be only products of suggestion. Gassner believed that health was restored when a possessing demon was cast out; Mesmer believed that illness arose from irregularities in magnetic fluid, and that health reflected its equilibrium; Puységur theorized that insanity was "disordered somnambulism," which could be cured by experiencing the proper kind.[36]

Finally, it was Puységur who discovered the seeming power of mesmerism over memory and identity.[37] The post-trance amnesia experienced by Victor Race became a normative expectation for other mesmerized subjects. Amnesia was not the only stunning display that Puységur's subjects manifested. While mesmerized, Victor Race began to diagnose illnesses, not only his own, but of other people who were not even in his physical presence. This feat was replicated by other mesmerized subjects, to the point that Puységur considered it a central feature of his own theories of mesmerism. As time went on, other people in the state of magnetic sleep appeared to be capable of telepathic and clairvoyant feats that they could not perform in their waking states. So striking were the talents and capabilities of magnetized individuals that they often seemed to behave as different people, speaking with a changed vocabulary and tone, as though they were of a different social class and character.[38]

During his public career, Mesmer had tried to shake off all association with the supernatural, insisting on the scientific and the physical basis of mesmerism. Although he never publicly credited Puységur with the discovery of magnetic sleep, Mesmer did meet Victor Race in 1784.[39] By the end of his life Mesmer may have incorporated Puységur's work into his reflections on mesmerism, and even acknowledged some of the apparently supernatural phenomena that he had previously rejected.[40]

Mesmer's name adhered to Puységur's practice of animal magnetism and persisted into the middle and even late nineteenth century; however, it is in Puységur's experiences that we have the origins of Trilby's dissociation of selves, her unmesmerized, talentless, working-class self on one hand, and her mesmerized virtuoso, who sang before kings. To be sure, Victor Race was not Trilby, and Puységur was not Svengali. When Race was taken to Paris in 1785, he was self-aware enough to diagnose his own

Figure 3 *Puységur with patients in Buzancy being magnetized by an elm tree. Lucien Laurent-Gsell, 1891, in Foveau de Courmelles,* L'hypnotisme, *Mary Evans Picture Library (maryevans.com).*

illness as resulting from Puységur putting him on public display.[41] Although Puységur seemed to believe that magnetic rapport gave him power "over" his subjects, he also recognized the will of his subjects over their own healing. He believed that their diagnoses of their ills and others' were superior to his own non-magnetized judgments. He even believed that it was possible for people to magnetize themselves.[42]

It is impossible to discount the good will of Puységur's involvement with mesmerism. Once he made his discoveries, he taught his techniques freely, and tried hard not to turn away anyone who requested his help. He is famous for an elm tree he placed in the public square and magnetized, which had the power to magnetize countless people simultaneously. He organized his own society to train magnetizers, which had by 1789 over 200 members. The French Revolution interrupted his practice and dissolved his society. He spent two years in prison. But he began practicing and publishing again through the first two decades of the nineteenth century.[43]

In 1818 he returned to his estate at Buzancy to magnetize Victor Race in the same cottage where the two men had made their great discovery more than 30 years before. When Puységur died in 1825, outliving Mesmer the wizard by only 10 years, his writings were forgotten for a few decades, as others stepped forward to claim mesmerism for themselves. The elm tree survived until 1940.[44] Still reputed for its healing power after more than a century, when it fell in a storm, local people hastened to gather up its pieces.

Notes

1 For a discussion of the desire of early magnetists to find precedence for their practices in pre-history see Ann Taves, *Fits, Trances, and Visions: Experiencing Religion and Explaining Experience from Wesley to James* (Princeton, NJ: Princeton University Press, 1999): 139.

2 For a deeper exploration of Mesmer's life and work see Frank Pattie, *Mesmer and Animal Magnetism* (Hamilton, NY: Edmonston Publishing, 1994); and Alan Gauld, *A History of Hypnotism* (Cambridge MA: Cambridge University Press, 1992).

3 Franz Mesmer, "Physical Medical Treatise on the Influence of the Planets," in Franz Mesmer, *Mesmerism: A Translation of the Original Scientific and Medical Writings of F. A. Mesmer*, trans. George Bloch (Los Altos, CA: William Kaufmann, 1980): 14.

4 See Frank Pattie, "Mesmer's Medical Dissertation and its Debt to Mead's De Imperio Solis ac Lunae," *Journey of the History of Medicine and Allied Sciences* 11 (1956): 275–287.

5 Vincent Buranelli, *The Wizard from Vienna* (New York: Coward, McCann & Geoghegan, 1975): 41.

6 Pattie, *Mesmer*, 80. According to Pattie this event was recorded in Mesmer's letters, though no contemporary record can substantiate it. He notes, however, that it was historically plausible for operas to have been staged there.

7 David A. Gallo and Stanley Finger, "The Power of a Musical Instrument: Franklin, the Mozarts, Mesmer, and the Glass Armonica," *History of Psychology* 3, no. 4 (2000): 326–343.

8 Franz Mesmer, "Dissertation on the Discovery of Animal Magnetism," in Mesmer, *Mesmer*, trans. Bloch, *Mesmerism*, 130.

9 Ibid., 48.

10 Cited by Pattie, *Mesmer*, p. 32.

11 Pattie, *Mesmer*, 50–52.

12 See Franz Mesmer, "Letter from M. Mesmer, Doctor of Medicine at Vienna, to A.M. Unzer, Doctor of Medicine, on the Medicinal Usage of the Magnet," in Mesmer, *Mesmer*, trans. Bloch, p. 23.
13 Henri Ellenberger, *The Discovery of the Unconscious* (New York: Basic Books, 1970): 54.
14 Ibid., 55.
15 Ibid., 56.
16 Ibid.
17 Ibid., 57.
18 For more on Gassner see H. C. Erik Midelfort, *Johann Joseph Gassner and the Demons of Eighteenth-Century Germany* (New Haven: Yale University Press, 2005).
19 See George Sarton, "Vindication of Father Hell," *Isis* 35, no. 100 (1944): 97–105.
20 Mesmer, "Dissertation on the Discovery of Animal Magnetism," p. 61.
21 The 1994 film, *Mesmer*, written by Dennis Potter and starring Alan Rickman in the title role, bluntly asserts that the blindness of Paradis was the result of incestuous assaults she suffered at the hands of her father, in combination with her mother's denial and failure to protect her. Although Mesmer accuses Paradis' parents of brutality, the incest was a modern addition, reflecting contemporary thinking about sexual trauma and its recent association with hypnotic recall. Pattie believes Paradis' blindness was likely organic, and that Mesmer's treatments were largely ineffective. See Pattie, *Mesmer*, 58–63.
22 Pattie, *Mesmer*, 61.
23 Mesmer, "Dissertation on the Discovery of Animal Magnetism," 67–70.
24 Ellenberger, *Discovery of the Unconscious*, 63.
25 Adam Crabtree, *From Mesmer to Freud: Magnetic Sleep and the Roots of Psychological Healing* (New Haven CT: Yale University Press, 1993): 23.
26 See Melvin A. Gravitz, "Mesmerism and Masonry: Early Historical Interactions," *American Journal of Clinical Hypnosis* 39, no. 4 (1997): 266–270.
27 See Pattie, *Mesmer*, 142–158.
28 For more on the Franklin Commission see "The 50th Anniversary Special Issue: Mesmer, Franklin, and the Royal Commission," *International Journal of Clinical and Experimental Hypnosis* 50, no. 4 (2002).
29 Pattie, *Mesmer*, 63. According to Pattie, who traced the story to its source, it is almost certainly apocryphal. See also Frank A. Pattie, "A Mesmer–Paradis Myth Dispelled," *American Journal of Clinical Hypnosis* 22 (1979): 29–31.

30 Buranelli, *The Wizard from Vienna*, 203–204. The original source of this story is Justinus Kerner (1786–1862) who heard the tale while visiting Meersburg after Mesmer's death. See Justinus Kerner, *Franz Anton Mesmer, der Entdecker des thierischen Magnetismus* (Frankfurt am Main: Literarische Anstalt, 1856).

31 See Robert Darnton, *Mesmerism and the End of the Enlightenment in France* (Cambridge, MA: Harvard University Press, 1968).

32 Ellenberger, *Discovery of the Unconscious*, 70. For his account of the mesmeric activities of the Puységur family, Ellenberger cites his personal communication with the Viscount du Boisdulier, a descendant of the Marquis de Puységur.

33 Ibid. See also Karol Weaver, *Medical Revolutionaries: The Enslaved Healers of Eighteenth-Century Saint-Domingue* (Urbana and Chicago: University of Illinois Press, 2006).

34 Amand M. J. de Chastenet, Marquis de Puységur, *Détails des cures opérées à Buzancy par le magnétisme animal* (Paris: n.p. 1784).

35 Cited by J. P. F. Deleuze, *Practical Instruction in Animal Magnetism*, trans. Thomas C. Hartshorn (New York: 1846): 214.

36 Amand M. J. de Chastenet, Marquis de Puységur, *Recherches, expériences et observations physiologique sur l'homme dans l'état de somnambulisme naturel, et dans le somnambulisme provoqué par l'acte magnétique* (Paris: Dentu, 1811).

37 Gauld, *History*, 44. Gauld wonders whether Victor Race has as much claim to be the inventor of "artificial somnambulism" as does Puységur.

38 Ibid., 60.

39 Ibid., 43.

40 See Franz A. Mesmer, *Memoir of F. A. Mesmer, Doctor of Medicine, on His Discoveries*, in Mesmer, *Mesmer*, trans. Bloch, 87–132.

41 Ellenberger, *Discovery of the Unconscious*, 72. For the full story, see Amand M. J. de Chastenet, Marquis de Puységur, *Mémoires pour servir à l'histoire et à l'éstablissement du magnétisme animal* (2d ed., Paris: Cellot, 1809): 39–52.

42 Apparently Mesmer had also experimented with mesmerizing himself. See Melvin A. Gravitz, "First Use of Self-Hypnosis: Mesmer Mesmerizes Mesmer, *American Journal of Clinical Hypnosis* 37 (1994): 49–52.

43 Amand M. J. de Chastenet, Marquis de Puységur, *Appel aux savans observateurs du dix-neuvième siècle, de la décision portée par leur prédécesseurs contre le magnétisme animal, et fin de la traitement du jeune Hébert* (Paris: Dentu, 1813).

44 Ibid. Ellenberger's source was a M. Guillermot, then Mayor of Buzancy. He further reported that a spring located at the site of the elm tree was still believed to have magical properties.

CHAPTER THREE

Magnetism and Hypnosis

During the early decades of the nineteenth century mesmerists in Europe were predominantly medical men engaged in a conflict of theory between "fluidists" who still maintained a belief in the physical reality of animal magnetism, and "animists" whose explanation for mesmeric phenomena was more psychological than physical. There were others who seemed to take an ambivalent attitude toward the existence of magnetic fluid. The unresolved question of *why* mesmeric techniques worked rarely interfered with the pragmatic fact *that* they seemed to work, but the tide was clearly turning against the belief in the physical existence of magnetic fluid.

Jose-Custodio de Faria (1756–1819) began in 1815 to offer demonstrations of animal magnetism in Paris to crowds of thousands. An ordained Catholic priest, Abbé Faria was born in Goa of Indo-Portuguese ancestry, and claimed to be of Brahmin caste. He spoke French badly, which added to his exotic presence, but it also made him easy prey for popular caricature. In his demonstrations he would cast his entire audience into a somnambulistic state with the barked command: "Sleep!" If it didn't work the first time, he would command it again, only louder.[1]

This technique met with such great success that he was accused of being a sorcerer. Faria never claimed to have any secret or power, however, and he specifically rejected the objective reality of magnetic fluid. He believed that the key was the belief and will of the subject. If subjects expected a magnetizer to have a special power, if they accepted the reality of magnetism, and if they thought that a particular object had been magnetized, then both magnetizer and magnet would have (or would appear to have) power over the subject. The real power, in Faria's view, was located in the subjects themselves.[2]

The most important insight made by Faria was his recognition of the significance of the mesmerist's suggestions, which seemed to have an effect on subjects when they were in a mesmeric trance, which he called "lucid sleep," but also when they were in their normal waking state. Faria believed that some people were better than others in achieving lucid sleep; he called these people "natural epoptes."[3] This term, like others that Faria introduced in his writings, did not catch on. The writings of two men who were introduced to mesmerism by Faria ended up having a more enduring influence on future generations of hypnotists. Ironically, one of these, General François Joseph Noizet (1792–1885), the author of an influential work on magnetic somnambulism, was a fluidist.[4] The other was physician Alexandre Bertrand (1795–1831), whose work is remembered for its emphasis on systematic empirical research and who was eventually to champion the more psychological view of magnetism.

Fluidism and Animism

Bertrand witnessed in 1819 a public demonstration of mesmerism near his birthplace of Nantes, and began lecturing on the subject that same year. He was able to demonstrate through experimentation what Faria had asserted, that the power of magnetism arose from the belief of the subject. He also found that this belief was susceptible to influence. Although the mesmerized subjects of a fluidist would experience the magnetic fluid as tangible and real, the subjects of animists would not.[5] In other words, Bertrand's findings indicated that the physical perception of magnetic fluid was itself a product of suggestion. This was not far from what the Franklin Commission had concluded, based on the same type of experiments that systematically manipulated the expectancy of the subjects. Bertrand, however, did not consider mesmerism as a whole to be discredited, as the Commission had done. Instead Bertrand followed Puységur in asserting that it was the altered state of magnetic sleep that was the defining characteristic of mesmerism, rather than the communication of magnetic fluid between mesmerist and subject. Bertrand studied the state of magnetic sleep in its historical context, and wrote about "epidemics of ecstasy" in previous eras, including religious experiences like possession, conversion, and exorcism as performed by Gassner.[6]

Another important animist during this period was Hénin de Cuvillers (1755–1841) whose work promoted the view that the phenomena associated with mesmerism resulted from a combination of suggestion and belief.[7] The shift from fluidist to animist explanations brought about a dramatic about-face in institutional attitudes toward mesmerism. The eighteenth century rejection of mesmerism by the mainstream French medical community had focused on refuting claims to the tangible existence of magnetic fluid, while remaining officially ambivalent to the results of mesmeric practice. Experiments performed by Joseph Philippe Francois Deleuze (1753–1835) and de Cuvillers, among others, convinced the Académie de Médecine in 1826 to take another look at the results produced by mesmerism. A new committee was formed. The report they produced in 1831 confirmed the reality of mesmerism's measurable effects including, most dramatically and convincingly, the possibility of painless surgical procedures.[8]

The new report of the Académie de Médecine was translated into English in 1833 by John Campbell Colquhoun (1785–1854), an Edinburgh gentleman and lawyer who had studied works on magnetism in both French and German. Colquhoun was the author of *Isis Revelata: An Inquiry into the origins, progress and present state of Animal Magnetism*, a book that would become one of the most accessible and popular treatises on magnetism for the English-speaking audience.[9] Colquhoun's work was not respected by scientific mesmerists, but it was widely read and imitated by nonmedical mesmerists and the masses of amateur enthusiasts to be found among humanists, novelists, and the general public of Victorian Britain.[10]

The flurry of mesmeric activity that took place in London in the late 1830s was a dramatic change from the first few decades of the nineteenth century, a period during which the mesmeric movement in Britain was all but nonexistent. Because mesmerism was routinely vilified or lampooned by the mainstream English medical community, the French commission's report had a significant impact. It even received serious review in the influential medical journal, the *Lancet*. The editor of the *Lancet* was Thomas Wakley (1795–1862), a savvy and ambitious man who employed his journal as a weapon to reform and police mainstream medicine in

Britain. Wakley would soon change his benevolent stance toward magnetism, but that was not to occur until the practice itself had made the leap across the Channel, and after one of the more colorful episodes of Victorian medical history had played out at University College Hospital in London, with Wakley taking an uncharacteristically central role.

The Channel-crosser in question was "Baron" Dupotet de Sennevoy (1796–1881). His title was more ornamental than actual, his formerly noble family having lost their fortune. Arriving in early summer of 1837, he set up shop and began to advertise his services as a mesmerist.[11] Employing a technique of guided meditation rather than direct suggestion, and adopting intimate postures and stylized patterns of touch, Dupotet produced dramatic effects in his subjects. By summer's end he was drawing crowds. He duly impressed a prominent doctor at London University, John Elliotson (1791–1868), who allowed him to mesmerize patients at University College Hospital.

During the 1830s, Elliotson had firmly established himself as a prominent and well-respected medical doctor. He was both a professor at London University (now University College) and a practicing physician at the University College Hospital. He imported to British medical practice from France new diagnostic techniques, drug treatments, and most famously, the stethoscope. He was also a close friend of Wakley, who frequently published in the *Lancet* accounts of Elliotson's lectures at the University hospital, including his less mainstream musings. Elliotson was a devoted phrenologist, becoming the founder and first president of the Phrenological Society in 1824.[12] Phrenology associated different areas of the skull with different emotional and cognitive phenomena, asserting that all mental faculties could be mapped to these specific "organs" in the brain. The system was introduced into Britain by Johann Spurzheim (1776–1832), who in 1825 gave 18 lectures disseminating the phrenological teachings of Viennese physician Franz-Joseph Gall (1758–1828).

Elliotson first encountered mesmerism in 1829 when he witnessed a demonstration by Richard Chenevix (1774–1830), a French chemist drawn to mesmerism by the work of Faria. This was before the release of the report by the Académie de Médecine, and though Elliotson was intrigued at that time, he was still building his career and pursuing his research in phrenology. He did not invest himself beyond publishing some positive commentary on the demonstration. It was the subsequent arrival of Dupotet in London in 1837 that was to be the tipping point for Elliotson's wholehearted engagement with mesmerism.

By inviting Dupotet into the University hospital to work with patients there, Elliotson lent to him his own not inconsiderable medical authority. Dupotet's demonstrations at the hospital were described in the *Lancet* in August of 1837 by an anonymous witness. The account was sympathetic, but ironic. Dupotet reacted to the tone in his published response. He defended mesmerism as serious science, and with an echo of Mesmer's hubris declared: "A new power is revealed to the world."[13] Meanwhile Dr. Elliotson, well known for his willingness to try alternative medical treatments, had begun his own experiments. He was interested in the use of mesmerism to treat disorders of the nervous system, including epilepsy and hysterical paralysis. Elliotson would swiftly eclipse Dupotet in Britain as the man of the times most associated with mesmerism. His reputation would also suffer the most through that association, and he would shortly resign under pressure from his positions at London University and Hospital.

Mesmerism at University College Hospital

The dramatic events of 1837 and 1838 revolved around two of Elliotson's inpatients at University College Hospital, Irish sisters, aged 15 and 16, by the name of Jane and Elizabeth O'Key.[14] Admitted as epileptic, a category that included what would decades later be understood as "hysterical" convulsions, the girls' presenting symptoms included dramatic uncontrollable fits. Elliotson believed these were the result of some physiological problem of the central nervous system, and so his first experiments were attempts to reduce their symptoms. He changed tactics when he discovered that he could also produce and control their "crises" through mesmerism. Although the O'Keys were not the only subjects of his research during this time, the dramatic changes they experienced while being mesmerized, particularly their shift to altered states of mind and personality, made them his star subjects for display. Elizabeth was publicly mesmerized at least 100 times over the space of a year. In addition to Elliotson's own detailed research notes, Elizabeth and Jane's "performances" were lavishly covered in the *Lancet*, accounts which also provide a detailed view of how the audience at the time was reacting to what they were seeing.

A writer for the *Lancet* tells us that the company present on the evening of Thursday, May 10, 1838 at University College Hospital in London included titled noblemen and several Members of Parliament. Elliotson brought Elizabeth O'Key to the central staging area, and began with a short lecture detailing the history of his own acquaintance with mesmerism, and the possibility of its scientific assessment through experimentation. As soon as he had finished his remarks, Elizabeth, who had been sitting passively, changed dramatically. She was fully alert, but appeared unaware of, or indifferent to, the gawking crowd that scrutinized her through spectacles and opera glasses:

> She then advanced and said, with innocent familiarity, and a peculiar and agreeable tone of voice, "Oh! How do ye?" to the Marquis of Anglesea, who sat immediately in front of her. "White trowsers. Dear! You do look so tidy, you do. What nice things. You *are* a nice man."[15]

Dr. Elliotson declared her to be in "the state of delirium." The demonstration drifted between Elliotson's sage commentary and Elizabeth's precocious outbursts. Some of what the O'Key sisters demonstrated Elliotson found useful to his specific research questions. He wanted to measure differences in magnetic force, and what factors might influence the relative power of various magnetic objects. He was interested in the possibility of mesmeric anesthesia and other supranormal functionings, like extraordinary strength and paranormal diagnostic abilities. The strange and often entertaining antics of the O'Key sisters strained his scientific agenda, however, a problem more obvious to witnesses than it seems to have been for Elliotson, who allowed the boundaries between his subjects and his audience to thin to nonexistence:

> Presently she whistled a tune clearly and correctly, and then rose to feel the shining boot of a gentleman who was sitting in the chair recently left by the Marquis, who had found, he said, the atmosphere too warm for him. While stooping at this time the writer twitched her hair, and pinched her neck, but she did not notice it,

> or evince the slightest symptom of pain. On rising she observed, "a nice large gentleman, with white legs."—"You are not so big," she said to his neighbor, "are you?"—"No, for that gentleman has the advantage of being stuffed?" "Stuffed? Pray with what? Is it with a good dinner? For that's the best of all good stuffing." Some visitor at this moment, out of her sight, passed his hand down behind her back, and thus instantly stupefied her. She fell backwards, and was caught by the nearest person.[16]

In their year on stage the O'Key sisters continued to sing, dance, speak impudently to visiting nobility and collapse cataleptically into their laps, let loose witty one-liners, and increasingly to exhibit complex dissociations of identity. Eventually they were channeling a "negro spirit-guide" with prophetic and diagnostic powers.[17] The demonstrations were attended as evening entertainment by London society, and even when critics attacked Elliotson, they were often admiring of the performance of the girls.

As the summer of 1838 wore on, the credulity of the medical community was wearing thin. A rumor circulated that the O'Key sisters had been members of Edward Irving's apocalyptic evangelic church at Islington Green.[18] This group was known for "speaking in tongues" and their involvement in this religious experience may in part explain the girls' dissociative expertise. The other influence upon the style of the sisters' interactions with the audience is likely to have been their exposure to working-class theatergoers of Covent Garden, who engaged in an easy and humorous give-and-take with the actors, interactions which became part of the show for the upper classes.[19]

The question at hand was whether the O'Key sisters were faking their performance while entranced or whether they were, as Elliotson claimed, mesmerized in the traditional fluidist sense, through the use of magnetized objects. Faced with increasingly hostile and incredulous medical peers who were encouraged into a frenzy by venomous publications in the *Lancet*, in August Elliotson finally agreed to let Wakley run his own experiments upon the girls. These experiments were not set up in a laboratory, but in Wakley's own home, and were conducted in the spirit of a criminal trial.[20] In the familiar expectancy-manipulating experiment, Wakley was able to mesmerize Elizabeth O'Key with "lead and a farthing," metal objects that were impervious to actual magnetization. She subsequently failed to be mesmerized by an actually magnetized nickel. Further tests were conducted on Jane O'Key, who likewise was not mesmerized by magnetized water, but did fall into trance after drinking ordinary water.[21]

Elliotson was a fluidist in his approach to mesmerism, in line with his commitment to phrenology. This attitude forced him to look for physical explanations for what others were free to perceive to be psychological phenomena. It also meant that he had to defend as legitimate products of animal magnetism (rather than of imagination or suggestion) all the behaviors of his subjects during trance. The weakness of this position had been demonstrated historically time and time again. It allowed detractors simply to question some phenomenon produced by mesmerism and thereby to discredit the entire practice.

The experiments were detailed precisely in the *Lancet* in an article that underscored Wakley's belief that mesmerism had been completely debunked. Wakley "contended that what had been done was, in his opinion, perfectly conclusive with reference to the character of the supposed phenomena, and that he did not consider that a single additional experiment could ever be necessary in connection with such an inquiry." Elliotson, however, was nonplussed: "Dr. Elliotson candidly admitted that he could not explain how the thing had occurred; it was most extraordinary, but still he had not the slightest doubt that the whole would yet admit of a satisfactory explanation."[22]

Wakley believed his experiments should have closed the book on magnetism, since the O'Key sisters had been exposed as deceitful, and Elliotson as a fool. Like many other magnetists before him, Elliotson was undeterred by the experiment's results. Although Elliotson did believe in the existence of some tangible "force" that had an independent effect on mesmerized subjects apart from will and imagination, he was not preoccupied with explaining or understanding it. He continued his work through the fall of that year, even allowing Elizabeth O'Key access to the men's wards at the hospital where she engaged in diagnosis while mesmerized, going so far as to predict imminent death in some of the patients. This was the last straw for the medical community. The O'Key sisters were expelled from the hospital. Elliotson was indignant, but resigned from both hospital and university under pressure, despite an 11th-hour majority vote by the student body in his defense.

Magnetism in Parlor and Sickroom

Elliotson had lost a big battle, but he was not in the least defeated. Though Elliotson was to be brutally attacked in medical journals, most bitterly and unrelentingly by Wakley, he continued to practice privately. Mesmerism was still enthusiastically embraced outside the medical establishment in Britain. It merely shifted from public to private venues, from a strictly scientific to a more popular context. This was possible because by the middle of the nineteenth century the imagination of the Victorians had become enthralled by mesmerism and its philosophical and medical possibilities. In parlor rooms and at sickbeds in private homes across Britain, experiments in mesmerism were taking place.[23]

The night that he tendered his resignation, Elliotson dined with Charles Dickens (1812–1870), a frequent witness to mesmeric demonstrations, who would eventually dabble in mesmerism himself.[24] Mathematician Ada Lovelace (1815–1852), social scientist Harriet Martineau (1802–1876), and poet Elizabeth Barrett Browning (1806–1861) were among the well-regarded public women whose took a private interest in mesmerism. Martineau was a prolific writer, producing over 50 books of fiction and non-fiction, and nearly 2,000 articles on environmentalism, education, economics, and social reform. Her translation of *Cours de philosophi positive* by Auguste Comte (1798–1857) facilitated the development of the discipline of sociology in the English-speaking world.[25] Much of this work she did from a sickbed; nearly one-third of her life she lived with debilitating pain, suffering from slow-growing uterine cancer, though many of her chronic symptoms had been thought to be hysterical in origin. In her ironic third-person autobiographical musings, Martineau reflects on the controversy surrounding her use of mesmerism to alleviate her symptoms:

> The immediate consequence of the whole business–the extension of the practice of mesmerism as a curative agent, and especially the restoration of several cases like her own–abundantly compensated Harriet Martineau for an amount of insult and ridicule which would have been a somewhat unreasonable penalty on any sin or folly which she could have committed. As a penalty on simply getting well when she was expected to die, the infliction was a curious sign of the times.[26]

Martineau's first treatment had been performed by the popular magnetizer Spencer T. Hall (1812–1885).[27] But it was her own maid and subsequently Mrs. Montague Wynyard, a "genteel woman's companion," who became her healers.[28] Letters from her houseguests attest to experimentation going on in her home. Elizabeth Barrett Browning, for example, who also suffered from chronic conditions that made her an invalid, described Martineau in 1844 in a letter expressing admiration for her friend:

> She is thrown into the magnetic trance twice a day; and the progress is manifest; and the hope for the future clear ... Is it not wonderful, and past expectation? She suggests that I should try the means–but I understand that in cases like mine the remedy has done harm instead of good, by over-exciting the system. But her experience will settle the question of the reality of magnetism with a whole generation of infidels.[29]

More skeptically, another literary houseguest, Charlotte Brontë, wrote in a letter to her sister Emily in 1851:

> You ask me whether Miss Martineau made me a convert to mesmerism? Scarcely; yet I heard miracles of its efficacy, and could hardly discredit the whole of what was told me. I even underwent a personal experiment; and though the result was not absolutely clear, it was inferred that in time I should prove an excellent subject.[30]

By all reports Martineau's household, organized around her sickbed, was an extraordinary and liberating one, which she wrote about in *Life in the sick-room, or, essays by an invalid*, a book that was widely read by the reform-minded.[31] It was, however, bitterly attacked by the medical establishment, which found it dangerously subversive for an invalid to speak authoritatively about herself, much less to direct her own healing.[32] Their established alternative in that era was hardly less dangerous. Ada Lovelace, who also suffered from uterine cancer, died of loss of blood, a consequence of the bloodletting that was offered to her as treatment.

Mesmeric Anesthesia

Despite the personal toll that his association with mesmerism caused to his own medical reputation, Elliotson continued actively to promote its use, creating in 1849 the London Mesmeric Infirmary. When his contributions are assessed retrospectively, it is clear that Elliotson was one of the first mesmerists to approach the medical effects of mesmeric techniques in a systematic and scientific way. Because of his insistence on the scientific basis for mesmerism, Elliotson was intolerant of the popular and eclectic versions that had begun to appear in Britain, and the writings that had become a fixture of Victorian popular culture. He was particularly critical of the writings of Colquhoun, who, it must be noted, was unimpressed in turn with Elliotson's phreno-magnetism.[33] Elliotson's journal, *The Zoist: A Journal of Cerebral Psychology and Mesmerism and their Applications to Human Welfare,* which ran from 1843 to 1856, had an orientation that was applied rather than strictly theoretical. Elliotson was interested in whatever worked to reduce human suffering, and was drawn to the possibility of using mesmerism to control pain.[34]

The hope of mesmeric analgesia had gained both popular and professional attention in Britain through the work of James Esdaile (1805–1855), a Scottish surgeon who had lived and practiced medicine in India. Esdaile had begun his experiments with mesmerism in 1845, in the Native Hospital of the village of Hooghly, near Calcutta.[35] He found his first patient in a local jail, Mádhab Kaurá, a man he described as a "hog-dealer, condemned to seven years' imprisonment, with labour on the roads, in irons, for wounding a man so as to endanger his life."[36] Kaurá suffered from enormous fluid-filled scrotal tumors. Esdaile had him brought to the charity hospital for surgery. After his patient had the fluid drawn out, he was in such a pitiful state that Esdaile decided to try to alleviate his pain through mesmerism, something he had only read about before. As Esdaile describes the scene:

> I placed his knees between mine, and began to pass my hands slowly over his face, at the distance of an inch, and carried them down to the pit of his stomach. This was continued for half an hour before he was spoken to, and when questioned at the end of this time his answers were quite sensible and coherent. He was ordered to remain quiet, and the passes were continued for a quarter of an hour longer–still no sensible effect.[37]

The weather was hot, and Esdaile grew tired of his efforts, which seemed at first to have failed. He sat beside Kaurá who was resting more quietly. The doctor ordered him to open his eyes, but when he did, he declared that there was smoke in the room. Encouraged, Esdaile persisted in his hand passes for another hour, until his patient's pain appeared to disappear completely: "his hands were crossed on his breast, instead of being pressed on the groins, and his countenance showed the most perfect repose."[38]

Esdaile tested this repose in typical Victorian stage-hypnosis fashion, by having him breathe and then drink ammonia, which he did without exhibiting distress. This convinced all witnesses of the reality and power of what they had done. Thus began an astonishing surgical practice, in which native mesmerists would stroke patients, sometimes for hours at a time, prior to going under Esdaile's knife. *The Zoist* carried accounts of these surgeries and in 1846 published a lengthy list of painless operations that Esdaile claimed to have carried out in an eight-month period. The list includes the amputation of an arm and a breast, the excision of a cataract, and the removal of 17 scrotal tumors weighing between 8 and 80 pounds.[39]

Esdaile testified that mesmerism produced fewer side-effects, and was less dangerous to his patients, than the new chemical anesthesia induced by ether and chloroform. Mesmerism fit Esdaile's philosophy of healing in which the doctor is secondary to nature. He believed it is the doctor's role merely to remove impediments to nature's own healing.[40] Documented cases of painless operations were persuasive even to skeptics back in Britain. Mesmeric anesthesia seemed to critics to be an effect beyond easy deception. Mainstream medical journals, with the exception of the *Lancet*, reviewed Esdaile's work favorably and with interest.

The prospect of reducing the pain of surgery was a preoccupying concern of another Scottish surgeon, James Braid (1795–1860). Braid rejected completely the existence of magnetic fluid, though he still maintained that the hypnotic induction of this state of "nervous sleep" was a physical process, and that it had the capability of ameliorating symptoms of physical ailments. Elliotson and Braid both suffered from the derisive skepticism of the mainstream medical community for their interest in mesmerism, and they shared the same contempt for stage hypnotists, humanist popularizers, and parlor-room mystics. Still, Elliotson and Braid were neither colleagues nor friends. They positioned themselves on opposite sides of the theoretical divide between fluidist interpretations of mesmerism and new neurological and psychological approaches that were to become influential in the development of modern hypnosis.

Neurohypnology

James Braid was born in Fifeshire, Scotland in 1795. He had studied medicine at Edinburgh University and became interested in mesmerism after seeing a performance in Manchester on November 13, 1841. The demonstration was presented by a traveling stage hypnotist from Switzerland, Charles Lafontaine (1803–1892). Child of a theatrical family, Lafontaine possessed the steely gaze of a Svengali-style mesmerist. He dressed all in black and sported an unfashionably long but dramatically dark beard. His style of demonstration inspired a generation of imitators who furthered a popular and profitable form of public entertainment in Britain. Lafontaine had a predilection for putting on stage subjects who would demonstrate insensibility to torturous pain. Famously, he had one of his subjects hold the live wires of a battery. To assure skeptics, one night he tested the battery on a fully conscious member of the audience who, it was reported, "gave a shout that we shall never forget as long as we live."[41] In addition to shocking his subjects, he also burned their fingers in candle flames, made them breathe ammonia, lanced them with pins, and inflicted other impressive torments on them, which the mesmerized subjects endured without apparent discomfort.

As Braid records his first encounter with mesmerism, he went to the demonstration by Lafontaine on the evening of November 13, 1841 a skeptic, "fully inclined to join with those who considered the whole to be a system of collusion or delusion, or of excited imagination, sympathy, or imitation."[42] Braid gives no details of the evening, only to say that his initial prejudices were confirmed. He was not impressed. Lafontaine, in his personal memoir published in 1866, gives a different account: "I put to sleep a number of persons who were well known residents of Manchester … I caused deaf mutes to hear, operated a number of different brilliant cures, and then retired to Birmingham.[43]

Braid was dismissive of all that he witnessed, but returned to another demonstration six days later where he glimpsed something he felt to be a "real phenomenon": the inability of mesmerized patients to open their eyes. Wanting to determine a physiological cause of this, Braid conducted a set of experiments of his own, using a good friend for his first subject, followed by his curious wife and one of his man-servants, all kept ignorant as to the nature of the experiment. As a result of his activities, Braid became convinced that the secret of mesmerism was connected to the eyes of the subjects and could be explained "on the principle of a derangement of the state of the cerebro-spinal centres, and of the circulatory, and respiratory, and muscular systems induced, as I have explained, by a fixed stare, absolute repose of body, fixed attention, and suppressed respiration."[44]

Braid began to publish his ideas as early as 1842.[45] His theory of eye-fixation specifically challenged the fluidist position that required stimulus from an external magnetized agent. Braid's argument was straightforward: the effects of mesmerism are due to the "physical and psychical condition of the patient," rather than the will of the mesmerist, the physical passes of his hands, or the power of a magnetized object. Braid asserted that mesmerism and the phenomena it produced occurred without "exciting in activity some mystical universal fluid or medium."[46]

With what he was convinced was a breakthrough discovery in hand, Braid began almost immediately to deliver public lectures and to give private demonstrations. Braid introduced his own terminology, including the words "hypnotism" and "hypnotize," adapted from *hypnos*, the Greek word for sleep. As early as 1821, French mesmerist Hénin de Cuvillers had suggested over 300 terms related to animal magnetism beginning with the prefix "hyno-", but Braid is recognized for crafting and popularizing the set of terms that would catch on, and become part of common shared usage.[47] Braid's most important and his only book-length publication, *Neurypnology, or the rationale of nervous sleep*, expanded on his new usage, and presented the results of his extensive experimentation.[48] As described at length in *Neurypnology*, his patients experienced cures or amelioration of symptoms in ailments ranging from rheumatism, to skin disorder, to backward curvature of the spine, to stroke-induced paralysis.

By the late 1840s, Braid was framing his theories in an explicitly psychological way, but always connected to specific physiological processes. He consistently induced in his subjects what he considered to be a special state of consciousness related to, but different from, ordinary sleep. This "nervous sleep," or hypnosis, was induced in discrete physiological stages, which Braid identified as "torpor," "catalepsy," and "anesthenia." By rejecting animal magnetism, but locating the phenomena associated with mesmerism in physiology, Braid was also distinguishing his theories from the arguments that were percolating in France, influenced by the work of Deleuze and Faria, which asserted that the subjects' expectation was the true engine at work, and that it was not necessary that they experience a physiologically and measurably "real" altered state.[49]

In general, Braid was dismissive of other mesmerists of nearly every other theoretical orientation. He expended considerable effort distinguishing his work from theirs, untangling the chronological appearance of particular insights and techniques, and portioning out credit and condemnation as strategically as he could. Under the circumstances of considerable professional hostility the only way he could regain the respect of the mainstream medical community was to distance it from the most significant points of controversy associated with mesmerism. To accomplish this Braid incorporated some aspects of mesmerism as practiced by animists under the term "hypnosis," while disdaining other traditional associations still held by fluidists as "mesmerism." In a letter to the *Lancet* he explains that he adopted the word hypnotism in order to "get rid of the erroneous theory about a magnetic fluid or exoteric (sic) influence of any description being the cause of the sleep. I distinctly avowed that *hypnotism* laid no claim to produce any phenomena 'which were not quite reconcilable with well-established physiological and psychological principles.'"[50]

In addition to insisting on nonmystical explanations for the phenomena that he produced in his subjects, Braid also attacked as non-credible fabrications any phenomena produced by mesmerists that could not be explained through his own theories. He did not reject outright the possibility of hypnotically induced clairvoyance, for instance, but only rejected its association with the paranormal, arguing that it was a form of ordinary perception honed through focused attention. He laid claim to the invention of induction techniques based on eye-fixation, which he believed produced more consistent results than mesmeric techniques which, when they worked, were likely to be *inadvertently* making use of eye-fixation. He makes this argument in an 1851 article in the *Monthly Journal of Medical Science*, where he takes on the

American mesmerists for borrowing his techniques without crediting him, and for misunderstanding the dynamics of their own practices. Braid believed that the process of focused attention, heightened through hypnosis, was enough to explain all the genuine physiological phenomena produced by mesmerists of all varieties.[51]

Braid died in 1860, but his terminology, his fixed-eye techniques, and his emphasis on clear stages of nervous sleep crossed over to France with Eugène Azam (1822–1899), a professor of medicine at Bordeaux. After finding a reference to Braid's *Neurypnology* and a description of his techniques, Azam began experiments of his own using Braid's approach.[52] Historians have suggested that a period of "Braidism" followed in France, but much of Braid's fame may be retrospective; the degree to which he directly influenced later hypnotic theory or merely foreshadowed it is contested.[53] To whatever extent Braid contributed to the intellectual developments that followed in France in the last decades of the nineteenth century, his resolute, if strategically self-interested, alteration of vocabulary coincided with a sea change in the grounds of debate.

From Magnetism to Hypnosis

For most of the nineteenth century in both France and Britain, the disagreement between fluidists and animists over the source of mesmerism's power gave shape to theoretical notions and controversies, including those surrounding the relationship between magnetizer and subject. If an external magnetic stimulus directed by the mesmerist was operating upon his subjects, then the relationship between them was constrained to a fairly narrow set of dynamics: there was an actor, the conductor of magnetic fluid, and someone who was acted upon, the recipient of the magnetic force. In a more immediate sense, someone was doing the touching, and someone was being touched.

The necessary intimacy of the drama of magnetism could not help but reflect preexisting cultural understandings of appropriate and inappropriate touch, understandings that mapped to multiple social hierarchies. It is no coincidence that women rarely were seen mesmerizing men; that members of the lower classes were not often in a position to demonstrate upon the upper class; and that patients were not mesmerizing their doctors. In India, where Esdaile trained his army of native mesmerists in a technique involving hours of compassionate stroking, the patients in nearly all cases were native, of similar or lower caste. An exception was occasionally made that transgressed both racial and social hierarchies, but ultimately the racist colonial cultural divide appears to have been too powerful. Soon after Esdaile's departure in 1851, the experiment of mesmerism in India was over.[54]

The issues surrounding the use of touch by mesmerists were culturally loaded and, not surprisingly, left them vulnerable to charges of sexual impropriety. These had been launched since Franz Mesmer first tried to cure the young pianist, Maria-Theresa Paradis. Stage hypnotists exploited the association to enhance personal presence. In Europe during the late nineteenth century, for instance, the successful Belgian-born stage hypnotist, Alfred Odonat, who went by the stage name Donato, employed his powerful gaze in a frankly sexual way.[55]

Although Braid the animist can most easily be distinguished from Elliotson the fluidist by their diametrically opposed convictions about the reality of magnetic fluid, Braid's more significant innovation was in technique. Because he induced hypnosis through eye-fixation, Braid did not have to touch his subject. In theory, at least, this allowed anyone to mesmerize anyone. In practice, the real shift was from a purely physiological to a more psychological view of mesmerism. It meant that the mesmerist was no longer a conductor of an external force. In the view of both proponents and critics, however, this did not necessarily mean that the mesmerist was without exceptional power.

Beginning with Faria in 1815, some animists had challenged the notion that the experiences of a mesmerized subject were due to the overpowering personal will of the mesmerist. Yet despite Faria's conviction that the subjects were really in charge, the charismatic strength of his own personality was a persuasive contradiction. The degree to which the will of the mesmerist was acting upon the subject still remained an issue. Even if the technique of induction did not involve intimate touch, the ubiquitous social differences between mesmerists and their subjects in both France and Britain in the nineteenth century were powerfully suggestive of innate personal differences in power of will and susceptibility between the mesmerized and those who mesmerized them, and the hypnotized and those who hypnotized them.

Figure 4 *Stage hypnotist Donato, suggesting to young men that they feel extremely cold. From* L'Illustrazione Italiana, *June 6, 1886, Mary Evans Picture Library (maryevans.com).*

Mesmerism did not simply disappear when hypnosis emerged; in fact their practices and techniques overlap in complicated and tangled ways. By inscribing his theories into language, Braid provided a linguistic divide that became increasingly useful to those who wanted to distinguish their own work from a century of bad press associated with magnets and invisible fluid. But hypnotism as Braid worked to define and disseminate it did not set off a revolutionary transformation of mesmerism in Britain, nor was it the only game in town. Elliotson's journal *The Zoist* was still the most important English language publication on mesmerism and its related ideas through the middle of the nineteenth century. Elliotson's approach, which was practical and medical, was not replaced by Braid's hypnosis; it would only lose its steam with the advancement of chemical anesthesia.

Implicit within the debate between fluidists and animists, more powerful than the issues relating to the relations between mesmerist

Figure 5 *James Braid hypnotizing through eye-fixation. Lucien Laurent-Gsell, 1891, in Foveau de Courmelles,* L'hypnotisme, *Mary Evans Picture Library (maryevans.com).*

and subjects, was the disagreement over the nature of magnetism and the source of its power. Elliotson's attachment to the physical reality of magnetism and his interest in phrenology made it difficult for him to tolerate the direction Braid was taking, toward psychological explanations of the phenomena that both mesmerism and hypnosis produced in subjects. Braid necessarily deemphasized the role of the brain as he explored the malleability of the human mind.

Elliotson and Braid were equally unsympathetic toward the spiritual versions of mesmerism being popularized by Colquhoun. Private séances were taking place in private homes, in parlor rooms and at bedsides across Victorian Britain, in versions much closer to what was going on across the Atlantic. In the United States spiritual philosophy and a new world view had become more important than the strictly medical and instrumental healing uses of the techniques, old and new.

The tension between Braid's hypnotic inductions, Elliotson's phreno-magnetic demonstrations, and Colquhoun's parlor-room séances was a result of their differing convictions about the source of it all. For Elliotson there had to be an external physical force, with measurable effects, following scientific laws. For Braid, the effects of hypnotic induction were still empirically measurable, but the engine was internal, perhaps electrobiological, but originating from within the subject. For Colquhoun and countless other "amateur" mesmerists of Victorian Britain, the source was supernatural, and investigations of the paranormal and lofty spiritual realms were therefore entirely appropriate.

Despite tremendous differences, these British variations had a powerful commonality: all three considered the induction of the trance state to be the one phenomenon that would determine whether a subject was mesmerized, or hypnotized, or not. Alterations of identity and personality became associated with the trance state, and ceased to be as remarkable as they were in the case of the O'Key sisters, who each had developed distinct mesmerized personalities. The trance states induced by Braid in his subjects did not typically reveal such elaborate content, but his new terminology and his approach to hypnosis were to make the trance state, some sort of dissociation from ordinary consciousness, the centerpiece of hypnosis. Although Braid believed suggestibility to be essential to the process, he never entertained the possibility that the trance itself might be another product of suggestion. Braid asserted that the failure, as he perceived it, of Faria and Bertrand to produce trance in all of their patients was clear evidence that their techniques were less effective than his own.[56]

Elliotson's defeat by Wakley was the last round in a long fight, and it represented one of the final and most publicized defeats for the fluidist position. But the passing of belief in magnetic fluid can almost be seen as a side note to the decisive victory of Puységur's style of mesmerism over Mesmer's. Puységur's had enshrined the trance as the aspect of mesmerism viewed to be the essential, even the defining, phenomenon produced through its techniques. And regarding the importance of the trance, Elliotson, Braid, and Colquhoun were in perfect agreement.

Notes

1 Gauld, *History of Hypnotism*, 274, citing Alexandre J. F. Bertrand, *Du magnétisme animal en France, et des jugements qu'en ont portés les sociétiés savants* (Paris: J. B. Bailliere, 1826): 247.
2 For a discussion of the importance of suggestion in Faria's approach to mesmerism, see Crabtree, *From Mesmer to Freud*, 122–123.
3 Gauld, *History of Hypnotism*, 274, citing José-Custodio de Faria, *De la cause du sommeil lucide ou étude de la nature de l'homme* (Paris: H. Jouve, 1906): 27
4 François Joseph Noizet, *Mémoire sur le somnambulisme et le magnétisme animal adressé en 1820 à l'Académie royale de Berlin* (Paris: Plon Frére, 1854).
5 Gauld, *History of Hypnotism*, 132, citing Bertrand, *Du magnétisme animal en France*, XIII–XV.
6 Ibid., 277, citing Bertrand, *Du magnétisme animal en France*, 311.
7 See Melvin A. Gravitz, "Etienne Félix d'Hénin de Cuvillers: A Founder of Hypnosis," *American Journal of Clinical Hypnosis* 36, no. 1 (1993): 7–11.
8 See Alison Winter, *Mesmerized: Powers of Mind in Victorian Britain* (Chicago, University of Chicago Press, 1998): 42.
9 John Campbell Colquhoun, *Isis Revelata: An Inquiry into the Origins, Progress and Present State of Animal Magnetism*, 2d ed., 2 vols. (Edinburgh: Maclachlan and Stewart, 1836).
10 See Fred Kaplan, *Dickens and Mesmerism: The Hidden Springs of Fiction* (Princeton, NJ: Princeton University Press, 1975): 18.
11 For a detailed account of Dupotet's activities, see Winter, *Mesmerized*, 42–48.
12 Kaplan, *Dickens and Mesmerism*, 13. See also Fred Kaplan, "'Mesmeric Mania': The Early Victorians and Animal Magnetism," *Journal of the History of Ideas* 35, no. 4 (1974): 691–702.
13 *The Lancet* September 4, 1837: 509.
14 See Winter, *Mesmerized*, 67–108, for a detailed account and analysis of the mesmeric performances of the O'Key sisters.
15 Ibid.
16 Ibid.
17 See Winter, *Mesmerized*, 90–93.
18 Ibid., 84.
19 Ibid., 85.
20 Ibid., 97. Winter suggests that Wakely had already decided the results before he began, so they weren't actually experiments but another kind of theater.
21 See *The Lancet*, Sept. 1, 1838.

22 Ibid.
23 See Alison Winters, "Emanations from the Sickroom," in Winters, *Mesmerized*, 214–245, for the definitive account of women's involvement with mesmerism in Victorian Britain.
24 Kaplan, *Dickens and Mesmerism*, 52.
25 August Comte, *The Positive Philosophy of Auguste Comte*, trans. Harriet Martineau (New York: Calvin Blanchard, 1855).
26 Harriet Martineau, *Autobiography, with Memorials*, vol. 2, ed. Maria Weston Chapman, 4th ed. (Boston: Houghton, Osgood and Co., 1879): 562–574. Written in 1855, the introduction to Martineau's memoir was originally published in the *London Daily News*, June 29, 1876.
27 For more on Hall see Gauld, *History of Hypnotism*, 204.
28 Winter, *Mesmerized*, 222.
29 Frederic G. Kenyon, ed., *The Letters of Elizabeth Barrett Browning* (New York: Macmillan, 1897): 184.
30 Elizabeth Gaskell, *The Life of Charlotte Brontë*, vol. 1. (New York: D. Appleton, 1857): 166.
31 Harriet Martineau, *Life in the Sickroom: Essays by an Invalid* (London: E. Moxon, 1844).
32 See Diana Postlethwaite, "Mothering and Mesmerism in the Life of Harriet Martineau," *Signs* 14, no. 3 (1989), 583–609. See also Alison Winter, "Harriet Martineau and the Reform of the Invalid in Victorian England," *The Historical Journal* 38, no. 3 (1995): 597–616.
33 See Gauld, *History of Hypnotism*, 207.
34 See John Elliotson, *Numerous Cases of Surgical Operations without Pain in the Mesmeric State with Remarks upon the Opposition of Many Members of the Royal Medical and Chirurgical Society and Others to the Reception of the Inestimable Blessings of Mesmerism* (London: H. Bailliere, 1843).
35 For a full discussion of the social and racial context behind Esdaile's presence in India, see Winter's chapter addressing the issue, "Colonizing Sensations in Victorian India," in Winter, *Mesmerized*, 187–212.
36 James Esdaile, *Mesmerism in India and its Practical Applications in Surgery and Medicine* (London: Longman, Brown, Green, and Longmans, 1846): 42.
37 Ibid., 43–44.
38 Ibid., 44.
39 See Winter, *Mesmerized*, 196 for the list originally published in "Accounts of More Painless Surgical Operations, Communicated by Dr. Elliotson," *The Zoist*, 3 (1846): 196–197.
40 See Winter, *Mesmerized*, 201.
41 Cited by Gauld, *History of Hypnotism*, 204, cited from a report in *The Times*, July 20, 1841.

42 James Braid, *Neurypnology*, reprinted in *Braid on Hypnotism: The Beginnings of Modern Hypnosis*, ed. Arthur Waite (New York: The Julian Press, 1960): 98.
43 Cited by Arthur Waite, "Biographical Introduction," in Braid, *Braid on Hypnotism*, 7. The original source is Charles Lafontaine, *Mémoires d'un Magnétiseur, par Ch. Lafontaine, suivis de l'examen phrénologique de l'auteur par le Docteur Castle*, vol. 1. (Paris, 1866). Waite cites long passages from Lafontaine's memoirs to debunk Lafontaine's claims to have been involved later in Braid's hypnotic experiments.
44 Braid, *Braid on Hypnotism*, 101–102.
45 See James Braid, *Satanic Agency and Mesmerism Reviewed, in a Letter to the Rev. H. McNeile, A.M. of Liverpool, in Reply to a Sermon Preached by Him in St. Jude's Church, Liverpool, on Sunday, April 10th, 1842* (Manchester: Sims and Dinham, Galt and Anderson, 1842). For a discussion of its significance see Crabtree, *Mesmer to Freud*, 158.
46 Braid, *Neurypnology*, in *Braid on Hypnotism*, 102.
47 See Crabtree, *Mesmer to Freud*, 158
48 James Braid, *Neurypnology; or the Rationale of Nervous Sleep Considered in Relation with Animal Magnetism. Illustrated by Numerous Cases of Its Successful Application in the Relief and Cure of Disease* (London: John Churchill, 1843).
49 See Braid, *Neurohypnology*, Braid, *Braid*, 88–90.
50 James Braid, "Mr. Braid on Hypnotism: To the Editor of *The Lancet*," *Lancet*, May, 1845. See also Winter, *Mesmerized*, 185.
51 Crabtree, *Mesmer to Freud*, 160, citing James Braid, *Electro-Biological Phenomena Considered Physiologically and Psychologically* (Edinburgh: Sutherland and Knox, 1851): 6.
52 Gauld, *History of Hypnotism*, 287, 364–369. Azam is best remembered for his early work with patients exhibiting symptoms of dissociation and multiple personality. See also Ellenberger, *Discovery of the Unconscious*, 136–138.
53 See Gauld, *History of Hypnotism*, 287–288.
54 For a discussion, see Winter, *Mesmerized*, 211–212.
55 For a description of a memorable encounter between Donato and the young Matisse, see Hilary Spurling, *The Unknown Matisse: A life of Henri Matisse: The Early Years, 1869–1908* (Berkeley: The University of California Press, 2001): 32.
56 See Braid, *Neurohypnology*, Braid, *Braid*, 88–90.

CHAPTER FOUR

Body and Soul

The United States was intellectually alive in the middle of the nineteenth century, fully engaged in religious revivals, progressive reforms, and spiritual movements whose members often dabbled in them all. Abolitionists, suffragists, and vegetarians rubbed elbows with homeopaths, phrenologists, and followers of the Swedish mystic Emanuel Swedenborg. Although there was as yet no formal discipline of psychology in the United States to receive and interpret mesmerism, there were widespread and hearty philosophical debates ongoing within both popular and ecclesiastical settings. When animal magnetism arrived on the western shore of the Atlantic, there was an audience ready for it.

Sporadic lectures on mesmerism were given in the United States during the first few decades of the 1800s. In 1829, for instance, a French teacher at West Point Military Academy who would make an important contribution to early hydrogeology, Joseph du Commun, also lectured on animal magnetism.[1] But the practice wasn't to attract popular attention until late 1837 when *Histoire Critique de Magnétisme Animal*, by Joseph Deleuze, was introduced to the magnetic community in the United States by its English translator, Thomas Hartshorn.[2] Published as *Practical Instruction in Animal Magnetism*, Hartshorn's book included in its appendix to the revised edition a collection of eyewitness testimony, not only of cures associated with mesmerism, but of episodes of clairvoyant and other psychic phenomena.[3]

This association with the paranormal would take on special significance in the United States where the medical aspects and healing properties associated with mesmerism were to be upstaged by its spiritual benefits. Mesmerism also aroused mystics and romanticists in Europe; however, the spiritual impulse there seems to have been more effectively dampened by rationalism and the rise of scientific positivism.[4] While Europeans tended to focus on the healing properties of mesmerism, in the United States it was other, more wondrous phenomena that caught the imagination, and the esoteric possibilities associated with achieving higher states of consciousness were eagerly investigated.

Mesmerism in the United States

European writers had warned about the dangers associated with the use of mesmerism outside the strict ethical guidelines of medical practice. Deleuze went so far as to suggest that only women should be magnetizers of other women, because of the danger of sexual exploitation that arose from the necessarily physically intimate relationship between a magnetizer and the subject.[5] In the United States the critics of mesmerism not only warned of sexual danger, but were particularly alarmed by spiritual dangers arising from the apparent loss of personal will, including the dire possibility of satanic possession. In American literature the perils of mesmerism were eloquently addressed in the writings of Nathaniel Hawthorne (1804–1864). In *The House of Seven Gables*, published in 1851, Hawthorne creates a mesmerist who controls a young woman and brings about her death.[6] In *The Blithedale Romance*, which came out the following year, he goes further to suggest that the power of a mesmerist could actually destroy its subject's soul.[7]

In addition to the concern over the spiritual dangers mesmerism presented, the popularization of mesmerism in the United States also differed significantly from its European manifestations in another significant way. In Europe the practice of mesmerism was a pastime of aristocrats, its demonstrations attended by the medically educated elite. From its popular beginnings in the 1830s in the United States mesmerism's most enthusiastic audiences and practitioners came largely from the middle class. Demonstrations occurred not in laboratories or at universities, but in private homes. American mesmerists were clergymen as often as they were practicing doctors. This is not to say that medical men were not intrigued by reports from abroad that mesmerism had powerful healing properties. There were American doctors who took up the study in the name of science. But Hartshorn's translation made mesmerism accessible to the lay person. This easy availability of technical knowledge was a boon to the people who became involved in mesmerism as entertainment, as well as those who viewed it as tool for spiritual development. In the end, mesmerism as medical research trailed a distant third.

Charles Poyen St. Sauveur (died 1844) is credited with inspiring the first real wave of popular interest in mesmerism, which he actively practiced in the United States from 1837 to 1838. Introduced to the phenomenon as a medical student in Paris, Poyen came across it again in the French West Indies. In late 1836 he arrived in Lowell, Massachusetts and began to offer lectures in mesmerism while championing its philosophy. Although he had no official credential to substantiate the title, Poyen referred to himself as "Professor of Animal Magnetism."[8] He was one of the first in what was soon to be a parade of traveling mesmerists demonstrating feats of magnetism across New England. He based his practice in Providence, Rhode Island, Hartshorn's hometown, which was to become "the Mecca of American magnetism."[9] His work was widely reported in press stories of his day. Poyen used volunteers from the audience in his demonstrations, as well as professional somnambulists who traveled with him. He reportedly succeeded in putting his subjects into trance about half the time.[10] If subjects wanted to be cured of physical ailments he would use the traditional "hand passes" associated with Mesmer, but healing was not the most spectacular of the effects of animal magnetism that he demonstrated. His subjects often appeared to be clairvoyant, a phenomenon that Poyen did not consider to be supernatural, but a common human capability.[11]

Apart from its spectacular aspects, Poyen's presentation of magnetism also struck a chord with his New England audience because it appealed to several strains of cultural thought simultaneously. In a brief but heated pamphlet war, Poyen defended another magnetizer, William Stone, who served as superintendent of New York public schools. Stone was an activist for compulsory public education as well as an abolitionist; his interest in magnetism was strongly tied to his philosophical and political orientation. When Stone began conducting demonstrations out of his home, these were attended by clergymen, businessmen, New York State senators, and even the governor of the state.[12]

By promoting the personal development of individuals, and by extension the perfectibility of society, mesmerism in the United States was particularly appealing to political dreamers and progressive reformers.[13]

Poyen returned to France in 1839, but in the decade that followed, magnetizers with clairvoyant somnambulist sidekicks took their shows on the road, giving demonstrations of the power of mesmerism to packed audiences across America. By 1843 there were some 200 professional magnetizers in Boston alone.[14] As its popular success grew, mesmerism attracted more interest from the medical establishment in the United States. The same lively intellectual climate that allowed mesmerism to thrive, however, also insured that it would only tread the waters of medical respectability. Through this period mesmerism remained entangled with intellectual innovations that were being explored at the margins of mainstream scientific research and medical practice.

Phrenomagnetism and Electrobiology

During the 1840s mesmerism collided with the practice of phrenology and emerged as a new medical movement. Phrenomagnetists believed that magnetic fluid could be directed at a particular part of the head and that this would draw from the subject symptoms associated with its phrenological "organ." Among the first proponents of phrenomagnetism in the United States were physician and teacher of medicine, Charles Caldwell (1772–1853), and his student Joseph Rodes Buchanan (1814–1899). Though Caldwell's father, an Irish immigrant and a devout Presbyterian, wanted him to become a minister, he ended up studying medicine at the University of Pennsylvania where, in 1796, he received his medical degree. In 1837 he moved to Kentucky and became the first professor of medicine at the Louisville Medical Institute. Caldwell was a powerful speaker and teacher as well as a prolific translator and writer. He had conferred with mesmerists in France and while he was in Paris learned of phrenology from Johann Spurzheim. After the introduction of phrenology into the United States by Spurzheim, who reputedly converted thousands as a result of lectures he gave in 1832, Caldwell was to become one of the champions of a hybrid practice combining the techniques of phrenology and mesmerism.[15]

Caldwell's book, *Facts in Mesmerism*, took a scientific view of the practice, and sought to answer the objections of skeptics through a clear presentation of the facts as he saw them.[16] He promoted the use of the term mesmerism, in preference to animal magnetism, because he believed the source of the technique's power was not physical but psychological in nature, having to do with the influence of the mesmerist, a reflection of his physical presence, as well as his will. Caldwell penned caustic rejoinders to his critics and set out to defend mesmerism from those who criticized it as dangerous or irreligious. He wanted to address religious ideas scientifically, promoting mesmerism as a "moral and religious engine of great power."[17]

If Caldwell was fascinated by the relationship of mesmerism to the human mind, Joseph Buchanan, son of philosopher Joseph Buchanan, was as captivated by the brain. A Kentucky native, Buchanan received his medical degree from the Louisville Medical Institute where he was mentored by Caldwell. Buchanan's interest in phrenology began with experimental investigations of the anatomy of the human brain. In 1841 he found that if he stimulated one particular spot on the temporal lobe of his subjects' brains with electromagnetic energy, he could induce them to have visions and to feel the presence of spirits. Sympathetic to the Spiritualist movement, Buchanan interpreted his subjects' experiences as authentic spiritual experiences, rather than hallucinations or products of imagination. He called this spot on the brain the "organ of spirituality."[18]

Buchanan was interested in establishing scientific bases for other apparently supernatural phenomena. His neurological principle of "impressibility," for instance, advanced the argument that although the social world imprints itself upon the brain in a physical way through the senses, the brain can also be impressed through nonphysical senses, such as clairvoyance or telepathy. Reciprocally, human beings also impress themselves upon the world, leaving a sort of psychic residue on everything they touch.[19] Buchanan coined the term *psychometry* to describe the process by which these impressions can be restored. He believed that certain talented individuals, when touching pieces of clothing from people not physically present, would be able to diagnose their illnesses; likewise, when holding an ancient artifact, they might attain knowledge of the civilization that created it. Buchanan's intellectual ambitions were wide-ranging; he eventually outlined a "neurological anthropology" in which philosophy, theology, and physiology could influence each other.[20]

Another man who claimed credit for combining phrenology with magnetism was Robert Collyer (1823–1912). An Englishman who had been exposed to mesmerism while studying medicine with John Elliotson in London, he, like Caldwell, learned about phrenology from Spurzheim in Paris. Collyer arrived in the United States in 1839. This was the year that Poyen left; Collyer swiftly took his place at center stage, popularizing mesmerism all across New England. Unlike Buchanan, who championed phrenomagnetism to the end of his career, Collyer was eventually to move beyond it. It is not hard to understand why phrenology would go by the wayside in the United States. It was a rigid system that located moral character in unchanging physiology. Mesmerism was always more compatible with philosophical systems that also allowed for unique development and personal transformation.[21]

In addition to the medical phrenomagnetists, there were non-medical men like James Stanley Grimes (1807–1903), John Boves Dods (1795–1872), and La Roy Sunderland (1803–1885) who were also traveling, lecturing, and writing to popular audiences about mesmerism, with and without the addition of phrenology, during this time. It has been argued that American mesmerists were engaged in a collaborative effort to construct a popular psychology that could explain religious and paranormal phenomena.[22] Although men like Grimes, Dods, and Sunderland did not conduct medical research nor direct the results of their investigations to the scientific community, they still employed scientific terminology to explain what they were doing. Grimes claimed that mesmeric phenomena were due to a combination of self-deception, a subject's belief, and a desire to conform; however, he, like most American mesmerists, could not let go of the physicality of the technique.[23] It was not the invisible power of magnets that intrigued him as much as the new invisible power found in electricity.

For many mesmerists phrenomagnetism gave way to new theories of electrobiology, and electric power replaced magnetic power as the key causal metaphor to explain illness and healing as well as the mysterious and otherwise inexplicable phenomena associated with mesmerism. Grimes, a lawyer who practiced in Boston and New York, coined the term *etherium,* which he described as "the natural substance occupying space which connects the planets and the earth and which communicates light, heat, electricity, gravitation, and mental emanations to one body from another and from one mind to another."[24] With echoes of Mesmer's hubris, Dods claimed that "there is but one cause of disease; which is the electricity of the system thrown out of balance."[25]

Dods, Grimes, and other electrobiologists produced in their subjects the symptoms and behaviors that would later become the main spectacles of stage hypnosis: catalepsy, insensitivity to pain, amnesia, and apparently involuntary actions out of character for the individuals who produced them. Although the demonstrations of the era anticipated and perhaps paved the way for the eventual use of hypnosis for pure entertainment, that was not what the electrobiologists thought they were up to. Dods was convinced that they were "riding on the glorious chariot of science."[26] Like Caldwell, he felt that mesmerism would provide scientific proof for key aspects of religious faith.

The preoccupation of American mesmerists with religion rather than medicine provides a striking contrast to the theories and practices of mesmerism originating in Europe. Rather than using mesmerism to heal the body, American mesmerists believed it was necessary to treat the whole person. The context in which one was magnetized was less clinical and more like a religious revival.[27] In fact, a significant number of mesmerists were themselves former revivalists, and even when they weren't, they still were likely to follow the New England revival circuit. Dods was typical of this group of men. He had been a Universalist minister in Provincetown, Massachusetts before becoming a mesmerist. He had previously abandoned his belief in the vengeful Calvinist God, preferring to preach the message that all were saved. When he found mesmerism, he left the Universalist church as well, but he did not leave behind the centrality of religion, even when he shifted to scientific terminology and explained his practice as "electric psychology."[28] Mesmerism provided its practitioners with a scientific basis for spirituality and a method of firmly connecting the mystical to the physical world.

Dods considered animal magnetism to be "the grand agent employed by the creator to move and govern the universe."[29] He didn't claim that mesmerism itself should be the basis for religion, nor was it to replace Christianity. He believed that mesmerism could both complement and explain religion. If God were connected to magnetic energy, then what mesmerism was doing was giving people a way to have direct contact with God. He believed that as an enhancement to the practice of Christian faith, mesmerism could be "a religious engine of great power."[30]

Mesmerism and Spiritualism

As the Second Great Awakening was winding down in the 1830s, Shakers, Adventists, Mormons, Communitarians, and Millenarians were still gaining converts. Mesmerism filled the same hunger for authentic spiritual experience that had inspired an array of religious movements. Many former revivalists took up progressive causes, becoming involved first in Universalism, then taking up mesmerism, and ending up at spiritualism. As a spiritual path mesmerism provided intense personal experience, both physical and spiritual, that could be attained without having to take on the weight of a creed.[31]

The most intellectually significant of the American mesmerists of the middle nineteenth century was La Roy Sunderland, whose career began quite typically. Sunderland had been a Methodist Episcopal preacher and revivalist through the 1820s, but became disenchanted with the revivalist road to spirituality after concluding that the experiences of the participants had a human rather than a divine origin.[32] He withdrew from his denomination and became an active abolitionist, helping to establish the Wesleyan antislavery movement. Like other former revivalists, he next found mesmerism, but then his story takes an unusual turn. At a demonstration in 1839 Sunderland recognized a mesmerized woman as someone he had previously "entranced" during a revival back in 1824. As Sunderland recalled, she recognized and corroborated their connection as well:

> She appeared to be in a state of ecstatic joy, when she grasped my hand and said "O, Brother Sunderland, this is the happiest state I was ever in. It is heaven. And do you remember how I went into this state under that powerful sermon you preached in our church in Scituate Harbor years ago? I was then 'caught up to Paradise,' as St. Paul was, and where I saw Jesus and all the angels so happy. Yes, Brother Sunderland and this is the same heaven—the same as when my soul was converted and filled with the love of God."[33]

It came to Sunderland that the woman had achieved an altered state of consciousness in both contexts, and that the two experiences must have some common source. From this insight he came to recognize the power of cultural expectations and the social effects of suggestion that work together to induce someone to enter into a trance state. For Sunderland the same process of "mental sympathy" could be observed at a revival and at a session of mesmerism.

Sunderland's career illustrates the engagement of mesmerists in the exploration of a swiftly expanding territory that lay somewhere between popular religion and popular psychology.[34] Sunderland coined the term *pathetism* to describe his version of magnetism. He had already rejected the materialist explanations of phrenology, so letting go of the reality of magnetic fluid was an easy step for him. His interpretation of mesmerism-related phenomena became increasingly less physiological and more undeniably psychological as his understandings progressed. In both private research and public demonstrations, Sunderland induced subjects to perform antics on stage, achieve catalepsy, and feel no pain when having their teeth extracted, but he concluded that none of these effects were due to his power, nor his will, nor even the relationship between himself and his subjects, but were essentially self-induced by the mesmeric subjects.[35]

Following his wholehearted immersion in mesmerism, Sunderland next became a Spiritualist, and he was not alone in this migration. It was a well-trodden path that led mesmeric clairvoyants toward second careers as Spiritualist mediums in the second half of the nineteenth century. The Spiritualist movement was never a unified religious movement, but included a gestalt of related activities that all claimed some relationship to the séances that began in Hydesville, New York in 1848 after the house of farmer John Fox was troubled by a poltergeist and his daughters found they could communicate with the ghost. The Fox sisters were to become the strange attractors for a chaotic and heterogeneous network of religious seekers of two main varieties, those who wanted to be mediums and to communicate with the spirits of the dead, and those who were seeking spiritual growth through contact with metaphysical worlds. Mesmerists who drifted to Spiritualism were usually of the second variety.

Like mesmerists, Spiritualists often saw their practices as compatible with their Christian faith, providing direct experience of what otherwise they could only understand intellectually. What mesmerism could contribute to Spiritualism was a scientific basis for their experiences.[36] Buchanan, the phrenomagnetist, served the Spiritualist movement well when he located in the human brain the phrenological organ for contacting spirits. From his own angle, Dods offered to his fellow Spiritualists the theory that poltergeists achieved physical presence through electricity. Sunderland too was initially captivated by the spiritual possibilities offered by Spiritualism, but he renounced it at the end of his life, dying a skeptic and an atheist.

Mesmerism and Swedenborgianism

A significant number of American Spiritualists became entangled with the teachings of Swedish philosopher Emanuel Swedenborg (1688–1771), whose mystical revelations led him to systematically reinterpret Christianity. Through 30 weighty volumes he detailed the development of the human soul through a hierarchy of spiritual planes. The esoteric results obtained by mixing magnetism, Spiritualism, and Swedenborgianism are illustrated most fully in the life of Andrew Jackson Davis (1826–1910), known as the "Seer of Poughkeepsie."

Davis's autobiography provides fascinating details of his early life, though as a whole it reads more like hagiography than biography.[37] The mythical life of Davis began in childhood when he precociously debated with his Calvinist teachers, arguing, as many Spiritualists did, against the brutal tenet of predestination, the idea that God had determined for all of us, before birth, whether we were to be damned or saved:

> Could a God of Love, knowing for certain that I would be miserable after death, bring me into existence? Yes, Uncle Isaac, that's what I want to know. I keep a-thinkin' in my brain that a God of Love and Wisdom is TOO GOOD to create anybody to suffer in hell for ever.[38]

After rejecting Calvinism, Davis passed through both Methodism and Universalism before finally embracing Spiritualism. The miraculous and supernatural events of childhood make his arrival there seem almost inevitable.

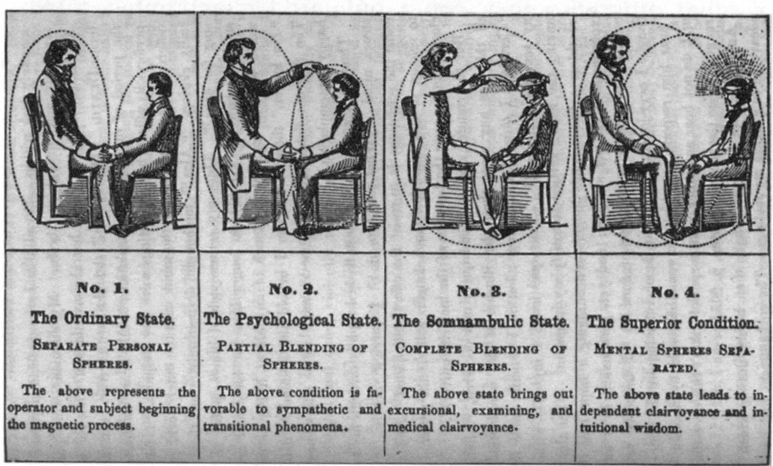

Figure 6 *The four magnetic states according to A. J. Davis. Illustration from Andrew Jackson Davis, 1857,* The Magic Staff.

Davis' life was changed irrevocably in 1843 when he was chosen out of the audience by traveling mesmerist, James Stanley Grimes, to come on stage as one of his magnetic subjects. Grimes failed to entrance him: "The professor went through a series of motions–resembling the 'presto change' of legerdemain performers–and then imperiously said: 'You can't open your eyes!' He was mistaken. I did open my eyes with perfect ease."[39] Davis, who was at the time working as a shoe store clerk, was still intrigued, and a few nights later he was successfully entranced by a local tailor by the name of William Livingston. Livingston duly discovered that Davis was clairvoyant, with the power to diagnosis illness at a distance.

The two men quit their jobs and for about 18 months Livingston mesmerized Davis on stage for the benefit of the curious and the ill. Slowly Davis became aware that his true calling was not to be a clairvoyant somnambulist, but a trance medium, as he increasingly found that he was able to bring back detailed messages, apparently from other worlds. He began to give lectures on spiritual philosophy while in a trance state.

Davis traded his tailor-turned-mesmerist, Livingston, for Dr. S. Silas Lyon, a professional mesmerist. The wisdom Davis received while entranced was carefully transcribed by a Unitarian minister, William Fishbough. This could not have been an easy job; Davis' book *Principles of Nature* (1847) was a hefty 786 pages long. The messages that Davis transmitted combined socialist idealism with progressive spiritual philosophy.[40] More than anything else, however, Davis' message was Swedenborgian, and this was no wonder, because as Davis eventually revealed, it was Swedenborg himself who was "coming through" to him. Swedenborg had appeared to Davis as early as March of 1844, alerting him to his important destiny as a medium and healer.

Davis' claim that he was, in modern terms, "channeling" Swedenborg might not have had much purchase, had he not received the initial and authoritative backing of George Bush (1796–1859), a professor of Hebrew and Oriental Literature at New York University, and a prominent Swedenborgian. In his book, *Mesmer and Swedenborg* (1847), Bush skillfully made use of mesmerism to provide scientific plausibility for Swedenborg's philosophical claims.[41] Although he was later to temper his enthusiasm, Bush initially gave credence to Davis's connection with Swedenborg, noting the sharp contrast in vocabulary, erudition, and demeanor between Davis in trance and Davis in waking life.[42] Bush also experimented with mesmerism on his own with great success. He records that his subjects often achieved states of mystical rapture, some even attaining the higher states of consciousness described by Swedenborg.[43]

Another of the sympathetic witnesses to Davis' trance sessions who was also involved with Swedenborgianism was mystic and poet Thomas Lake Harris (1823–1906), the founder of the utopian Brotherhood of New Light Community. Harris shared with Davis the belief that spiritual truths should be experienced directly: "to believe in God is but to believe that the spirit which we feel flowing into ourselves flows from an Infinite Existing Source."[44] This direct personal experience of the divine is what mesmerism was able to contribute to the spiritual seekers of the era.

Davis engendered as many skeptics as followers, among them Edgar Allen Poe (1809–1849) who produced a series of short stories during the 1840s that addressed mesmerism, including "Mesmeric Revelation," "Tale of Ragged Mountain," and "Mesmerism in Articulo Mortis."[45] In "Mesmeric Revelation," Poe transmitted ideas found in the popular book, *Facts in Mesmerism*,[46] written by English poet and amateur mesmerist, the Rev. Chauncy Hare Townshend (1798–1868). Poe's prose in the piece was so

Figure 7 *While being mesmerized by C. H. Townshend, a young woman mesmerizes her sister. Illustration from Chauncey Hare Townshend, 1844,* Facts in Mesmerism, *Mary Evans Picture Library (maryevans.com).*

pedagogical in style that some literary commentators have interpreted this as an indication that Poe believed mesmerism allowed its subjects to achieve transcendental insight; others are convinced of his cynicism.[47] Certainly Poe was unimpressed by Swedenborgian thought as he had witnessed it being channeled through the trances of Andrew Jackson Davis: "There surely can*not* be more things in Heaven and Earth than are dreamt of (oh, Andrew Jackson Davis!) in *your* philosophy."[48]

New Thought and Christian Science

In addition to its influence on Spiritualism, mesmerism is also recognized for its influence on the development of two other religious movements in the United States: New Thought and Christian Science. Both of these can be traced through the same intellectual lineage to the work of a man who, much like Davis, began his career in the audience of a lecture hall. It was in 1836 that Phineas Parkhurst Quimby (1802–1846) heard a demonstration offered by Charles Poyen in Belfast, Maine. Quimby became a loyal follower of Poyen, studying the techniques of magnetism until he had mastered them and could begin to travel and teach on his own. He first employed Lucius Burkman, a clairvoyant telepath with the seeming ability to diagnose illness, as his somnambulist.

Quimby by all accounts was a sincere and tireless healer. In 1865 he treated 12,000 people through a combination of techniques. Some echoed traditional practices of mesmerism: he would give subjects magnetized water to drink. Others were idiosyncratic: with the help of Burkman, he implanted healing images telepathically into the minds of his subjects. The key moment in Quimby's career occurred when he came to believe that Burkman was not actually diagnosing disease, but was only reading the minds of the subjects, and relating what *the subject believed* to be the cause of a disease. He observed that it didn't matter what medicine was prescribed. If the subject believed it would work, the medicine would provide the cure. It was a short step from these insights to a philosophical position on illness that we today recognize as acknowledging both the physiological effects of psychological stress and the efficacy of placebo treatment on a wide range of psychological and physical ailments.[49]

What makes Quimby's style of cure most interesting is that he accompanied all of his physical and psychic ministrations with simple directed conversation. As Quimby explained the dynamics of illness, someone who is suffering from a physical ailment is "deceived into a belief that he has or is liable to have a disease, the belief is catching, and the effects follow from it."[50] Quimby came to believe that disease was simply the product of wrong thinking. It followed that truth would be the cure. It has been cogently argued that historians of psychology are remiss not to consider Quimby a pioneering psychotherapist, and that what he created was actually a popular psychology based on self-spirituality.[51] He explained that he was talking people out of their belief that they were ill, but not any talk would do:

> I sit down by a sick person, and you also sit down. I feel her trouble and the state of her mind, and find her faint and weary for the want

> of wisdom. I tell her what she calls this feeling that troubles her; and knowing her trouble, my words contain food that you know not of. My words are words of wisdom, and they strengthen her while, if you speak the same words, and the sound should fall on the natural ear precisely as mine, they are only empty sounds, and the sick derive no nourishment.[52]

As "the father of self-help psychology," he fits more closely with the mesmerists whose interest was less paranormal than philosophical.[53] Systems of "self-help" that were developed during the nineteenth century promoted individual change through a process of transforming self-concept, while simultaneously revising one's understanding of the world. Both Caldwell and Buchanan expressed in their scientific convictions an optimistic faith in progress and the ability of individuals to improve themselves, their relationships, and even society.[54] For Quimby, the symptoms associated with the mental condition that came to be understood as hysteria was not a neurological problem, but an error in worldview. Quimby, along with other mesmerists of his time, believed that worldview could be modified and lead to positive health effects. In short, Quimby believed the heart of his job as a healer was to reeducate the sick.[55]

As Quimby's understanding of disease and healing developed, he found he no longer needed the traditional associations of mesmerism. He dispensed with the terms, many of its techniques, and even dismissed his somnambulist, Burkman. In an article about Quimby's practice that ran in *The Bangor Jeffersonian* it was noted that "his first course of treatment of a patient is to sit down beside him, and put himself *en rapport* with him, which he does without producing the Mesmeric Sleep."[56] Quimby referred to what he was doing as "mind cure philosophy," a train of thought which was to become influential in the development of the ecumenical movement in the United States known as New Thought, an anti-dogmatic approach to religious life that promoted direct personal experience of the divine.

Quimby's legacy has been complicated by a split between his followers, some like Warren Felt Evans (1817–1889), Julius Dresser (1838–1893), and Anneta Seabury Dresser (1844–1935) who embraced his anti-ecclesiastical approach, and one in particular who set out to create a new religious institution. In 1862 Quimby treated Mary Patterson, better known by her married name, Mary Baker Eddy (1821–1910). She would become the founder of

Christian Science, a religion identified with its approach to healing based on faith rather than medical intervention. Eddy was an invalid when she came to Quimby suffering from chronic and painful ailments. He healed her of her symptoms and inspired her to begin her own career in mental healing. After Quimby's abrupt and premature death in 1866, Eddy soon set off on her own path. Much of the controversy over her relationship with Quimby has to do with conflicting assessments of his influence upon her.

After Quimby's death, Eddy was not the only follower to move forward into public prominence. Evans was a prolific writer, and the Dressers eventually settled in Boston where they continued to teach mental healing in the style they had learned from Quimby. The Dressers accused Eddy of distorting Quimby's teachings and claiming his ideas for her own. Their son Horatio Dresser (1866–1954) published *The Quimby Manuscripts,* which sought to establish the relationship between Quimby and Eddy by providing evidence of their intellectual connections.[57]

Eddy's defenders believed *The Quimby Manuscript* to be a pointed hoax concocted just to discredit her. From Eddy's perspective, her early relationship with Quimby was irrelevant: she had rejected his teachings in key ways, and had every right to move forward with her own system. Certainly her theology bore little resemblance to what Quimby had taught. Eddy claimed Quimby's healing of her was only temporary, the result of theological error, and that her real healing was accomplished through Jesus and the intervention of the Bible. The development of Christian Science therefore followed from this personal religious experience of healing, and not from her relationship with Quimby.[58] Eddy took a hard line against mesmerism, not denying its reality or power, but emphasizing its malicious possibilities. Christian Scientists would also reject the new theories of hypnosis soon to come across the ocean, even continuing to do so after her death.[59]

The controversy over the nature of Eddy's intellectual connection to Quimby has persisted into the present day, not only in the contrasting historical narratives offered by the defenders and detractors of Christian Science, but also in academic disagreements about how to credit the creation and development of New Thought. The movement was philosophically more compatible with the earlier ideas of Quimby, but some of its early teachers, like Emma Curtis Hopkins (1853–1925), were closely involved with Eddy before breaking away.[60]

The story of mesmerism in the United States arguably could cease prior to the war between New Thought and Christian Science over the legacy of Phineas Parkhurst Quimby.[61] By the end of his life Quimby was no longer a mesmerist, just as those who found their way to Spiritualism often left mesmerism behind them. The era of the traveling mesmerist ended in the middle of the nineteenth century in America, as the techniques of mesmerism dissolved into Spiritualist and other religious practices; popular ideas about mesmerism, however, remained in the public consciousness.

From Body to Soul

The idiosyncratic expressions of mesmerism in the United States in the nineteenth century are frequently left out of summary histories of hypnosis, which tend to focus on the scientific and medical practices of mesmerism taking place at the same time in France and Britain. It is true that the intellectual lineage from mesmerism to hypnosis can be drawn more neatly if its detour into American spirituality is judged to be peripheral to the narrative. Without this piece of the historic puzzle, however, it becomes more difficult to understand the remarkable resurgence of hypnosis in the United States in the twentieth century in both popular and medical forms.

Ideas about the relationship between mesmerist and subject, changes in assumptions about the nature of mesmerism, and powerful assertions about the power of mesmerism over identity all came into play as the mesmerists of the nineteenth century in the United States dramatically shaped images of hypnosis that would appear in popular culture, psychology, and spiritual practice throughout the twentieth century. Unlike their European counterparts, American mesmerists often came from the middle and working classes. Their subjects were liable to be of the same social class as themselves, allowing for relationships of unusual equality between mesmerists and their somnambulists, who often worked as partners. Andrew Jackson Davis was a shoe salesman, and his mesmerist a tailor, though he left his tailor behind when he became the Seer of Poughkeepsie.

The emphasis of nineteenth century American mesmerism on individual growth and personal spiritual transformation served to some extent to level hierarchical social relationships between members of different social classes and between men and women, at least within white, Anglo-Saxon, Protestant America. The enthusiastic participation and leadership of women in the Spiritualist movement reflected new access to sources of spiritual authority that opened up to them in the nineteenth century.[62] Rather than being seen as simply weak or gullible, somnambulist subjects, much like Spiritualist mediums, were admired within their communities for the spiritual aptitude that allowed them to acquire secret knowledge.

American mesmerists who were medical doctors were often drawn to phrenology, a system that inscribed social hierarchy into biology and so limited the possibility of social mobility; in contrast, the spiritual mesmerists had as their sources of authority spiritual forces that were not constrained by traditional hierarchies. With a few key exceptions, mesmerists were less interested in demonstrating their power of will over others than in enabling others, as a minister does, to share a common experience, and to enter into a community of like-minded searchers. American mesmerists in the nineteenth century were looking for a more directly powerful and spiritually authentic experience than mainstream philosophical systems, religious or political, could offer them.

In contrast to the prevailing European notions regarding the nature of mesmerism, in the United States its key purpose was spiritual rather than medical, even when physical healing was involved. Puységur's contention that the trance state is the essential feature of mesmerism was transferred in its entirety to the United States, and was for the most part left unchallenged. What the nature of that trance should be was understood quite differently depending upon the context of the mesmeric event: was it to be an evening of entertainment or a séance? Differences in the expectation of the subjects and the suggestions given by the mesmerizer would ensure that Spiritualists would be contacting the dead, while Swedenborgians would produce esoteric philosophy. Sunderland, who passed through it all and died an atheist, has been singled out by historians, among all the sundry American mesmerists, for having understood that a combination of suggestibility and expectation linked together the experiences of revivalists and mesmerists, their ecstatic converts, and somnambulist subjects.[63]

The effects of nineteenth century American mesmerism on twentieth century hypnosis stem mainly from a shift in emphasis from phenomena associated with the body to those associated with the mind and the soul. The twentieth century association of hypnosis with dramatic changes in identity had significant precedent in the parlor séances of the century before. By the time Andrew Jackson Davis was channeling Swedenborg as the Seer of Poughkeepsie, the association of mesmerism with such dissociations was widespread and uncontroversial. The debate over the significance of these and other trance states would soon take center stage back across the Atlantic in France in a famous conflict between the hypnotists of the Nancy School and those associated with the asylum and teaching hospital, the Salpêtrière.

Notes

1 Joseph Commun, "On the Cause of Freshwater Springs, Fountains, etc. ...," *American Journal of Science* 14 (1828): 174–176. For significance of Commun's lectures on mesmerism see Edward John Nygren, "Ruben Peale's Experiments with Mesmerism, *Proceedings of the American Philosophical Society* 114, no. 2 (1970): 100–108.

2 Joseph Deleuze, *Histoire Critique de Magnétisme Animal*, 2 vols. (Paris: Mame, 1813); Joseph Deleuze, *Practical Instruction in Animal Magnetism*, trans. Thomas C. Hartshorn (Providence: B. Cranston, 1837).

3 Joseph Deleuze, *Practical Instruction in Animal Magnetism*, trans. Thomas C. Hartshorn (New York: D. Appleton and Co, 1846).

4 Ellenberger, *Discovery of the Unconscious*, 86, 91.

5 Deleuze, *Practical Instruction*, 1846: 163–164.

6 Nathaniel Hawthorne, *The House of Seven Gables* (Boston: Ticknor, Reed & Fields, 1851).

7 Nathaniel Hawthorne, *The Blithedale Romance* (Boston: Ticknor, Reed & Fields, 1852). For more on Hawthorne and the influence of mesmerism on his writing, see Maria M. Tatar, *Spellbound: Studies on Mesmerism and Literature* (Princeton: Princeton University Press, 1978).

8 Robert C. Fuller, *Mesmerism and the American Cure of Souls* (Philadelphia: University of Pennsylvania Press, 1982): 17. See Charles Poyen, *Progress of Animal Magnetism in New England* (Boston: Weeks, Jordan, and Co., 1837).

9 Gauld, *History of Hypnotism*, 181.

10 Fuller, *Mesmerism and the American Cure of Souls*, 18.

11 Ibid., 2.

12 Ibid., 23. See William Stone, *Letter to Dr. A. Brigham on Animal Magnetism* (New York: George Dearborn, 1837).

13 Ibid., 21.

14 Gauld, *History of Hypnotism*, 185.
15 Spurzheim died unexpectedly the same year; his followers attributed his death to dedication and exhaustion. See John D. Davies, *Phrenology, Fad and Science: A Nineteenth Century American Crusade* (New Haven: Yale University Press, 1955).
16 Charles Caldwell, *Facts in Mesmerism: And Thoughts on its Causes and Uses* (Louisville: Prentice and Weissinger, 1842).
17 Fuller, *Mesmerism and the American Cure of Souls*, 62–64.
18 Joseph R. Buchanan, "Spirituality—Recent Occurrences," *Buchanan's Journal of Man* (New York: 1850): 489.
19 See Joseph R. Buchanan, *Outlines of Lectures on the Neurological System of Anthropology as Discovered, Demonstrated and Taught in 1841 and 1842* (Cincinnati: n.p., 1854): 40.
20 Ibid. See also Fuller, *Mesmerism and the American Cure of Souls*, 53–54.
21 Ibid., 51.
22 Ibid., 55; Taves, *Fits, Trances and Visions*, 202.
23 Fuller, *Mesmerism and the American Cure of Souls*, 56–57. See also James Stanley Grimes, *The Mysteries of the Head and the Heart Explained* (Chicago: Sumner and Co., 1875).
24 Cited by Fuller, *Mesmerism and the American Cure of Souls*, 60. See James Stanley Grimes, *Etherology, and the Phreno-philosophy of Mesmerism and Magic Eloquence: Including a New Philosophy of Sleep and of Consciousness*, 2d ed., ed. W. G. Le Duc (Boston: Munroe, 1850): 18.
25 Fuller, *Mesmerism and the American Cure of Souls*, 88. Also see Gauld, *History of Hypnotism*, 187. Gauld refers to electrobiological theories as "gobbledy-gook," but he credits them with producing in their subjects all the phenomena associated with modern hypnotism, in both its stage and clinical aspects.
26 Cited by Fuller, *Mesmerism and the American Cure of Souls*, 67.
27 See Taves, *Fits, Trances and Visions*, 132–133.
28 Fuller, *Mesmerism and the American Cure of Souls*, 85.
29 Ibid., 86.
30 Ibid., 89.
31 Ibid., 79–80.
32 Gauld, *History of Hypnotism*, 288.
33 Cited by Taves, *Fits, Trances, and Visions*, 144.
34 Taves, *Fits, Trances, and Visions*, 124. See also Fuller, *Mesmerism and the American Cure of Souls*. Fuller's central thesis is that mesmerism laid a path for a psychological "cure of souls."
35 See La Roy Sunderland, *The Trance and Correlative Phenomena* (Chicago: James Walker, 1868): 109–110.
36 For a discussion, see Taves, *Fits, Trances, and Visions*, 167–168.

37 Andrew Jackson Davis, *The Magic Staff: An Autobiography of Andrew Jackson Davis* (New York: J. S. Brown & Co., 1859).

38 Ibid., 161–162.

39 Ibid., 201–202.

40 For a detailed discussion of Davis's message and its relationship to transformation in the social world, see Catherine L. Albanese, "On the Matter of Spirit: Andrew Jackson Davis and the Marriage of God and Nature, *Journal of the American Academy of Religion* 60, no. 1 (Spring, 1992): 1–17.

41 George Bush, *Mesmer and Swedenborg; Or, The Relation of the Development of Mesmerism to the Doctrines and Disclosures of Swedenborg* (New York: John Allen, 1847). Some controversy has raged over what influence the genealogical connection between the Swedenborgian George Bush and the presidential Bushes (they are first cousins, several times removed) might have on President George W. Bush's Middle Eastern policy. See George Bush, *The Life of Mohammad* (New York: J. & J. Harper, 1830). In this book, George Bush, the Swedenborgian, describes Islam as a "horrid superstition" and the prophet as an "Imposter." For the U.S. government's response to the issue, see http://usinfo.state.gov/media/Archive_Index/Life_of_Mohammed_Book_NOT_Authored_by_Grandfather_or_Ancestor_of_President_Bush.html.

42 Taves, *Fits, Trances, and Visions*, 170.

43 George Bush, *Mesmer and Swedenborg*, 17.

44 Thomas Lake Harris, quoted by R. Laurence Moore, *In Search of White Crows* (New York: Oxford University Press, 1977): 12.

45 *The Complete Works of Edgar Allan Poe*, ed. James A. Harrison (New York: Crowell, 1902).

46 Chauncy Hare Townshend, *Facts in Mesmerism, or Animal Magnetism. With Reasons for a Dispassionate Inquiry into It* (London: Baillerie Press, 1844).

47 Compare, for instance, Fuller's view of Poe's cynicism in Fuller, *Mesmerism and the American Cure of Souls*, 36–37, with a contrasting analysis in Tatar, *Spellbound*, 197–199.

48 *Complete Works of Edgar Allan Poe*, XIV, 173.

49 Fuller, *Mesmerism and the American Cure of Souls*, 120.

50 Cited by Fuller, *Mesmerism and the American Cure of Souls*, 121.

51 See Fuller, *Mesmerism and the American Cure of Souls*, 128–136.

52 Annetta G. Dresser, *The Philosophy of P. P. Quimby* (Boston: George H. Ellis, 1895): 50.

53 Fuller, *Mesmerism and the American Cure of Souls*, 118.

54 Ibid., 67.

55 Ibid., 129–130.

56 Dresser, *The Philosophy of P. P. Quimby*, 23.

57 Horatio Dresser ed., *The Quimby Manuscripts: Showing the Discovery of Spiritual Healing and the Origin of Christian Science* (New York: Thomas Y. Crowell, 1921).

58 See Robert Peel, *Mary Baker Eddy: The Years of Trial* (New York: Holt, Rinehart and Winston, 1971): 208–209.

59 See, for example, Sue Harper Mims, "Jesus in Christian Science," *The Christian Science Journal* (October, 1902).

60 Eddy excommunicated her in 1887, and again in 1888 along with Julius Dresser. For a full discussion of the context of the controversies surrounding Quimby, Christian Science, and New Thought, see Taves, *Fits, Trances, and Visions*, 213–225; and Eric Caplan, *Mind Games: American Culture and the Birth of Psychotherapy* (Berkeley, University of California Press, 1998): 65–88.

61 This controversy gains its association with the history of mesmerism through the classic narrative of mesmeric history by Frank Podmore, *From Mesmerism and Christian Science* (London: Methuen, 1909). For an interesting account of the relationship of the controversy to the development of New Thought, see Taves, *Fits, Trances, and Visions*, 222–225.

62 For a thorough analysis of the role of women in the Spiritualist movement, see Ann Braude, *Radical Spirits: Spiritualism and Women's Rights in Nineteenth Century America* (Boston: Beacon Press, 1989).

63 In his history of hypnosis Gauld doesn't place Sunderland alongside the other American mesmerists, but presents him separately, in a section on precursors to the late nineteenth century hypnotic movement in France. Taves makes Sunderland a central figure in *Fits, Trances and Visions*, as well.

CHAPTER FIVE

Salpêtrière and Nancy

The remarkable mainstream success of hypnosis as a medical technique in France during the last decades of the nineteenth century is due in part to the reputation lent to it by Charles Richet (1850–1935), a well-respected doctor who would serve as professor of physiology at the Faculty of Medicine in Paris. In the early twentieth century Richet was awarded the Nobel Prize in recognition of his pioneering research on anaphylaxis. In the 1870s he was experimenting with techniques associated with both mesmerism and hypnosis.

Although Richet was likely to be familiar with Braid's new techniques of inducing trance through eye-fixation, Richet experimented with hypnosis in medical settings using traditional mesmeric techniques, including the hand passes introduced by Franz Mesmer a hundred years before. He first published his results in 1875, describing a variety of hypnotically induced phenomena, including hallucinations, non-volitional behaviors, and post-hypnotic amnesia.[1] What Richet's subjects did *not* regularly experience was the catalepsy that Braid had considered to be the final "stage" of the hypnotic process, and that other magnetizers were producing.[2] During the same period, for example, Carl Hansen (1833–1897), a magnetic demonstrator from Denmark who traveled across Europe, from Sweden, Denmark, and Finland, to Russia, Austria, and Britain, consistently put subjects into cataleptic states.

Hansen was recognized for invoking impressive muscular rigidity in his hypnotic subjects, going so far as to place them like a bridge across the tops of two chairs and to climb on top of them.[3] He inspired an army of imitators across Europe who pushed the envelope on the range of physical feats that hypnosis could induce.

Hypnosis in the German-speaking world was dominated in this era by stage performers who were more interested in phenomenological and theoretical issues than medical or therapeutic ones. This was not the case in France, where a dramatic application of hypnosis in a public health setting was about to occur.

Hypnosis at the Salpêtrière

In 1862 a celebrated clinical neurologist, Jean-Martin Charcot (1825–1893), became Chief of Medicine at the Salpêtrière women's asylum. The Salpêtrière had a colorful history in France, serving successively and sometimes simultaneously as a prison, poorhouse, and old folk's home in addition to housing the developmentally, neurologically, and mentally ill. During Charcot's tenure the Salpêtrière was going through dramatic institutional transformation. As part of its modernization it became a teaching institution with a new focus on research. It ceased to admit poor, chronically ill, or pregnant women, and began to welcome a patient population composed of thousands of elderly and mentally ill women, including at any one time a few hundred children, some of whom would spend their entire lives there, first as inmates and later, sometimes, as staff.[4]

In 1886 its campus included 45 large buildings and 60 smaller ones. Its amphitheater could hold an audience of 500 people who would come to hear medical lectures and to see demonstrations and medical procedures performed upon its inmates. Charcot described the Salpêtrière in 1862 as a kind of museum:

> The clinical types available for study are represented by numerous examples, which enables us to study categoric disease during its entire course, so to speak, since the vacancies that occur in any specific disease are quickly filled in the course of time. We are, in other words, in possession of a sort of museum of living pathology of which the resources are great.[5]

Charcot's involvement with the Salpêtrière was as lifelong as that of many of his patients. Beginning as a medical student there in 1849, he was Chief of Medicine for 30 years, remaining in the post until his death in 1893. Although Charcot is most frequently associated with hypnosis, he had made substantial contributions

Figure 8 *Charcot demonstrating at the Salpêtrière. Lucien Laurent-Gsell, c. 1878, in Foveau de Courmelles,* L'hypnotisme, *Mary Evans Picture Library (maryevans.com).*

to medical knowledge of pulmonary and kidney disease. He also developed protocols for neurological diagnosis, which goes far to explain why, when placed in charge of a ward filled with women who suffered from convulsions, Charcot was interested to know which of the women suffered from neurological epileptic conditions, and which from convulsions arising from hysteria. Hysterics in the Salpêtrière had seemingly learned from the epileptics how to have "epileptoid" attacks.[6]

Inspired by the work of Richet, during the late 1870s Charcot began an active study of hypnosis with his hysterical female patients. Much as Braid had done, Charcot identified stages of hypnosis that he was able to observe in all of his patients. During the stage of "Catalepsy" his subjects still responded to physical suggestion, obeying the hypnotist like automatons. When they entered the stage of "Lethargy" they became insensible, and were no longer responsive to suggestions. In the final stage of "Somnambulism" they became capable of conversation, and could respond to suggestion. They did so with autonomy and enthusiasm. Every Tuesday morning at the Salpêtrière Charcot examined patients in front of an audience that included doctors,

Figure 9 *Hysterics at the Salpêtrière entering hypnotic trance following an unexpected noise. Engraved from a photo, 1877, in Paul Regnard,* Sorcellerie, Magnétisme, Morphinisme, Délire des Grandeurs, *Mary Evans Picture Library (maryevans.com).*

students, members of the press, and the curious public, frequently demonstrating his ability to draw them through the three stages of *Grande Hypnotisme.*

Charcot followed up his weekly demonstrations with lectures on Friday mornings. He was an effective teacher, sporting a dramatic mustache, speaking with theatrical flair, and making use of the new technology of photographic projection to great effect. Not all descriptions of his teaching style are flattering, however. Charcot was also known as the "Napoleon of Neurosis," a nickname explicated by Leon Daudet (1867–1942), a one-time medical student at the Salpêtrière and later the author of *Les Morticoles,* a novel satirizing the medical profession of his day, and savaging Charcot, in particular, through its characterization of a sadistic doctor.[7] In his memoirs, Daudet recalled that Charcot, "although his forehead was too low, had the features of a stout Napoleon. I fancy that this resemblance, which he accentuated, influenced his habit and his career. I never knew a man who tyrannized more those about him. One could see this at a table, when he kept glancing suspiciously at his students and reprimanding them harshly."[8]

During Charcot's weekly presentations to the public, his most important and infamous subject, Blanche Wittman, sometimes referred to as a "prima donna" of hysterics, could always be counted on to put on a good show.[9] Of course, the "shows" were perceived differently by the medical men of their day than by their critics. Axel Munthe (1857–1949), a Swedish doctor who was practicing medicine in Paris, described with disdain Charcot's amphitheater filled to the eaves with voyeurs entertained by the sight of a hypnotized woman eating charcoal she believed to be chocolate, rocking a top hat following the suggestion that it was a baby, and barking on all fours on the floor like a dog.[10]

The behaviors associated with the three stages of hypnosis were familiar to Charcot as symptoms of hysteria, an illness that was understood during this period to be a neurological disorder brought about by a physical or psychic trauma in those individuals who inherited a predisposition to the disease.[11] It was diagnosable through the behavioral patterns it produced: hallucinations, organic manifestations of illness, and epileptic-like seizures followed by periods of delirium and sensibility. Charcot initiated a journal, *Photographic Iconography of the Salpêtrière*, which from 1877 to 1880 documented each stage of the hysterical crisis. Likewise the journal photographed and commissioned etchings of Wittmann and her fellow hysterics in each of the stages of *Grande Hypnotisme*.[12]

Given such dramatic and visual evidence, it would have been difficult to dispute that the identifying characteristics of the hypnotic state as described and demonstrated by Charcot at the Salpêtrière, and the prevailing diagnostic symptomatology of hysteria, were all but identical. Charcot's explanation for this correspondence was straightforward but soon to become controversial: both hysterics and hypnotizable subjects were susceptible to suggestion because hypnotism was a manifestation of hysteria.

Charcot had completed his definitions of the three stages of hypnosis by 1882 when he presented his research to the *Académie des Sciences*. He was inducted as a member the following year, achieving for a time the professional respect that had sadly eluded Franz Mesmer a century before. Charcot and his followers at the Salpêtrière, however, were soon to become embroiled in an intellectual battle with another set of researchers and practitioners, known collectively as the "Nancy School." It was a battle that would significantly diminish their legacy.

The Nancy Approach to Hypnosis

The father figure of the Nancy School, Ambroise-Auguste Liébault (1823–1904), had been born in a French village near Nancy, becoming a doctor in Strasbourg in 1850. He stumbled across an old book on animal magnetism and began to experiment with it as a treatment for his patients, who were typically poor but suffered from a wide range of physical ailments, from arthritis to tuberculosis. Liébault's method involved the physical touch characteristic of earlier generations of magnetism, in combination with suggestions that his subjects should sleep, as was characteristic of more recent hypnotic models and techniques. As a witness to Liébault's practice recalled:

> The patients told to go to sleep apparently fell at once into a quiet slumber, then received their dose of curative suggestions, and when told to awake, either walked quietly away or sat for a little to chat with their friends, the whole process rarely lasting longer than ten minutes ... No drugs were given, and Liébault took special pains to explain to his patients that he neither exercised nor possessed any mysterious powers, and that all he did was simple and capable of scientific explanation.[13]

As late as the 1880s Liébault still referred to a "nervous force" reminiscent of the old magnetic fluid, but he was persuaded to give up the conviction by his friend and colleague, Hippolyte Bernheim (1840–1919), after Bernheim re-created the classic placebo-controlled experiments to show that unmagnetized water was just as effective as magnetized water, if the subject believed it to be magnetized.[14] A professor of medicine at Nancy, Bernheim visited Liébault in 1882 before initiating his own study of hypnosis. His public career was launched in 1886 with the publication of his first critique of Charcot's work. The "Nancy School" came to be defined in large part by its rejection of the *Grande Hypnotisme* practiced at the Salpêtrière.

The pamphlet war that ensued between the two groups of hypnotists was bitter. The Salpêtrière position, by then institutionalized and mainstream, was that hypnosis was an abnormal state associated with hysteria, characterized by three clearly defined stages. Bernheim, the upstart, denied the association between hysteria and hypnosis, claiming that the hypnotic state was not pathological and that suggestibility was a normal human capacity. To make the point that anyone can be hypnotized, Bernheim deliberately preferred men for his research subjects because they typically were not considered to suffer from hysteria to the same degree as women. Under attack, the Salpêtrière supporters countered that the real problem was that Bernheim had not correctly diagnosed his subjects.

Following Liébault and Braid, Bernheim recognized "degrees" of hypnosis but he understood these to be different depths of suggestibility rather than discrete states of consciousness of the type described by Charcot. Bernheim declared that although he could not confirm Charcot's three stages by observation, he could produce them by suggestion.[15] The charge that the supposedly universal stages of *Grande Hypnotisme* were merely products of suggestion proved to be the undoing of Charcot when the dynamics of life within the Salpêtrière came to light.

Opinions both then and now differ as to whether the hysterical subjects featured in Charcot's weekly demonstrations were faking their performances outright, or if they were unconsciously fulfilling the expectations of their doctors and peers. Perhaps staff members, from malice, or from ignorance, were training hysterical subjects how to behave. Dardot's account makes a suggestion in the direction of the latter, recalling that Charcot "could not stand stupidity. But his need for domination caused him to eliminate the more brilliant of his disciples, so that in the end he was surrounded by mediocre people."[16] It is not possible to know to what degree Charcot was aware that he was suggesting to his subjects that they should produce the particular behaviors that he expected to see. Even in the absence of explicit suggestions, details regarding animal magnetism were common knowledge in mainstream French popular consciousness. Certainly everyone working with Charcot at the Salpêtrière had intimate knowledge of all the particulars of the three expected stages.

Critical but sympathetic accounts written by Pierre Janet (1859–1947), who became supervisor of the Psychological Laboratory at the Salpêtrière in 1889, explained what he believed had occurred in the Salpêtrière under Charcot. According to Janet, the three stages were products of deliberate training by student magnetizers, likely without the knowledge of the master. Charcot's error arose from his desire to come up with a classification for hysterical diseases that would be as universally applicable as the diagnostic categories for neurological diseases that he had previously developed. To accomplish this goal, he necessarily oversimplified the conditions he was describing. His error was compounded, Janet more critically suggested, by a lack of interest in the individual lives of his subjects.[17]

Despite growing criticism of Charcot's demonstrations with hysterics, defenders of Charcot rejected Bernheim's position with the not unreasonable argument that if the stages of hypnosis were simply products of suggestion, then all measures of hypnosis must be products of suggestion, and if this is so, then how can it ever be determined if someone is hypnotized or not?[18] This was a conundrum tangled enough to cause Liébault and Bernheim to part ways. Although Liébault also rejected the three stages as defined by Charcot, he did see hypnotic sleep as a necessary aspect of hypnotic healing; to Bernheim the trance state was just another product of suggestion.

By the 1890s *Grand Hypnotisme* was no more, and Charcot's approach had been displaced by a "hypnotherapeutic" movement which asserted that hypnosis was a method of curing disease through psychological means. As for Blanche Wittmann, she was to live at the Salpêtrière for 17 years, from 1878 to 1895. In her final years she became a member of the staff, no longer a hysterical patient. She eventually died of radiation exposure, suffering multiple amputations, the result of working in the radiation clinic.[19]

The Nancy School approach to hypnosis which spread across Europe and the United States beginning in the 1890s was understood to be a psychologically oriented rather than physiological approach to the phenomenon, although differences of opinion remained in consideration of its relationship to pathology. The lingering ambiguity can be seen in the shifting views of Janet. Initially he shared with Charcot the belief that hypnosis was an abnormal state, a type of hysterical somnambulism. His subjects at the Salpêtrière demonstrated a wide range of symptoms associated with hysteria including delirium, hysterical paralysis, automatic writing, dissociations of identity, and somnambulistic speech. He didn't believe that these were simply products of his own suggestion. Why did suggestive statements have power only over certain people? Janet answered this question by theorizing that the diminished consciousness of hysterics lacked some critical cognitive functions. It followed from this explanation that only hysterics were hypnotizable.

Eventually the doctors at the Salpêtrière who followed Charcot, including to some extent Janet, moved in the direction of the Nancy position, accepting that normal, healthy people could also be hypnotized and induced to exhibit all the symptoms of hysteria. Still, Janet never lost his interest in what he considered to be pathological expressions. Charcot's more enduring influence on Janet came from the implications arising from his work, that thoughts can become dissociated from conscious awareness. Both Janet's understanding of dissociation and Freud's subsequent theory of the unconscious owe much to the work of Charcot at the Salpêtrière.

The Fall of Hypnosis

Having been defined in its opposition to the Salpêtrière, the Nancy School dissipated as a discrete intellectual entity once the battle had been won. Historians of hypnosis are in disagreement about the degree to which hypnosis use among mainstream medical practitioners declined following the intellectual victory of the Nancy School.[20] Bernheim's theoretical positions on hypnosis did appear more extreme as time went on, giving ammunition to its skeptics. Content at first to overturn the three stages as defined by Charcot, but still believing that "nervous sleep" could increase the susceptibility of a subject to suggestion by the hypnotist, Bernheim eventually rejected his own view. His research had convinced him that people are just as suggestible when they are wide awake as they are when they are in a hypnotic trance. Infuriating friends, colleagues, enemies, and critics alike, he was to declare at a conference in Moscow in 1897, "*Il n'y a pas d'hypnotisme*–there is no such thing as hypnotism."[21]

By asserting that all induction techniques were useful only to the degree that it was suggested to the subjects that they were useful, and that every phenomenon produced by hypnosis was a product of suggestion, Bernheim had peeled the onion of hypnosis as far as he could go, and concluded that the onion consisted of peels all the way down. His view triggered the question that the defenders of the Salpêtrière had anticipated: If everything produced by hypnosis is only a product of suggestion, then how can hypnosis be measured at all? Now Bernheim seemed to be answering the question in the way they had feared, by claiming that hypnosis did not exist. Certainly skeptics were eager to interpret Bernheim's view in this way, just as the Franklin Commission and Wakely had done. If some phenomenon or other was shown to be a product of suggestion, this provided a basis to challenge mesmerism or hypnosis as a whole.

There had always been researchers and clinicians, however, who were not bothered by the idea that the key to hypnosis was suggestion and imagination, and whose focus was on the pragmatic successes of the techniques. As early as 1785, after the Franklin Commission dismissed the realities of animal magnetism, Charles D'Eslon responded wryly, "If the medicine of the imagination is the most efficient, why do we not make use of it?"[22] In a similar spirit, the preface to Alexandre Bertrand's 1823 book, *Traite du Somnambulisme*, was titled, "How the author came to realize that animal magnetism does not exist."[23] This early work of Bertrand found its way into the hands of Joseph Delboeuf (1831–1896), a rationalist philosopher turned experimental psychologist.[24] Sixty-eight years after Bertrand, and six years before Bernheim, Delboef penned his own article entitled "*Comme quoi il n'y a pas d'hypnotisme*" ("So it turns out there is no hypnosis") (1891), in which he presented his conviction, based on his own research, that subjects were susceptible to suggestion regardless of whether they were induced into trance.[25]

Delboef visited both the Salpêtrière and Nancy, developed his own experimental research, and provided critical challenges to the assertions of both schools of thought. He claimed that nonhysterical subjects could be induced to produce all the Salpêtrière phenomena, which meant that they must be due to suggestion, not psychopathology, and certainly not the power of magnetic fluid. Delboeuf published details of his visit to the Salpêtrière in 1885. He was harshly critical of the experimental conditions he found there, particularly the lack of care to isolate experimental subjects from the conversation of the experimenters about what was supposed to be happening to them.[26]

Delboeuf was more sympathetic to the Nancy position than to the Salpêtrière, and he was also more influential upon it, and upon Bernheim in particular. The declarations of the nonexistence of hypnosis from Delboef and then Bernheim were intended to be both provocative and ironic. While many theorists of the time simply integrated the consensus about the power of suggestion into their ideas about the trance, conceptualizing hypnosis as some sort of state of heightened suggestibility, those who dispensed with the trance completely were left with suggestion alone as the key explanatory factor of all phenomena related to hypnosis.

The person other than Bernheim (signifying the entire Nancy School) who is said to be responsible for the fall of hypnosis from prominence at the turn of the century is Sigmund Freud (1856–1939). After studying with both Charcot and Bernheim in the late nineteenth century Freud initially made hypnosis a central aspect of his clinical technique. Freud's association with Joseph Breuer (1842–1925) centered upon his interpretations of Breuer's work with his most famous patient, Bertha Pappenheim, known pseudonymously as Anna O., whose case they described in a co-authored 1893 publication.[27] The case has received substantial academic attention because Breuer's narrative of its facts, as taken up by Freud, provided an empirical basis for psychoanalysis. Bertha was diagnosed as a hysteric and was hospitalized multiple times during the years in which Breuer worked with her. He later claimed that her symptoms disappeared as a result of hypnotic regression in which she traced backwards the traumatic circumstances that had given rise to them, experiencing "catharsis" each time a memory was brought forward into consciousness.

The details of her case and the treatment she received have been significantly contested, and the various influences upon both Breuer and Pappenheim investigated.[28] Breuer's interest in hypnosis seems to have been set off by the work of neurologist Moriz Benedikt (1849–1920), whose own experiments with the technique began in the period of intense interest in hypnosis whipped up by the stage hypnotist Carl Hansen. Vienna in 1880 has been described as suffering from a "veritable attack of mesmero-hypnotic fever."[29] In his autobiography, even Freud claims to have been introduced to hypnosis by Hansen, though this may well have been a retrospective confabulation.[30] Like Blanche Wittmann at the Salpêtrière, Pappenheim began producing her hysterical symptoms at a time when knowledge of what those symptoms should be was already in the popular consciousness. It has been suggested that just as Wittman provided Charcot with perfect demonstrations, Pappenheim was a perfect hysteric patient, giving Breuer what he wanted to see, producing all the symptoms that his diagnosis required.[31]

Freud soon rejected hypnosis as a technique in favor of his own psychotherapeutic techniques, particularly free association. The hypnosis that Freud abandoned, it must be noted, was not Bernheim's peeled-onion version. Hypnosis, for Freud, still referred to the induction of a somnambulistic trance state related to, but unlike, normal sleep.[32] In Freud's view the trance was not a product of suggestion, as theorists of Nancy claimed, but essential to hypnosis. Although eschewing somnambulism, he incorporated into his practice other techniques long associated with both mesmerism and hypnosis, including rapport, touch, and the liberal application of suggestion, both intentional and unintentional. Freud's work with his patients also led in some cases to "catharsis," an experience not so removed from the crisis invoked by Mesmer more than a century before.

Given the centrality of Freud's influence on the field, his professional choice to "abandon" hypnosis by that name had the effect of keeping it out of mainstream practice for half a century. Practically speaking, maintaining the hegemony of psychoanalysis required a marginalization of other significant figures and their writings within the canonic history of psychoanalysis and psychiatry. This does not, however, mean that they ceased to work or had no followers. The influence of Liébault, the kindly father of the Nancy School, for example, can be discerned through the turn of the century into the twentieth, in the work of Albert Moll (1862–1939) in Germany, Julian Ochorowicz (1850–1917) in Poland, Henri Forel (1848–1931) in Switzerland, Vladimir Bechterev (1857–1927) in Russia, Milne Bramwell (1852–1925) in Britain, Emile Coué (1857–1926) in France, and Morton Prince (1862–1939) in the United States.

The turn of the century was also marked by an astonishing international collaboration of practitioners, researchers, and scholars from a variety of disciplines whose interests and inclinations were influenced by, and overlapped with, those of Janet. Their work is directly connected to the dramatic resurgence of mainstream interest in hypnosis that occurred during the second half of the twentieth century. They were engaged in a common quest to understand human consciousness, in a train of intellectual thought that continued outside the psychoanalytic mainstream.

Hypnosis outside the Mainstream

Spiritualism had arrived in Britain from the United States in the 1850s, and had been well established there for 20 years when minister-turned-medium William Stainton Moses (1839–1892) became the subject of scientific investigation. He produced through automatic writing 24 volumes of "spirit teachings" over a decade beginning in 1873. An Oxford graduate with an impressive personal presence, Moses attracted scientific attention because he was not a flim-flamming stage medium of the kind proliferating throughout Europe and the United States during that period. Frederic W. H. Myers (1843–1901) and Edmund Gurney (1847–1888) began their study of Moses in 1874. By 1882 when the Society for Psychical Research was initiated in Britain, however, Myers and Gurney had already left spiritualism behind them.

As the mission statement of the Society for Psychical Research explained, they were interested in "the study of hypnotism and the forms of so-called mesmeric trance, with its alleged insensitivity to pain; clairvoyance and other allied phenomena."[33] Henry Sidgwick (1838–1900), a professor of moral philosophy at Cambridge, was its first president. The secretary for the committee on mesmerism within the Society was prolific author Frank Podmore (1856–1910), though most of its hypnosis research during the late nineteenth century was done by Gurney and Meyers, both separately and in fruitful collaboration. Gurney, the experimenter, was fascinated by telepathy while Myers, the theorist, was equally intrigued by dissociation. In their experiments they found ordinary people capable of a range of hypnotic abilities, including automatic writing, a phenomenon that intrigued them both.

Some of Gurney's experiments, for which he employed a stage hypnotist to induce his subjects into trance, involved post-hypnotic phenomena and what he perceived to be two stages of hypnotic memory: an alert and a deep stage.[34] Myers had rejected the concept of discrete stages of hypnosis as they were understood at the Salpêtrière, and he disagreed with Janet's focus on the pathological expressions of hysterical subjects. But neither was Myers ready to accept the strong Nancy position and attribute the hypnotic trance completely to suggestion. Myers believed that hypnosis was associated with a change in states of consciousness, but he was convinced that dissociation was a normal cognitive function:

> I hold that each of us contain the potentialities of many different arrangements of the elements of our personality, each arrangement being distinguishable from the rest by differences in the chain of memories.[35]

Gurney died suddenly in 1888, an accidental death caused by an overdose of the chloroform he used to relieve the pain of neuralgia he suffered in his face, though rumors suggested suicide. After Gurney's death, Myers continued his study of the phenomena of automatic writing and multiple personality disorder, making use of Janet's paradigm of alternative consciousness to develop a comprehensive theory of personality.[36]

Janet had theorized that painful experiences and other fixed ideas can become split off and "dissociated" from ordinary consciousness. Because of their isolation, they may manifest as hysterical symptoms. Myers was less interested in pathological expressions of dissociation. In his theoretical scheme he referred to ordinary human consciousness as the "supraliminal self." This privileged personality is the one with which we usually identify, but it is not necessarily our primary consciousness, and certainly not the only one, as he famously explained: "I accord no primacy to my ordinary waking self, except that among my potential selves this one has shown itself the fittest to meet the needs of common life."[37]

According to Myers, while we are asleep the functions of the "subliminal self" take over. All the wonders associated with mesmerism and hypnosis are also functions of that subliminal consciousness, of which our ordinary self is typically unaware. The hypnotic process allows communication between the subliminal and supraliminal selves. Myers believed that in a mentally healthy person, the boundary between subliminal and supraliminal is opaque; mental illness arises when material from the subliminal gets through to the supraliminal in a disorganized way. Still he believed that there was nothing structurally different about the consciousness of a dissociative hysteric from the consciousness of everybody else.[38]

This view was also growing in France, promoted by Richet and further developed by Alfred Binet (1857–1911). Binet had been a student and defender of Charcot, but broke off his relationship with his teacher and left the Salpêtrière in 1891 after being convinced by the trenchant criticisms launched by Delboeuf. Binet's 1896 book, *On Double Consciousness*, provided experimental evidence that healthy people could produce the same dissociative states as hysterics and that he could, through suggestion, get them to suppress knowledge associated with their primary personality, and begin to exhibit multiple personalities.[39]

In 1889 Janet published his work, *L'automatism Psychologique*, which examined the multiple personalities of Léonie Leboulanger, a woman who had also been studied by Richet.[40] Janet never completely lost his image of dissociation as pathological, but elsewhere in Europe and the United States it was the non-pathological view, shared by Myers in Britain and Binet in France, that flourished. In Germany, the neo-Kantian philosopher Max Dessoir (1867–1947) developed a system like Myers of "over consciousness and under consciousness" and argued in his work, *Das-Doppel-Ich*, that everyone has the potential of having multiple selves.[41] In the United States, William James (1842–1910) built on the work of the Europeans Janet, Myers, Binet, and Dessoir. In his voluminous *Principles of Psychology*, published in 1890, James lent support to the view that human consciousness may be considered multiple by definition, because of the way that cognitive functions are separated from one another in consciousness.[42]

In the career of William James, godson of the transcendentalist Ralph Waldo Emerson and son of Henry James, the eccentric Swedenborgian theologian, the American story of mesmerism reconnects to the European. European ideas about hypnosis arrived at the turn of the century to an America that already had its own indigenous proto-psychotherapeutic traditions. James was an important figure in the New Thought Movement, for example, which had originated in the activities of the magnetizing healer Phineas Parkhurst Quimby. James once declared New Thought to be America's "only decidedly original contribution to the systematic philosophy of life."[43]

James' career at Harvard spanned the years 1873 to 1907. With the international circle of extraordinary individuals that surrounded him, his intellectual contributions to pragmatist philosophy, epistemology, philosophy of religion, history, and aesthetics are widely celebrated. James created the first laboratory of experimental psychology in the United States, but he was also a founding member of the American Society for Psychical Research. James became convinced of the possibility of spiritualism after a séance with trance medium Leonora Piper (1859–1950) whom he judged, among the many notoriously shady mediums of his day, to be the genuine article. In a well-remembered lecture he gave in 1890 he explained her importance: "To upset the conclusion that all crows are black, there is no need to seek demonstration that no crows are black; it is sufficient to produce one white crow; a single one is sufficient."[44]

The issue of the paranormal created a chasm between otherwise compatible theories and experimental methodologies. During the 1890s and through the turn of the century, researchers and theorists continued to use scientific methods to explore the connections between hypnosis and paranormal phenomena, some as believers and some as raging skeptics. Others, like Myers, aspired to neutral observation. Although he had given up his focused research on spiritualism and its mediums, Myers did not discount the claims of spiritualists that some influence originating somewhere other than within the personality of the medium might be occurring.[45] What distinguished Myers from other spiritualists was his desire to establish this empirically.[46]

Skeptics and believers were connected in a body of research that attempted to explain the processes at work, regardless of the larger religious questions that they evoked. Richet, for instance, who had been studying the material evidence of ectoplasmic appearances during séances, did not think that they provided proof for survival after death; paranormal feats attributed to spirits might also have psychic, rather than other-worldly causes. Albert Moll, the German psychiatrist who was best known for his pioneering sex research, and was more aligned to the ideas of Nancy, became an enthusiastic debunker of spiritist mediums. In his writings, Moll also explored the differences between mesmerism and hypnosis.[47]

Hypnosis had not replaced mesmerism at the end of the nineteenth century, but still existed alongside it. Julian Ochorowicz argued that magnetic sleep and hypnotic sleep were distinct phenomena, and that magnetism was the more powerful and practical technique.[48] There also remained overlapping features between the two traditions and techniques: Gurney, for example, retained a belief that some aspects of the hypnotic induction were physical, rather than psychological. In the United States, Thomas Jay Hudson (1834–1903), the author of a runaway bestseller, *The Law of Psychic Phenomena*, put forth the unusual argument that mesmerists were also mesmerizing themselves. In this state of "double subjectivity" distance healing became possible through telepathic transmission. This can't occur in hypnosis, he reasoned, because only the subject is effectively entranced.[49]

The first decades of the twentieth century saw the continued publication of books that dealt with many of these issues; there was concentrated interest in questions arising from the dissociations of personality that manifest themselves both in spirit mediums and in those who exhibit multiple personalities. Swiss psychologist Théodore Flournoy (1854–1921) published his landmark book, *From India to the Planet Mars* (1900), a detailed account of French psychic Helene Smith (1861–1929) who claimed to be communicating with Martians.[50] He did not accept her experiences at face value, but was fascinated by the cognitive processes that would allow her to experience such creative dissociations of personality. Flournoy's work was influenced by James, and he would later be a significant mentor to Carl Jung (1875–1961).

Another man in James' circle, Harvard-educated physician Morton Prince, visited Charcot at the Salpêtrière. In 1906 he published *Dissociation of a Personality*, his famous study of the multiple personalities of Clara Norton Fowler, referred to in publications as Sally Beauchamp.[51] Prince distinguished between human subconscious, which he called "co-conscious," and the unconscious, which he defined as being without consciousness. The concept of co-consciousness suggested that multiple consciousness exists and functions simultaneously with ordinary consciousness, with and without our awareness. Along similar lines Boris Sidis (1867–1923), the Russian-born American psychiatrist, in *The Psychology of Suggestion* (1911) distinguished between a "waking" and "subwaking" self, and asserted that the uncritical sub-waking self is susceptible to suggestion, that it can gain autonomy and even "take over" the body.[52] Many of these studies found renewed relevance in the late twentieth century, when multiple personality disorder found itself back in the clinical, laboratory, and media spotlights.

From Salpêtrière to Nancy

The conflict that had so defined hypnosis at the end of the nineteenth century, the rivalry between the Salpêtrière and Nancy, may appear to have disintegrated all in a moment and to have taken mainstream practice of hypnosis along with it. In fact, the stages of hypnosis as defined by Charcot proved to be a straw man. The demise of *Grande Hypnotisme* did not set off a catastrophic end to the practice of hypnosis, nor did it bring consensus to the theoretical landscape. After the "victory" of Nancy, recognition of the significance of suggestion became widespread; however, a significant gap still remained between those who judged the hypnotic trance state to be an epiphenomenal product of suggestion, and those who retained a conviction that it was an explanatory phenomenon in need of continued study.

The approach of the first group was represented by the research of Bernheim and Delboeuf, and later in the writing and clinical practices of Coué and Bramwell, who once proclaimed that "the production of a preliminary imitation of sleep is not necessary, and is simply waste of time.[53] Many of their ideas anticipate what would half a century later reappear as the social psychological or "non-state" approach to hypnosis.

The views of the second group are most closely associated with Janet, who became heir to Charcot's position as director of research at the Salpêtrière, but it also included many of the students of Liébault. Arguably, most of the people active in hypnosis research at the end of the nineteenth century and into the twentieth were part of this lively community of researchers, some who had been associated with the Salpêtrière and some with Nancy. What they all had in common was an active engagement with the study of human consciousness.

By the end of the first decade of the twentieth century the most important controversy swirling around hypnosis was occurring *within* this community, involving the pointed question of whether or not intelligent acts require consciousness. There were three prevailing answers to this question.[54] Those who believed that intelligent acts do not require consciousness correspondingly hypothesized a human subconscious which was also *un*conscious. This was the position that mainstream psychologists in Europe were taking. "Unconscious cerebration" was a physiological rather than a cognitive explanation, a view that gained steam as psychiatry turned away from hospital clinics in France, looking increasingly toward university laboratories in Germany for direction.

The other two positions had in common the belief that intelligent acts do require consciousness; both hypothesized the existence of some kind of subliminal consciousness that is dissociated from ordinary consciousness and operates independently from it. If there are co-consciousnesses split off from one another, each with its own "memory chains," as Myers had postulated, this would explain personality development through time and the apparent accumulation of memory by channeled spirits and multiple personalities. Those like Janet who perceived these processes of dissociation to reflect some type of pathological condition tended to be physicians. Others, while embracing the reality of dissociative processes, understood them to reflect more generally upon ordinary human consciousness. This was the position reflected in the work of Myers, Binet, and James, a view that came to be associated with popular rather than medical thought.

Since the winners of wars get to narrate the events and the Freudian subconscious won the day, Janet and other prominent psychiatrists were written out of the history, at least until the late twentieth century. Janet continued his practice, his writing, and his use of hypnosis until his death in 1947, but his place in the canon of psychological thought was not established until 1970, in large part as a result of Henri Ellenberger's influential history, *Discovery of the Unconscious*.[55] The career of Prince, who created the Harvard Psychiatric Clinic in 1927, and trained many of the men who would take hypnosis research into the twentieth century, has not been as successfully redacted.

Those who took the third position fared even worse. Despite dedicated research alongside and in collaboration with mainstream scientists, Myers and other psychical researchers with educational backgrounds in the humanities were swiftly marginalized and even dismissed as naïve amateurs. Only in the past few decades has credit been given to these early psychical researchers for their substantial contributions to experimental and statistical methodology.[56] Even James and Flournoy, who were widely respected mainstream figures, have been described as being left in a kind of "academic limbo."[57]

James' legacy is immense and his reputation easily survived the retrospective embarrassment of his involvement with paranormal research. Most people forgive it as part of his interest in religion more broadly, though this interpretation may have had the effect of blurring his substantial involvement in the birth of experimental psychology in the United States. Likewise, Richet's Nobel Prize for the discovery of anaphylaxis seems to have provided him with a halo that excused, but also contributed to an erasure of, his enthusiastic and professionally satisfying "thirty years of psychical research," the title of a book that he dedicated to Myers.[58] A thorough professional biography of Richet, published in a series dedicated to Nobel Prize winners, dispatches those 30 years in only eight words, listing his "interest in spiritualism" among his "recreations." There is no mention of his lifelong contributions to the scientific study of hypnosis.[59]

Groups and individuals whose explorations of hypnotism were spiritual rather than medical, or private rather than institutional, or who operated unnoticed at the edge of academe, continued their work unperturbed by the sudden and, as it turned out, temporary loss of attention by mainstream medical, psychoanalytic, and psychological communities. The history of hypnosis provides ample illustration of how the boundary defining respectable scientific inquiry is continuously redrawn.

Notes

1 Charles Richet, "Du somnambulisme provoqué," *Journal d'anatomie et physiologie* II (1875): 348–378.
2 Gauld, *History of Hypnotism*, 300.
3 Ibid, 303.
4 For a detailed history of the Salpêtrière see Mark Micale, "The Salpêtrière in the Age of Charcot: An Institutional Perspective on Medical History in the Late Nineteenth Century," *Journal of Contemporary History* 20, no. 4 (1985): 703–731.
5 Cited by Sander Gilman, *Seeing the Insane* (New York: J. Wiley, 1982): 194.
6 Ellenberger, *Discovery of the Unconscious*, 90.
7 Léon A. Daudet, *Les Morticoles* (Paris: Bibliotèque-Charpentier, 1894).
8 Léon A. Daudet, *Memoirs of Leon Daudet*, trans. Arthur Kingsland Griggs (New York: Dial Press, 1925): 133.
9 Ellenberger, *Discovery of the Unconscious*, 99.
10 See Axel Munthe, *The Story of San Michele* (London: John Murray, 2004).
11 See Mark Micale, *Approaching Hysteria* (Princeton, NJ: Princeton University Press, 1995).
12 See Gilman, *Seeing the Insane*, 194–204.
13 This account by Milne Bramwell cited by Clark Hull, "Hypnotism in Scientific Perspective," *The Scientific Monthly* 29, no. 2 (1929): 154–162.
14 Gauld, *History of Hypnotism*, 324.
15 Ibid., 329.
16 Cited by Gauld, *History of Hypnotism*, 92.
17 See Pierre Janet, *Psychological Healing* (London: George Allen & Unwin, 1925): 186–192.

18 Gauld, *History of Hypnotism*, 331.
19 For more on Wittman and the treatment of hysteria at the Salpêtrière, see Micale, *Approaching Hysteria*.
20 See Gauld, *History of Hypnosis*, 559–561.
21 Hippolyte Bernheim, *L'hypnotisme et la suggestion* (Paris: O. Doin, 1897): 9.
22 Alfred Binet and Charles Féré, *Hypnotism* (New York: D. Appleton, 1888): 17.
23 Alexandre Bertrand, *Traité du somnambulisme et des différentes modifications qu'il présente* (Paris: Dentu, 1823).
24 Joseph Delboeuf, "La mémoire chez les hypnotisés," *Revue philosophique* 21 (1886): 441.
25 Joseph Delboeuf, "Comme quoi il n'y a pas d'hypnotisme," *Revue de l'hypnotisme* 6 (1891–1892): 129–135.
26 Joseph Delboeuf, *Le magnétisme animal: à propos d'une visite à l'école de Nancy* (Paris: F. Alcan, 1889): 7. For more on Delboeuf, see Alan Gauld, "Joseph Delboeuf (1831–1896): A Forerunner of Modern Ideas on Hypnosis," *Contemporary Hypnosis* 14, no. 4 (2006): 216–225.
27 Sigmund Freud and Josef Breuer, "Üeber den psychischen Mechanismus hysterische Phänomene," *Neurologische Centralblatt* 12 (1893): 4–10, 43–47.
28 See Borch-Jacobsen, *Remembering Anna O.*, 64. Borch-Jacobsen credits his analysis to Uffe Hansen, *Hypnotisoren Carl Hansen og Sigmund Freud* (Copenhagen: Akademisk Forlag, 1991).
29 Ibid., 65.
30 Ibid.
31 Ibid.
32 Sigmund Freud, "On Psychotherapy" (1905), In *The Standard Edition of the Complete Psychological Works of Sigmund Freud*, vol. VII (1901–1905). *A Case of Hysteria, Three Essays on Sexuality and Other Works* (London: Random House, 2001): 255–268.
33 Crabtree, *From Mesmer to Freud*, 270.
34 Gauld, *History of Hypnotism*, 391.
35 Ibid., 332, 395.
36 Crabtree, *From Mesmer to Freud*, 328.
37 Cited by Taves, *Fits, Trances, and Visions*, 257.
38 For a discussion see Crabtree, *From Mesmer to Freud*, 335.
39 Alfred Binet, *Alterations of Personality: On Double Consciousness* (London: Chapman and Hall, 1896).
40 Pierre Janet, *L'automatisme psychologique: essai de psychologie expérimentale sur les formes inférieures de l'activité humaine* (Paris: F. Alcan, 1889). For an analysis see Edward M. Brown, "Pierre Janet and Félida Artificielle: Multiple personality in a nineteenth century guise," *Journal of the History of the Behavioral Sciences* 39 (2003): 279–288.

41 Max Dessoir, *Das-Doppel-Ich* (Leipzig: Gunther, 1890).
42 William James, *Principles of Psychology*, 2 vols. (London: Macmillan, 1890).
43 William James, *The Varieties of Religious Experience: A Study in Human Nature* (New York: Longmans, Green & Co. 1902): 88–89.
44 For a discussion see Laurence, *In Search of White Crows*.
45 Crabtree, *From Mesmer to Freud*, 258.
46 Frederic W. H. Myers, *Human Personality and its Survival of Bodily Death* (New York: Longmans, Green & Co., 1903).
47 Albert Moll, *Der Hypnotismus* (Berlin: Fischer, 1889).
48 Julian Ochorowicz, *Mental Suggestion* (New York: Humboldt, 1891).
49 Thomas Hudson, *The Law of Psychic Phenomena* (Chicago: A. C. McClurg, 1898). Discussed in Crabtree, *From Mesmer to Freud*, 279. The book sold over 100,000 copies.
50 Theodore Flournoy, *From India to the Planet Mars: A Study of a Case of Somnambulism*, trans. Daniel B. Vermilye (New York and London: Harper & Brothers, 1900).
51 Morton Prince, *Dissociation of a Personality* (New York: Longmans, Green & Co., 1906).
52 Boris Sidis, *The Psychology of Suggestion: A Research into the Subconscious Nature of Man and Society* (New York: D. Appleton, 1911).
53 Cited by Gauld, *History of Hypnotism*, 564.
54 This analysis, cogently presented in Taves, *Fits, Trances, and Visions*, 259–260, originated with Hugo Munsterberg, a colleague of William James at Harvard.
55 See Ian Hacking, *Rewriting the Soul: Multiple Personality and the Sciences of Memory* (Princeton, NJ: Princeton University Press, 1995): 44–45.
56 See, for example, Ian Hacking, "Telepathy: Origins of Randomization in Experimental Design," *Isis* 79, no. 3 (1988): 427–451.
57 Taves, *Fits, Trances, and Visions*, 260.
58 Charles Richet, *Thirty Years of Psychical Research*, trans. Stanley de Brath (New York: McMillan, 1923).
59 "Charles Richet: The Nobel Prize in Physiology or Medicine 1913," in *Nobel Lectures, Physiology or Medicine 1901–1921* (Amsterdam: Elsevier Publishing, 1967).

CHAPTER SIX

Laboratory and Clinic

During the 1890s Joseph Jastrow (1863–1944), who was to be the founder of the Department of Psychology at the University of Wisconsin, was conducting research on hypnosis, investigating the mechanisms of voluntary and involuntary behavior, and the processes of self-deception and self-control. As the century turned, he continued to be fascinated by everyday dissociations of mental processes, including daydreaming, slips in attention, and perceptions of involuntariness for behaviors actually under conscious control.[1]

Born in Poland, Jastrow did his doctoral work at Johns Hopkins, where he became a student of Granville Stanley Hall (1844–1924), the pioneer of American psychology and first president of the American Psychological Association. Jastrow admits, however, to have been more influenced by philosopher Charles S. Peirce (1839–1914) who encouraged him toward experimental psychology, and invested him with a love of logic.[2] Jastrow was also to become a close friend and a colleague of William James, who cited him frequently in his *Principles of Psychology*. More tellingly perhaps, James and Jastrow shared the same doctor during the recuperative summers spent together on the coast of Maine in the 1890s where they were both recovering from depression and exhaustion.[3] Their friendship flourished despite James' inquiries into spiritualism. Jastrow was a skeptic of metaphysical phenomena and spent much of his later career analyzing the human proclivity for what he saw as "cultish" beliefs.[4]

At the University of Wisconsin, where Jastrow was head of the psychology department, he taught a long-running course on the medical uses of hypnosis. The course would eventually be taken over by his most celebrated student, Clark Leonard Hull

(1884–1952). Jastrow and Hull were famously critical of each other's personal styles and professional choices.[5] Hull had studied mining engineering before switching to psychology and always identified strongly with his role as a laboratory scientist. Completing his doctoral work in 1918, Hull became an avowed behaviorist, narrowing the acceptable analysis of human beings to what he could observe, analyze, and preferably communicate mathematically. This effectively put out of bounds inquiry into "mentalist" internal processes.[6] Jastrow, in contrast, was a vocal anti-behaviorist, who employed a literary style in both his personal and professional writings that revealed deep, and perhaps frustrated, artistic sensibilities. Although both men were afflicted with notable professional arrogance, the differences between Jastrow and his student Hull foreshadow conflicts emerging over hypnosis much later in the century between practitioners and laboratory researchers and, more subtly, between those who celebrate a connection to William James within their intellectual lineage and those who do not.[7]

Hypnosis Research in the Early Twentieth Century

From World War I until the 1950s in the United States the most significant professional work associated with hypnosis was experimental rather than therapeutic in nature. While Hull's centrality within the mainstream story of the development of modern hypnosis has been long settled, Jastrow is generally left out.[8] Even at the time, he seems to have been underappreciated. His salary at Wisconsin was woefully low, and he was forced onto the lecture circuit to support his family. In the end he became a successful and active contributor to the American self-improvement and self-help traditions. After retiring from academic life, he published many successful books written for a lay audience, and hosted a radio show offering psychological advice.[9]

Hull's career provides a dramatic contrast. His central position in the story of twentieth century hypnosis is due to his own substantial labors, but also to the rapid success of behaviorism in establishing itself as the mainstream train of thought within American psychology. This gave him a professional advantage over those whose interest in hypnosis appeared to be looking backwards to the concerns of the nineteenth century, but Hull also took an active part in shaping the collective history of hypnosis and his own place within it.

In 1929 Hull left Wisconsin and began what would be a 23-year tenure at the Institute of Psychology at Yale University. His most famous student at Yale was Kenneth W. Spence (1907–1967), who would extend Hull's theoretical work on conditioning and learning. In 1929, however, Hull was still riveted on hypnosis. He published an article in *Scientific Monthly*, entitled "Hypnotism in Scientific Perspective," in which he set out a terse and unsentimental narrative. Anticipating and perhaps laying groundwork for his influential book, *Hypnosis and Suggestibility*, which came out in 1933, his rhetorical strategy was to construct an uncompromising boundary between the rational and the mystical and, by association, between the experimental and the clinical:

> All sciences alike have descended from magic and superstition, but none has been so slow as hypnosis in shaking off the evil association of its origin. None has been so slow in taking on a truly experimental and genuinely scientific character.[10]

The narrative does the work of separating Hull's approach to hypnosis from nearly everything that had come before him. After giving a nod to Mesmer, he traces his own intellectual tradition from Braid in Britain, and Faria in France, followed by Noizet, Bertrand, and Liébault, leading to Bernheim and finally Coué, though he is hardly effusive in his praise of any of these men:

> The century since 1825 has shown a remarkable sterility in this field. Almost nothing of significance has been accomplished during this period except the very gradual correction of errors which originally flowed directly from bad experimental procedures.[11]

Describing Bernheim's use of controls in his experiments to attack the work of Charcot, Hull goes on to decry what he sees as the lack of trained scientific investigators in the history of hypnosis. His objection to the century of research and practice on mesmerism and hypnosis arises from his belief that scientific research should be conducted in a laboratory:

> The dominant motive throughout the entire history of hypnotism has been clinical, that of curing human ills. A worse method for the

> establishment of scientific principles among highly elusive phenomena could hardly have been devised.[12]

Finally, calling for more rigorous application of experimental methods, Hull predicts a future for hypnosis within the scientific mainstream.

Though he subsequently moved on to other research interests, Hull is recognized for his significant contributions to the contemporary scientific study of hypnosis, particularly his development of the first scales for measuring suggestibility, and other instruments necessary for empirical study of the phenomena long associated with hypnosis. Hull's rigorous experimental work demonstrated, among other things, that hypnosis had no relationship with sleep, and that it did not foster any particularly spectacular, much less paranormal abilities in its subjects. He was, however, able to document the validity of other traditional hypnotic phenomena, including hypnotic anesthesia.[13]

Also doing experimental research in this area was Frank A. Pattie (1901–1999) who published in 1937 a study on hypnotically induced tactile anesthesia.[14] During the 1920s, Pattie received an A.M. from Harvard and completed his doctoral work at Princeton. He briefly returned to Harvard to teach before taking a position at Rice University in 1929. In 1947 he was recruited by the University of Kentucky where he spent the remainder of his professional career. He continued his intellectual pursuits after his retirement to the end of his life. Pattie is best known for his over 40 years of dedicated research on the life of Franz Mesmer which culminated in the 1994 publication of *Mesmer and Animal Magnetism: A chapter in the history of medicine.*[15]

Pattie was one of a group of hypnosis and personality researchers who were connected to Morton Prince at Harvard during the 1920s, a group that included William Sentman Taylor (1894–1976), Paul Campbell Young (1892–1991), and Henry Alexander Murray (1893–1988). Taylor was the first to graduate, receiving his Ph.D. from Harvard in 1921, going on to teach abnormal psychology at Smith College where he worked from 1926 to 1962. Young's doctoral dissertation, completed in 1923, was the first systematic experimental research on hypnosis to be completed at Harvard.[16] He moved on to become the head of the psychology department at Louisiana State University where he worked from 1925 to 1960.[17]

Murray's connection to hypnosis research at Harvard is more circuitous. Murray earned his M.D. at Columbia College of

Physicians and Surgeons in New York in 1919. While he was subsequently working toward a Ph.D. in biochemistry at Cambridge University in England during the 1920s, he traveled to Zurich and began a lifelong friendship with Carl Jung, a meeting that also influenced the turn in his career trajectory toward psychology.[18] After completing his doctoral work in 1927, Murray became an instructor at Harvard under Prince's supervision. The directorship of the Harvard Psychological Clinic that Prince had founded eventually passed to Murray, though he had never actually had formal training in psychology. Reflecting his diverse academic background, Murray's approach to the experimental laboratory was interdisciplinary by nature, and he shifted its focus from consciousness studies as favored by Prince, to his own intellectual preoccupation with personality.[19]

Murray was to author an important book about the career of Prince,[20] but he earns his real significance within the history of hypnosis for a different reason. Murray's eclectic approach to psychology caught the attention of the young Robert Winthrop White (1893–1988), whose research was more directly influential upon the development of hypnosis in the twentieth century. White had initially entered the Harvard doctoral program in 1928, the same year as B. F. Skinner, but after feeling his incompatibilities with the lab-intensive experimental technique of Edwin G. Boring (1886–1968), left the program for a teaching position at Rutgers. He returned three years later to work with Murray with whom he shared a preference for qualitative methods and a particular interest in "life-history" data.[21]

Murray had, after Prince's death, turned the energies of the Harvard Psychological Clinic to a massive study of personality, which became the basis of a landmark book.[22] White's participation in the project, which became his dissertation research, involved a study on hypnotic receptivity. Eventually replacing Murray as director of the Clinic, White continued his research on hypnosis for a few more years, a body of work that was to have enduring effect on the study of hypnosis through the second half of the twentieth century.[23] Uncomfortable with experimental research, however, White eventually shifted his attention to the study of personality, establishing a close personal and professional relationship with Gordon Allport (1887–1967), who would become a well-regarded social psychologist and personality theorist.

Hypnosis Research during the World Wars

William McDougall (1871–1938) was another significant presence at Harvard during the 1920s. He taught alongside Morton from 1920 to 1927 before moving to Duke University. Intellectually McDougall considered himself to be a student of William James, and found more to admire in the work of Janet than in Freud. He consistently opposed behaviorism, and was distressed by its growing prominence in American psychology. In his characteristically blunt and colorful way, he termed behaviorism "a most misshapen and beggarly dwarf."[24]

Born in England, McDougall's early education was broad, encompassing biology, geology, physiology, anatomy, and finally anthropology, the study of which he concluded with a formative stint of field research in Borneo. Rather than pursuing anthropology in his gradate studies, however, he returned to medical school, read William James and was immediately captivated by psychology, eventually becoming in 1900 a lecturer in psychology at University Hospital in London. He accepted a position at Oxford in 1904 where he remained until World War I.[25]

During the war McDougall drove an ambulance as a private in the French army; afterward he was commissioned a major in the British Royal Army Medical Corps where he worked with war-related mental disorders, employing hypnotic techniques in his treatment. Though he was influenced by Freud, McDougall also rejected key aspects of the creed. He described the war experience in his autobiography:

> Hypnosis proved very useful as a method of exploration but was not always indicated or feasible. Sympathetic rapport with the patient was the main thing, not a mysterious "transference" of a mythical "father-fixation" of the "libido"; but under the circumstances, a very natural and simple human relation. It is true that I felt like the father of a multitude of helpless children, hopelessly stumbling on the brink of hell.[26]

A more significant influence on McDougall's professional trajectory was British military psychiatrist W. H. R. (William Halse Rivers) Rivers (1864–1922), whom he had accompanied in 1898 on an anthropological expedition to the Torres Straits.

Rivers, who is remembered for his pioneering of cross-cultural psychological research,[27] became a lecturer in psychological and experimental psychology at Cambridge. He is recognized for his substantial contributions to the development of modern traumatology, shifting the theoretical paradigm of war-related mental illness from physiological to psychological trauma. Although Rivers also had been influenced by Freud, his work on trauma rejected the Freudian explanatory mechanism of infantile sexuality, looking instead to the repression of the horrors of the battlefield experience itself as the cause of mental distress.[28] Rivers employed hypnosis in his work with soldiers suffering from traumatic amnesia. His unique combination of experiences, from anthropology to war psychiatry, brought him to the realization that suggestion was the key to healing:

> Both faith and suggestion are of the greatest importance in psycho-therapeutics. It is undoubtedly to them that the remedies employed by the savage and barbarous peoples owe their efficacy, and they continue to be operative in the most modern forms of medicine.[29]

McDougall was in the United States when Rivers died. He continued his research on hypnosis, writing books on social psychology and abnormal psychology, and participating in the scientific study of psychic phenomena as well; in his autobiography he refuses to apologize for his own "thirty years of Psychical Research."[30] He is equally unrepentant about his attachment to a belief in the hereditary nature of group differences. McDougall confessed himself to have been unaware that addressing the racial question in the United States would stir up such a "hornet's nest."[31] The media antagonism generated by the support his work offered to eugenicist policies was to dog the public reception of his publications on all topics for the rest of his career. He ended his autobiography with a wistful and strangely naïve confession: "I have not been able to acquire James' magic touch which made all his readers his friends."[32]

McDougall died before World War II. Following him, the most significant work on hypnosis in Britain was accomplished beginning in the early 1940s by Hans Jürgen Eysenck (1916–1997), Walter Desmond Furneaux, and Hamilton Bertie "Tony" Gibson (1914–2001). Eysenck had arrived in England from Nazi Germany in 1934, and received his Ph.D. from London University in 1940. During the war he worked at the Mill Hill emergency hospital and, along with Furneaux, conducted substantial hypnosis research from the psychology department of the hospital. Meanwhile Gibson, a political anarchist, spent much of the war in prison as an unregistered conscientious objector. At Mill Hill Eysenck was investigating the reliability of psychiatric diagnoses.[33] The results of his study gave him a lifelong and vocal distrust of clinical psychology. After the war the trio of Furneaux, Gibson, and Eysenck studied hypnosis together and separately at the Institute of Psychiatry in London.

Later in his career Eysenck added to an already controversial reputation by engaging in the scientific study of astrology and parapsychology, at the same time that Gibson, who was largely responsible for the founding in 1978 of the British Society of Experimental and Clinical Hypnosis, had become an enthusiastic skeptic. In addition to being recognized as a major figure in the development of British psychology, outside the psychological and psychiatric community Eysenck is best remembered for his controversial belief in the power of racial heredity and its effects on intelligence. Both McDougall and Eysenck continue to be esteemed by the contemporary eugenics movement as intellectual martyrs; critics of the eugenicist tradition are significantly less flattering in their evaluations of their legacies.

Departing from the genetic determinism of McDougall and Eysenck, back in North America one of McDougall's own students of hypnosis at Harvard was to contribute a critical understanding of social factors that might influence racial measures, particularly economic and educational stratification.[34] This was George Hoben Estabrooks (1885–1973), a Canadian-American psychologist who received his doctorate at Harvard in 1926 after spending three years in Oxford as a Rhodes Scholar. Estabrooks was for many years chairman of the Department of Psychology at Colgate University, where he conducted research on hypnosis. He was a prolific, articulate, and eventually a popular writer as well. He is credited with the production of the first recorded hypnotic induction; it was released as a Victrola record.

Estabrooks launched himself into celebrity status for his relationship to the United States government during World War II, ostensibly "hypnoprogramming" government agents for intelligence operations and other government service. He discussed the possibility and advocated such a use of hypnosis in the chapter on "Hypnotism in Warfare" included in his 1943 book, *Hypnosis*.[35]

Estabrooks revealed his "super spy" work to the public in 1971, providing detailed descriptions of his method for programming double agents which involved the deliberate iatrogenic development of multiple personalities.[36] While one personality would remain loyal to the United States, a secondary personality could take on the philosophical beliefs of the organization he was to infiltrate and be completely loyal to it, unaware of the existence of the other personality that would willingly betray all of his secrets. It has been difficult for historians to assess the veracity of his claims, given the wide disagreement among hypnosis researchers about their theoretical validity.

The more mundane uses of hypnosis in the military that had become common following World War I were taken up in World War II. American army psychiatrists working in the field and military hospitals, like their British counterparts, were routinely trained in the use of hypnosis.[37] Colonel M. Ralph Kaufman, the chief neuropsychiatric consultant for the U.S. Army in 1944, for instance, helped to establish a psychiatric field hospital in the Philippines that relied on hypnosis for the rehabilitation of its psychological casualties. The success of hypnosis in the Philippines led to its battlefield use in 1945 during the Okinawa campaign.[38]

The successful therapeutic application of hypnosis by military physicians and psychotherapists during the two World Wars is one of the two most significant factors in the resurgence of interest in clinical hypnosis within the professional mainstream in the second half of the twentieth century. The other is the psychotherapeutic work of Milton Erickson (1902–1980) and his followers, whose innovations in the clinical practice of hypnosis would help to restore its popular fascination. Erickson's techniques, creative and sometimes controversial, enlivened traditional methods and powerfully influenced theorists and practitioners who worked from the margins to the mainstream of the psychotherapeutic world.

Psychological Healing in the Early Twentieth Century

When Erickson began his investigations of hypnosis as an undergraduate student at the University of Wisconsin in the 1920s, there was no formal clinical hypnosis training available to him there.

He ended up turning this historical circumstance into a fortuitous opportunity to create his own system of hypnotic psychotherapy. In fact the field of clinical hypnosis was not empty at all. It is only that many of the early practitioners of what may be termed psychotherapy operated outside the mainstream, finding it necessary to sustain their activity through popular interest and support. The politically and spiritually progressive H. Addington Bruce (1874–1959), for example, published two popular books, *The Riddle of Personality* in 1908 and *Scientific Mental Healing* in 1911, which explored hypnosis as well as the idea that the unconscious gives access to metaphysical realities and truths.[39] Directing his book to the lay reader, Bruce was tapping into the spiritual self-help tradition that had its roots in the nineteenth century, but which blossomed fully by the end of the twentieth.

The most cohesive "psychotherapeutic" initiative at the turn of the century was the Emmanuel Movement, which emerged as a mainstream response to Christian Science and New Thought, and other spiritual groups that mainline Protestants viewed as "healing cults." In a calculated attempt to undercut the appeal of the various mind-cure healing traditions, the Emmanuel Movement was a serious attempt to synthesize progressive mainline Christianity with the new psychological ideas about human consciousness.[40] Beginning in 1906, physicians began to appear in the Emmanuel Episcopal Church, under the guidance of its rector, Rev. Dr. Elwood Worcester (1862–1940). Worcester, in coordination with Dr. Joseph Pratt of Massachusetts General Hospital, made a cooperative "outreach" to the tuberculosis-ridden Boston slums.

By 1909 the Emmanuel Movement could be found in Brooklyn, Buffalo, Philadelphia, Detroit, Seattle, and San Francisco, and internationally in Britain, Ireland, Australia, South Africa, and Japan. Its religious sponsors now included Baptists, Presbyterians, Congregationalists, Universalists, and Unitarians, and the Catholic Church had even expressed some interest in similar ideas. Although the popularity of the movement was largely over by 1912, it would continue in Boston even after Worcester's death in 1929.[41]

The fledgling movement had enemies, however, and not only the Christian Scientists whose methods and philosophy they were trying to repudiate and replace. The mainstream medical and psychological community, which had been initially supportive of the Emmanuel Movement's psychotherapeutic innovations, within a few years circled the wagons around healing, both physical and mental, as their own professional territory. By withdrawing their participation, they killed what they had helped to create.[42] As Bruce read the situation in 1909, because mainstream medical doctors and even psychologists were looking for physiological explanations for psychological distress, those who were interested in the idea of psychotherapeutics were "studiously ignored."[43]

The Emmanuel Movement is periodically rediscovered by historians and credited for its many innovations, including the invention of both lay and group therapies. In its humane treatment of indigent alcoholic men, the movement was influential upon Bill Wilson, the founder of Alcoholics Anonymous. Other popular self-help programs and spiritual therapies that became widespread in the late twentieth century have their roots in the wide intellectual circle that can be drawn around William James at the beginning of the century. The work of Ira Progoff, M. Scott Peck, and Rollo May, for example, are all connected to nineteenth century healing traditions in which both mesmerism and hypnosis had played key roles.

In a parallel track, approaches associated with Norman Vincent Peale and his "Power of Positive Thinking" can be traced in an intellectual line back to Bernheim and Delboeuf through the "Neo-Nancy" work of Emile Coué (1857–1926). Trained in hypnosis by Liébault, Coué developed the "Coué method" of self-hypnosis which became hugely popular after the 1920 publication of his book *Self-mastery through Conscious Autosuggestion*, in which he laid out his basic technique:[44] Coué is most famous for his self-conditioning mantra, "*Tous les jours à tous points de vue je vais de mieux en mieux*"; "Day by day, in every way, I am getting better and better." Inventing the first "affirmation," Coué inspired an entire tradition of psychological self-improvement based on hypnotic auto-suggestion.

The Resurgence of Clinical Hypnosis

When Erickson attended the University of Wisconsin, the attitude of the medical profession toward healing of psychological disorders had already reverted to a physiological, somatic, and increasingly behavioral view of symptom treatment, which left little opening for clinical applications of hypnosis to operate. In summaries of the history of hypnosis Erickson is frequently named a student of Hull, leaving the impression that there was some type of mentoring relationship between them. The situation was significantly more complicated than that. Although the work of both Hull and Erickson would become tremendously influential during the same period, their success was unrelated to any intellectual or personal relationship between them. It was Jastrow who found Erickson to be a promising student, who encouraged and supervised some of his earliest formal experimental research, sometimes conducted without Hull's knowledge or approval.[45]

The exact details of the first interactions of Erickson and Hull are historically unresolved. According to Erickson, it was his own experimentation with hypnosis as an undergraduate student that first introduced Hull to the phenomenon, though Ernest Hilgard investigated this during the 1980s and was unable to find any confirmation of it in Hull's writings.[46] Regardless, their professional relationship began when Erickson, still an undergraduate, was invited by Hull to appear in a graduate seminar on hypnosis he was holding at the University of Wisconsin during the 1923–24 academic year. Erickson shared with the students his personal investigations into hypnosis, which sparked debate about the nature of hypnosis and its attendant phenomena. The course appears to have been successful, and it led to Erickson's involvement in experimental studies conducted by Hull. What it did not do was foster a fruitful collaborative relationship between them.

Erickson's objections to Hull's approach to hypnosis as well as his experimental style were immediate. Hull was working on establishing a standardized technique for hypnotic induction as a feature of his experiments. According to Erickson, Hull ideally would have liked to induce hypnosis through a phonograph recording that would insure the same instructions with the same inflections were used on every experimental subject. In Erickson's view, Hull appeared to "disregard subjects as persons, putting them on a par with inanimate laboratory apparatus, despite his awareness of such differences among subjects that could be demonstrated by tachistoscopic experiments." This is the reason Erickson gives for not consulting Hull when he began to conduct formal hypnosis experiments on his own, with Jastrow's support.[47]

Hull was even more unimpressed with Erickson. Not only did Erickson reject the necessity of standard inductions, he employed a highly personal and completely idiosyncratic method of inducing subjects into a trance state. His techniques, which would become the hallmark of Ericksonian psychotherapy, were apparent even in his first investigations. For example, Erickson experimented with hypnosis on a graduate student he names "Miss O," during a classroom seminar. He re-created in her the anger patterns of her childhood tantrums in which she typically would storm away from her parents. By having her storm in and out of the classroom, he was able to induce in her what he judged to be a productive trance state. Characteristically, it was more of an experiment in psychotherapy than hypnosis per se, but he was delighted by his success and eager to continue along this line.

Hull did not experience the same delight. As Erickson records the fallout, "the entire sequence of events was disturbing and obviously displeasing to Dr. Hull, since he felt that the importance of suggestion and suggestibility and the role of the operator in trance induction were being ignored and bypassed, with the result that this approach to a study of hypnosis was then abandoned in the University of Wisconsin seminars."[48] After going through his old notebooks of unpublished research, Erickson shared this story in 1964 in an article in *The American Journal of Clinical Hypnosis*. Readers didn't get to hear what happened next until 1967 when he continued the narrative, describing the results of his ongoing work with Miss O., who had, Erickson recalls, "volunteered for continued experimental work with the author."[49] Here Erickson does gives Hull some credit for inspiring his research: "the rejective attitude of Clark L. Hull toward the author's first experimental study of the nature of hypnotic phenomena stimulated still further investigation." It is perhaps not surprising that the two men soon experienced what Erickson calls "considerable estrangement" over their theoretical differences.[50]

From Erickson's earliest experiments it is possible to glimpse the characteristics of what would develop into an influential school of "Ericksonian" psychotherapy, a tradition that continues to be taught and practiced into the twenty-first century. Erickson received his medical degree at the Colorado General Hospital. Beginning in 1930 he was the chief psychiatrist of the Research Service of the Worcester Massachusetts State Hospital. He also taught at Wayne State University College as well as Michigan

State University at East Lansing before health issues caused his move to Phoenix, Arizona in 1948, where he set up a successful private practice. His Arizona home was to become a Mecca for aspiring Ericksonian psychotherapists and other mythopoeic pilgrims.

The Rise of Popular Hypnosis

Erickson's approach to hypnotic induction is often described as nondirective and naturalistic. He believed that the induction should be a highly personal process, ideally never conducted the same way twice. In his "utilization" technique, for instance, the clinician will "utilize" whatever the patient provides in the way of feelings, thoughts, behaviors, and beliefs. Among his other pioneering psychotherapeutic techniques, Erickson made use of paradox, humor, reframing, confusion, surprise, double-binds, metaphors, and the patients' own resistance. In teaching his approach to psychotherapy, he often employed the use of stories from his own life and practice.

For example, Erickson credited many of his insights and abilities to the substantial physical challenges and limitations he suffered in childhood, which included dyslexia, color blindness, tone deafness, and an excruciating rehabilitation from childhood polio contracted at the age of 17, which left him with post-polio syndrome. These sensory limitations, he believed, increased the sensitivity of his other senses, some quite subtle. For instance, although Jastrow tested Erickson and found him in the "lower one percentile of those who appreciated music or rhythm," his hearing range was above average for the very top and bottom of the normal range. This odd combination, Erickson believed, allowed him to become keenly aware of other people's breathing patterns.[51] He learned through trial and error that he could manipulate people's breathing, and then their speaking patterns, by pacing their breathing, and altering his own. He later discovered that he could use this technique as a hypnotic trance induction in clinical settings as well. He records the pertinent reflection of a 5-year-old patient who told Erickson that while his mother sang him to sleep, "you bweath me to sweep."[52]

This type of anecdote became a central teaching tool in Ericksonian psychotherapeutic training. In addition to Erickson's own writings, successful and increasingly popular publications by and in collaboration with his students, including Jay Haley and Ernest Rossi among others, contain many now classic stories of Erickson employing his techniques with astonishing success. Erickson is recognized for his contributions to the development of brief therapy, family therapy, systems-oriented therapy, solution-focused therapy, ordeal therapy, the psychobiological therapy developed by Rossi, and the neurolinguistic programming initiated by John Grinder. He was also a major influence across disciplines, most notably through his relationships with Virginia Satir, Margaret Mead, and Gregory Bateson. Generally speaking, Erickson contributed to a popular awareness of hypnosis, which dovetailed with efforts by increasing numbers of hypnosis practitioners, who were conducting their work both within and outside of the professional mainstream.

By the late 1940s hypnosis had become front page news, gaining attention from public and professionals alike. This occurred in part because of a wider explosion of interest in mental health disorders and treatments. The membership of the American Psychological Association increased from 3,000 in 1940 to 16,000 by 1950. Through the fifties, a spate of new psychological journals appeared, including the *American Journal of Clinical Hypnosis*, the *Annual Review of Hypnosis Literature*, the *Journal of Clinical and Experimental Hypnotism*, and the *Journal of Hypnosis and Psychology in Dentistry*. During this time hypnosis also took off within the eclectic and burgeoning field of "self-help" therapies.

Andrew Salter (1914–1996), who began a clinic to teach self-hypnosis,[53] Clark Bellows, who created the Institute of Applied Hypnotherapy, and Harry Arons, the author of the 1948 *Master Course in Hypnotism* and founder of the Association for the Advancement of Ethical Hypnosis, were among the rising number of hypnotic practitioners who contributed to the use of hypnosis outside of the mainstream, as a popular form of therapy. Public interest drove many nonprofessional practitioners out of the margins of culture and into the media limelight. Franz Polgar, Walter Gibson, Melvin Powers, and John Garrett were all stage hypnotists who drew substantial media attention and gained celebrity status. In 1949, Polgar hosted a 10-minute hypnosis demonstration, "Fun with the Mind," on CBS, which ran directly after the evening news. The public was arguably more interested in the use of hypnosis for therapy rather than entertainment, however, and hypnosis during this period has been described as the "lowbrow" version of psychoanalysis.[54]

At the sensational end of popular interest, the potential use of hypnosis for brainwashing began to grow in the public awareness after World War II, and took off during the Korean War. The apparently unlimited power of hypnosis as a tool for political interference, propaganda, and mind control was to become one of the anxious preoccupations of the Cold War era. The novel *The Manchurian Candidate* by Richard Condon, published in 1959, both expressed and disseminated the fear that our soldiers might have been or would be brainwashed while in enemy hands, becoming stealth Communists, with secret commands buried in their minds, which could later be triggered.[55]

Hypnosis researchers offered contradictory opinions regarding the possibility of using hypnosis to force people to commit criminal acts against their will. In his 1956 book *The Rape of the Mind*, Columbia University Professor of Psychology Joost Meerlo argued that Communist brainwashing, which he termed "mind-killing," was connected to the larger process of mass hypnosis that was occurring as a result of modernization and industrialization.[56] Cold War worries about the dangers of Communism leaked into popular views of hypnosis and it was increasingly portrayed as dangerous. Television and radio stations were pressured into limiting or canceling programs that dealt with hypnosis, because of fears that subliminal Communist messages were being delivered to the American public. Publications with titles like *Communism, Hypnosis and the Beatles* communicate the odd mixture of paranoia and fascination that characterized popular awareness of hypnosis, and that provided the backdrop for research and clinical practice during the final decades of the twentieth century.[57]

From Laboratory to Clinic

The supposed gap of half a century between the nineteenth century investigations of hypnosis of Bernheim, Janet, Prince, and James and the "golden age" of hypnosis that began in the 1960s may be largely attributed to a kind of historical rounding error. The last generation of nineteenth century hypnosis researchers and practitioners lived well into the twentieth century, continuing their research, writing books, and most importantly, training students, who then trained others in turn. The generation of hypnosis researchers who were engaged in their mature professional work beginning in the 1950s and 1960s had in many cases begun that work decades before.

The relative absence of institutionally driven clinical hypnosis prior to Erickson is usually attributed to the predominance of Freudian psychoanalysis, which marginalized not only hypnotic techniques, but also the mythopoeic approach of Jung that took inspiration from and had as its key sources the work of Flournoy and James.[58] But the overwhelming predominance of hypnosis laboratory research over clinical practice during the first half of the twentieth century can also be traced back to the aftermath of the victory of the Nancy School over Charcot's Salpêtrière at the end of the nineteenth century, and the new consensus on the central role of suggestion in the production of hypnotic phenomena.

A resolution had never been achieved, however, on the relationship of trance to the processes of suggestion. For the admirers of the work of Bernheim and Delboeuf, the trance was just another product of suggestion; those who were intrigued by the work on dissociation being done by Janet in France, and by James and Prince in the United States, among others, were more inclined to interpret the appearance of a trance state in a causal or explanatory way. This is the train of thought that led hypnosis to be understood, in shorthand definition, as a "state of heightened suggestibility."

The wrenching emotions that Hull and Erickson experienced in their disastrous academic relationship were an inheritance from battles that had preceded them but had never been resolved. Hull's preferred narrative of the history of hypnosis jumped directly from Bernheim to himself, with only the briefest nod to the self-help regimen of Coué. Although Hull did not completely discount the reality of the hypnotic trance state, his understanding of what that might be included a wholehearted rejection of the theories of dissociation proposed by Janet, James, and Prince, along with the association of their work with spiritualism, clairvoyance, telepathy, and multiple personality.

Hull's "dismay and discomfort" with the classroom experimentation of Erickson was not only a reaction to its lack of scientific precision, but also to its blurring of the boundaries between laboratory and clinic. Hull perceived the blending of religion and science that was prevalent in psychotherapeutic methods available during the first decade of the twentieth century to be a powerful threat to the development of scientific hypnosis. The failure to police that boundary could only lead to a persistence of the "evil association" of hypnosis with magic and superstition that had led to what he saw as the useless intellectual indulgences of James and Prince.

The chasm of professional inclination and differing ambitions that lay between Hull and both Jastrow and Erickson was deep. On one side there was the behaviorist, disinterested in the clinical ramifications of his research, dismissing the work of James and his intellectual circle, and lacking curiosity about the subjective experience of the "trance." Hull's contributions to hypnosis research centered on his development of rigorous scientific instruments and methods. He was proved to be correct that professional medical respect for hypnosis would follow from such a path. The substance of his research questions initiated crucial theoretical discussions, still continuing into the twenty-first century, having to do with suggestibility and hypnotic responsiveness.[59] If only one name is given for the most significant figure in hypnosis research in the first half of the twentieth century, invariably that will be Hull, and justifiably so.

On the other side of the chasm there were men like Jastrow and Erickson who shared interest in practical applications of hypnosis research. In his own corner of the new psychologically savvy world, Jastrow would become the host of a self-help radio show; Erickson would found a school of psychotherapy. They were both intellectually and, in the case of Jastrow, personally connected to James. More significantly, they were both fascinated by dissociative states, Jastrow by their spontaneous everyday occurrences and Erickson by their deliberate induction.

While the image of the hypnotist for Hull was an objective scientist, for Erickson the hypnotist was a subjective, intuitive, and frankly powerful character. Erickson accused Hull of treating a hypnotic subject as a piece of laboratory equipment, just another experimental variable. He was not the only researcher of the tim[illegible] to feel that way. White moved on from hypnosis to personali[illegible] research in part because he was uncomfortable with the narr[illegible] ness of the laboratory relationship between hypnotist and su[illegible] Eric[illegible] rejected the experimental approach, but then emb[illegible] [illegible]o deeply into his psychotherapeutic techniqu[illegible] [illegible]n looking at Ericksonian psychotherapy to [illegible]

While for Hull the appearance of a trance state was a variable to be accounted for, Erickson made it central to his investigations and pursued its therapeutic value as far as he could take it. His followers went further still. For Erickson, hypnosis *was* the trance; he blurred the distinctions between processes and products of suggestion almost completely. Between these two dramatic extremes, hypnosis theorists, researchers, and clinicians who studied with them and followed them would have to position themselves, and carve out territories for their own inquiries and applications. Within the intellectual landscape mapped out during the first half of the twentieth century, in the second half, hypnosis theory, research, and practice were soon, and extravagantly, to thrive.

Notes

1 Joseph Jastrow, *The Subconscious* (New York: Houghton Mifflin, 1907).

2 Joseph Jastrow, "Joseph Jastrow," in *A History of Psychology in Autobiography*, vol. 1, ed. Carl Murchison (New York: Russell & Russell, 1961): 135.

3 Ibid., 150.

4 Joseph J. Jastrow, *Fact and Fable in Psychology* (New York: Houghton Mifflin, 1901).

5 See Clark L. Hull, "Joseph Jastrow: 1863–1944," *The American Journal of Psychology* 57, no. 4 (1944): 581–585. Even Hull's published obituary for Jastrow is laced with left-handed compliments.

6 See Rodney G. Triplet, "The Relationship of Clark L. Hull's Hypnosis Research to his Later Learning Theory: The Continuity of his Life's Work," *Journal of History of the Behavioral Sciences* 18, no. 1 (1982): 22–31.

7 For an account of the legacy of James among hypnosis researchers see John F. Kihlstrom and Kevin M. McConkey, "William James and Hypnosis: A Centennial Reflection," *Psychological Science* 1, no. 3 (1990): 174–178.

8 Even Jastrow's papers were misplaced after his death. For the story of how his personal papers languished in a basement of Duke University ntil Arthur Blumenthal unearthed them for the 50th anniversary of iversity of Wisconsin's Department of Psychology, see Arthur umenthal, "The Intrepid Joseph Jastrow," in *Pioneers in Psychology*, imble, Gregory A., Wertheimer, Michael and Charlotte White ngton: American Psychological Association & Lawrence Associates, 1991): 75–87.

9 Ibid.

10 Clark L. Hull, "Hypnotism in Scientific Perspective," *The Scientific Monthly* 29 no. 2, (1929): 154–162.

11 Ibid., 160.

12 Ibid.

13 See Hull, Clark L. *Hypnosis and Suggestibility: An Experimental Approach* (New York: Appleton-Century-Crofts, 1933).

14 Frank A. Pattie, Jr. "The Genuineness of Hypnotically Produced Anesthesia of the Skin," *American Journal of Psychology* 49, no. 3 (1937): 435–443.

15 Pattie's exceptional collection of primary and secondary sources related to Mesmer, including 50 volumes published prior to 1800, was acquired intact in 1992 by Princeton University Library. For an assessment of Pattie's contributions, see William E. Edmonston, "Frank A. Pattie, PhD: In Memoriam," *American Journal of Clinical Hypnosis* 43, part 2, no. 2 (2000): 105–106.

16 Paul C. Young, "An Experimental Study of Mental and Physical Functions in the Normal and Hypnotic States," *American Journal of Psychology* 36, no. 2 (1925): 214.

17 Young was interviewed by Jack Fiser in 1980 for the T. Harry William Center for Oral History Collection at Louisiana State University. The five-hour interview covers his experiences while head of the Department of Psychology at LSU during the 1920s and 1930s.

18 Jung is credited for encouraging an extramarital relationship between Murray and Christiana Morgan (1897–1967), which continued until her death by suicide in 1967. In 1938 they developed together the Thematic Apperception Test (TAT). Although it was first known as the Morgan–Murray Thematic Apperception Test, it later became credited to only Murray and the "staff of the Harvard Psychological clinic." For Murray's explanation of this, see Henry A. Murray, "Dr. Henry A. Murray replies (Letter to the editor)," *Second Century Radcliffe News* 6, no. 1 (1985): 2.

19 Rodney G. Triplet, "Henry A. Murray. The Making of a Psychologist?" *American Psychologist* 47 no. 2 (1992): 299–307.

20 See Henry A. Murray, "Morton Prince: Sketch of his Life and Work," *Journal of Abnormal and Social Psychology 52* (1956): 291–295.

21 Robert W. White, *Lives in Progress: A Study of the Natural Growth of Personality*. 3d ed. (New York: Holt, Rinehart and Winston, 1975).

22 Henry A. Murray, *Explorations in Personality: A Clinical Study of Fifty Men in College* (New York: Oxford University Press, 1938).

23 See Robert F. Bale and others, "FAS Memorial Minute: Robe[illegible] Winthrop White," *Harvard University Gazette*, May 23, 2[illegible] available online at: http://www.hno.harvard.edu/gazette/2002/0[illegible] 18-memorialminute.html.

24 Cited in Frank Pattie, "William McDougall: 1871–1938," *American Journal of Psychology* 52, no. 2 (1939): 307.
25 See also William McDougall, "William McDougall," in *A History of Psychology in Autobiography*, vol. 1, ed. Carl Murchison (New York: Russell & Russell, 1961): 191–233.
26 McDougall, "William McDougall," 211.
27 For an account of Rivers' life and anthropological career, see Richard Slobodin, *W. H. R Rivers: Pioneer Anthropologist, Psychiatrist of the Ghost Road* (New York: Sutton, 1997).
28 See Allan Young, "W. H. R. Rivers and the War Neuroses," *Journal of the History of the Behavioral Sciences* 35, no. 4 (1999): 359. Young disputes the traditional association of Rivers as a Freudian, since he differed with Freud at so many key points. In his approach to memory and healing, he followed Janet more than Freud.
29 Cited by Young, W.H.R. Rivers, 375.
30 McDougall, "William McDougall," 221–222.
31 Ibid., 213.
32 Ibid., 223.
33 See Claire Hilton, "Mill Hill Emergency Hospital: 1939–1945," *Psychiatric Bulletin* 30, no. 3 (2006): 106–108.
34 George H. Estabrooks, "That Question of Racial Inferiority," *American Anthropologist* 30 (1928): 470–475.
35 George H. Estabrooks, *Hypnotism* (New York: E.P. Dutton, 1943).
36 George H. Estabrooks, "Hypnosis Comes of Age," *Science Digest*, April, 1971: 44–50.
37 Robert Genter, "'Hypnotizzy' in the Cold War: The American Fascination with Hypnotism in the 1950s," *Journal of American and Comparative Cultures* 29, no. 2 (2006): 154–169.
38 Ralph M. Kaufman and Lindsay Beaton, "A Psychiatric Treatment Program in Combat," *Bulletin of the Menninger Clinic* 11, no. 1 (1947): 411–421.
39 See H. Addington Bruce, *The Riddle of Personality* (New York: Moffat, Yard & Company, 1908); and H. Addington Bruce, *Scientific Mental Healing* (Boston: Little, Brown & Co., 1911).
40 For a full account of the Emmanuel Movement, see Caplan, *Mind Games* 117–148.
41 See Raymond J. Cunningham, "The Emmanuel Movement: A Variety of American Religious Experience," *American Quarterly* 14, no. 1 (1962): 48–63.
42 See Sandford Gifford, *The Emmanuel Movement The Origins of Group Treatment and the Assault on Lay Psychotherapy* (Boston, MA: Harvard University Press, 1997).
I. Addington Bruce, "Mental Healing of To-day," *Outlook* XCIII 909): 32; cited in Cunningham, "The Emmanuel Movement," 49.

44 Emile Coué, *Self-mastery through Conscious Autosuggestion* (New York: American Library Service, 1922).
45 Milton H. Erickson, "Initial Experiments Investigating the Nature of Hypnosis," in *The Nature of Hypnosis and Suggestion: The Collected Papers of Milton H Erickson on Hypnosis*, vol. 1, ed. Ernest L. Rossi (New York: Irvington Publishers, 1980): 4. Originally published in *The American Journal of Clinical Hypnosis* 7 (1964): 152–162.
46 Ernest R. Hilgard, *Psychology in American: A Historical Survey* (Forth Worth, TX: Harcourt Brace Jovanovich, 1987).
47 Erickson, "Initial Experiments," in *The Nature of Hypnosis*, 4.
48 Ibid., 15.
49 Milton H. Erickson, "Further Experimental Investigation of Hypnosis: Hypnotic and Nonhypnotic Realities," in *The Nature of Hypnosis and Suggestion*, 18. Originally published in *The American Journal of Clinical Hypnosis* 10 (1967): 87–135.
50 Ibid., 39.
51 Milton H. Erickson, "Respiratory Rhythm in Trance Induction: The Role of Minimal Sensory Cues in Normal and Trance Behavior," in *The Nature of Hypnosis and Suggestion*, 363.
52 Ibid., 361.
53 Andrew Salter, "Three Techniques of Autohypnosis," *Journal of General Psychology* 24 (1941): 423–438.
54 Genter, "Hypnotizzy," 160.
55 Richard Condon, *The Manchurian Candidate* (New York: McGraw Hill, 1959).
56 Joost A. M. Meerlo, *The Rape of the Mind: The Psychology of Thought Control, Menticide, and Brainwashing* (New York: World Publishing Co., 1956).
57 David A. Noebel, *Communism, Hypnotism and the Beatles: An analysis of the Communist use of music – the Communist master music plan* (Christian Crusade Publications, 1965).
58 Sonu Shamdasani, *Encountering Hélène: Théodore Flournoy and the Genesis of Subliminal Psychology* (London: Routledge, 1994). See also Ronald Goldsmith, "The Life and Work of Théodore Flournoy," Ph.D. thesis, Michigan State University, 1979.
59 See Hull, *Hypnosis and Suggestibility*. See also Kenneth W. Spence, "Clark Leonard Hull: 1884–1952," *The American Journal of Psychology* 65, no. 4 (1952): 639–646.

CHAPTER SEVEN

State and Trait

As hypnosis moved back into the mainstream after World War II, researchers and clinical practitioners soon clashed over the same questions that Bernheim and his opponents had so provocatively framed during the nineteenth century: Which aspects of hypnosis are essential, and which are products of suggestion? If even the hypnotic trance is a product of suggestion, then where does that leave hypnosis? Hull's investigation of the matter measured the effects of suggestions with and without a formal hypnotic induction. What he found was that hypnotic and non-hypnotic responsiveness to suggestion were highly correlated. The effect of the ritual induction of hypnosis was "far less than the classical hypnotists would have supposed had the question ever occurred to them."[1] This correlation has since demonstrated itself to be highly robust.[2]

Focusing on the relatively small effect that the hypnotic induction seemed to have on suggestibility, Hull accepted the trance as a causal factor which begged some explanation. In his seminal 1941 article, Robert W. White (1904–2001) offered one, and in so doing, defined the contours of the debate for decades to follow.[3] White argued that hypnotic subjects were sensitive to the wishes of the hypnotist, and would respond to unspoken as well as deliberate suggestions: "Hypnotic behavior is meaningful, goal-directed striving, its most general goal by the subject being to behave like a hypnotized person as this is continuously defined by the operator and understood."[4]

In this articulation, White provided a starting place for what would eventually be the "social cognitive" view of hypnosis; however, like Hull, White also believed that hypnotic behavior was produced within an altered state of consciousness that included measurable cognitive changes. The contested terrain of hypnosis during the second half of the twentieth century, following the work of Hull and White in the 1930s to 1940s, would center on the balance between these two ideas. To what extent is the altered state a causal or explanatory factor for other hypnotic phenomena, or should the altered state itself be understood as another product of suggestion?

Neodissociation Theory

Beginning in the 1950s and continuing into the 1970s, the views of researchers, theorists, and practitioners of hypnosis, particularly in the United States, became polarized into two opposing positions characterized by their attachment to either "altered state" or "non-state" theories. Altered state theorists, generally speaking, set out to explain at least some aspects of hypnosis (e.g., increased suggestibility) as due to the presence of a trance state; in contrast, non-state theorists looked to cognitive and social behavior to completely explain hypnotic phenomena.

The most influential of the early state theorists was Ernest Ropiequet Hilgard (1904–2001), whose professional career began at Stanford University in 1933, after completing his doctoral work, on conditioned responses in learning, at Yale under the supervision of Raymond Dodge (1871–1942). In partnership with his wife, Josephine Rohrs Hilgard (1906–1989), whose landmark interview research identified an important link between imaginative involvement and hypnotizability, and with the support of colleague Andre M. Weitzenhoffer (1921–2005),[5] he set up the Laboratory of Hypnosis Research in Stanford, serving as its director from 1957 until 1979. In the early years of the Laboratory, Hilgard and Weitzenhoffer developed the widely used "Stanford Scales" of hypnotic susceptibility that are still the gold standard measures of susceptibility.

Hilgard later developed "neodissociation theory" through which he explored the hypothesis that the human mind is composed of multiple cognitive systems, organized in a hierarchy and controlled by an "executive ego."[6] He proposed that cognitive subsystems carry out habitual actions that are activated by that central control system, but once they are activated, the subsystems do their work with little interference from the executive ego. This is the reason why, for instance, we might be surprised to find ourselves driving to the store along our habitual route, even though it had been our original intention, when we got in the car, to go to the bank.

According to Hilgard, hypnotic suggestions are accompanied by a division of the executive ego into two parts separated by an amnesic barrier. This results in the subjective feeling that hypnotic responses are not volitional, although this is not actually the case. For example, in response to a typical "ideomotor" suggestion to lift or bend an arm, the executive ego must intentionally activate it for the arm to move. When the central control system is dissociated, however, the amnesiac barrier prevents the executive ego from being aware of its own command.[7] In Hilgard's theory, dissociation is not unique to hypnosis, but also describes a variety of mundane experiences as well (e.g., unintentionally driving home, when one was intending to drive to a less usual destination). For this reason, it is no longer considered strictly as an altered state theory. The terms "state" and "non-state" were gradually replaced by the more descriptive terms "special process" and "sociocognitive" in the 1980s.

Empirical evidence for Hilgard's model has been sought in the phenomenon of the "hidden observer," a self-aware part of consciousness that remains immune to suggestion during a hypnotic induction. Hilgard first demonstrated the phenomenon of the hidden observer in a subject who had responded to the suggestion that he was completely deaf.[8] Despite having no startle response to loud noises, the subject nonetheless responded to what Hilgard said next: "Although you are hypnotically deaf, perhaps there is some part of you that is hearing my voice and processing the information. If there is I should like the index finger to rise as a sign that this is the case."[9] The rising finger of the subject indicated to Hilgard the existence of some dissociated, "hidden" part of the subject that remained fully aware during a hypnotic procedure. The existence of a hidden observer is important for neodissociation theory in that it provides direct empirical support. Not surprisingly, the hidden observer phenomenon became the subject of many studies, in the context of a wide variety of hypnotic responses, and the results have been used both to support neodissociation theory, and to critique it.[10]

One clear strength of the theory is that it proposes the same underlying mechanism to produce a range of hypnotic phenomena. The model accounts for hypnotic analgesia, for instance, through the mechanism of the dissociation of the central control system. It is not that the pain is not being experienced, but only that the pain is only perceived by the dissociated part of the ego, the part that is evoked during hypnosis as the hidden observer.[11] Similarly, amnesia in a subject also can be explained by the dissociation of the executive ego into a part that receives the output from a memory substructure, and another part that has no apparent access to the memory.

Altered State Theories

An influential altered-state theorist, and a colleague of Hilgard's, Kenneth S. Bowers (1937–1996), came to believe that the postulation of an amnesic barrier as an underlying mechanism revealed a weakness of the neodissociation model. The problem, according to Bowers, is that the approach attempts to explain commonplace phenomena (like driving unintentionally to the store) through a relatively rare one – the spontaneous creation of an amnesiac barrier.[12] Research indicates that suggested amnesia is successful in no more than 25% of hypnotized subjects.[13] Bowers developed his theory of "dissociated control" to address this problem and it emerged as a critical alternative to Hilgard's neodissociation perspective.[14]

Receiving his doctorate in clinical psychology from the University of Illinois in 1964, Bowers spent his professional career at the University of Waterloo in Ontario, Canada, but was twice a visiting scholar at Stanford early in his career, working closely with Hilgard, and he returned to Stanford in 1983 as a Visiting Professor. Bowers, Eric Z. Woody, and other proponents of the dissociated control approach employ the term dissociation to describe a different mechanism than did Hilgard. As they use the term, dissociation does not refer to a divided executive ego, but rather a disengagement of subsystems from conscious control.[15] That separation means that "subsystems of control can be directly and automatically activated, instead of being governed by high level executive control."[16] In this view, hypnotic subjects in this state function rather like people suffering from frontal lobe disorders.[17]

Most recently, neodissociation theory has also been extended in significant ways by John F. Kihlstrom, who has addressed the types of dissociation that may occur in the context of hypnosis: dissociations between experience and memory, and between pain and the experience of pain, for instance.[18] He is also recognized for incorporating new models of cognitive psychology into hypnosis theory and research, including memory models and difference between procedural and declarative knowledge.[19]

Kihlstrom completed his doctoral work in personality and experimental psychopathology in 1975 at the University of Pennsylvania, where he taught until 1987; he has since continued his work at the Universities of Arizona, Yale, and Berkeley. Appealing for tolerance and inclusivity across the state/non-state divide,[20] Kihlstrom's attachment to the "state" tradition appears to arise from his identification with an intellectual lineage that leads back to William James.[21] His interest in cultivating the center ground may be reflective of the collegial relationship he enjoyed with his graduate mentor, Martin T. Orne (1927–2000).

Orne began his investigation of the subjective experiences of hypnotic subjects in the 1950s. Born in Vienna, he received a medical degree from Tufts in 1955 and in 1958 earned his doctorate in psychology from Harvard, where he had been a student of Robert White. Orne spent 32 years as professor of psychology and psychiatry at the University of Pennsylvania where he developed his phenomenological, or interactive, model of hypnosis. Orne's approach is sometimes misjudged by state theorists to represent the non-state position, and by non-state theorists to be supporting a state view. In fact, the model deliberately incorporates aspects of both, and focuses particularly on differences between hypnotic and waking cognitive activities.[22]

Important theorists continuing to work in this area include Peter W. Sheehan and Kevin M. McConkey.[23] Sheehan's mentor at the University of Sydney was John Philip Sutcliffe (1926–2000), the most important figure in the birth of experimental hypnosis research in Australia. Sutcliffe's Ph.D., which he completed in 1959, was supervised by Robert White in Boston, Hans Eysenck in London, and A. Gordon Hammer (1914–1999) in Sydney. Hammer and Sutcliffe were to educate an entire generation of Australian hypnosis researchers who dispersed diaspora-like across the planet, including Sheehan, Fred Evans, and Campbell Perry (1937–2003), who also worked with Orne at the University of Pennsylvania.[24] Australian hypnosis researchers are recognized in particular for their contributions to methodological and experimental design in hypnosis research.

Sheehan's contextual model, for example, highlights the interactive and reciprocal relations at work in the hypnotic context, shedding light on the "fine-grained variation" in responsiveness to suggestions among very highly suggestible participants.[25]

In a similar vein, McConkey, who was Sheehan's student, and worked with Perry and Jean-Roch Laurence at Concordia during the 1980s, has studied variables in hypnotic responses, examining the meaning that subjects place on the hypnotist's communications, and the idiosyncratic ways in which they cognitively process suggestions. The work of Sheehan and McConkey is related to other interactional approaches to hypnosis that consider multiple, dynamically interacting determinants of hypnotic responding. Australian psychologists Amanda Barnier and Richard Bryant, both students of McConkey, have continued this tradition and focused on posthypnotic amnesia and emotional responses during hypnosis, respectively, and forged productive collaborations with researchers in the United States. Graham Jamieson, another of Sheehan's students, now at the University of New England (Australia), teamed with Erik Woody, at the University of Waterloo (Canada), to elaborate the cognitive-neuroscience underpinnings of dissociative control theory, and collaborated with the prolific neuroscientist John Gruzelier of Imperial College, London, to study the relation between hypnosis and frontal lobe function.

Another approach to altered states theories of hypnosis emerged from the psychodynamic tradition. Erika Fromm, Michael Nash, and Elgan Baker described how hypnosis could be understood in terms of modern psychodynamic theory, emphasizing the ability of hypnosis to increase the availability of imagination, fantasy, and other primary process thinking. Erika Fromm (1909–2003) received her Ph.D. from the University of Frankfurt, and emigrated from Nazi Germany to the Netherlands and then to the United States in 1938. She became a professor of psychology at the University of Chicago the following year, where she was an inspiring teacher who trained many practitioners of hypnosis, and, in collaboration with Michael Nash, introduced hypnotic methods to a new generation of psychodynamic therapists. Nash completed his doctoral work with Steven Jay Lynn at Ohio University, and then established an active laboratory at the University of Tennessee. Nash contended that hypnosis engenders a special state of psychological regression with specific properties that include an increase in primary process material, more spontaneous and intense emotion, unusual body sensations, the experience of nonvolition, and the tendency to develop a special rapport with the hypnotist. Elgan Baker received his Ph.D. from the University of Tennessee in 1976, and is a member of the faculty in the Department of Psychiatry at Indiana University School of Medicine. Baker described how hypnosis could be understood in terms of object relations theory, and applied to the treatment of serious personality disorders, including borderline personality. His work integrates psychoanalytic theory with hypnotic phenomenology.

Non-State Theories

The history of the sociocognitive perspective begins with Theodore R. Sarbin (1911–2005) who, as early as 1950, first challenged the traditional association of hypnosis with the hypnotic trance state, particularly the presumption that it functions as a causal factor in the experience of hypnotic suggestibility. In general, theorists who take a "non-state position" may accept dissociation as a descriptive, but not an explanatory phenomenon. They maintain that subjects' beliefs, expectations, and imaginings about hypnosis, and their interpretations of the suggestions of the hypnotist, are sufficient to explain hypnotic response.

After receiving his doctorate from Ohio State University in 1941, Sarbin became a research-oriented clinical psychologist. Working at UC Berkeley from 1949 until 1969 and then at the UC Santa Cruz until 1976, he was recognized for his development of "role theory" with applications across the field of psychology. Analyzing hypnosis as social psychological behavior, he applied role theory to the study of hypnosis, looking at the relationship between hypnotist and subject and identifying the implicit and explicit scripts that each would follow. In this view it is not the hypnotic induction that produces a response in a subject, but the belief that the response is an appropriate one for a hypnotized subject to produce. People who display arm catalepsy in response to a hypnotic suggestion are more likely to do so if they have been told that this is something that hypnotized subjects typically do, for instance.[26]

Sarbin deliberately used the term *role taking* as opposed to *role playing* because he did not intend to imply that subjects were only pretending to experience hypnosis. According to Sarbin, subjects may be completely unconscious of the role they are taking on. Noting individual differences in the ability to take on the hypnotic role, however, he found that acting students responded better to hypnotic suggestions than science students, for example.[27] Sarbin continued to pursue a narrative, dramaturgical model throughout his career, and with colleague William C. Coe (1930–2004) identified a range of variables that affect hypnotic responsiveness, including those associated with knowledge, expectations, and imagination. Sarbin coined the evocative term "believed-in imaginings" to describe the spontaneous distortions of reality that can occur both within the hypnotic context and in ordinary life.[28] Generally speaking, role theory analyzes the experiences of a hypnotic subject as a performance within an active, collaborative, and imaginative relationship, not essentially different from the dynamics of non-hypnotic relations.

Although influenced by Sarbin's approach to hypnosis, Theodore X. Barber (1927–2005) criticized its logical circularity, since hypnotic responsiveness is used both to indicate the presence of a hypnosis state and is also explained by it.[29] Working for 35 years at the Medfield Foundation and Cushing State Hospital in Massachusetts, Barber conducted an extensive series of studies during the 1960s and early 1970s.[30] He concluded that hypnotic responses were strongly correlated to an even wider array of factors, including attitudes, expectancies, the wording and tone of suggestions, motivations, the definition of the situation as "hypnosis," suggestions for relaxation, the wording of the inquiry with which the response is assessed, and the behavior adopted by the experimenter.

In contrast to other sociocognitive theorists, Barber is noted for emphasizing individual differences in imaginative ability as one of the key determinants of hypnotic responsiveness.[31] For Barber, the bottom line, however, is that hypnosis can have positive therapeutic outcomes regardless of the innate hypnotic ability of a subject, and regardless of whether the subject experienced a dissociated state.[32] In his later work, he suggested that different individuals may respond to hypnotic suggestions according to their own distinctive personal style; although some people respond dissociatively, others do not.[33]

Combining and extending both Sarbin's role theory and Barber's cognitive behavioral theory, the work of Nicholas P. Spanos (1942–1994) was to become one of the most influential sociocognitive approaches to hypnosis at the end of the twentieth century. Spanos began his prolific career working with Barber at the Medfield Foundation before moving to Carleton University in Ottawa in 1975. The research of Spanos and his colleagues, including John Chaves, who also worked with Barber at the Medfield

Foundation, focused on social psychological processes, particularly the dynamics of communication that lead subjects to understand their role as a hypnotic subject, and to interpret hypnotic suggestions in certain ways.[34]

Spanos coined the term "special process" as an alternative label for altered state theories, to reflect their shared premise that hypnotic behavior is essentially different from non-hypnotic behavior, because it is produced by a trance state or through a related process of dissociation.[35] Social psychological (or cognitive-behavioral) theories, in contrast, seek to explain hypnotic behavior using the same variables that account for non-hypnotic behavior.

Analyzing the hidden observer phenomenon in this way, Spanos argues that unless the hidden observer exists independently of the participant's expectations and the instructions used to communicate with it, the appearance of the hidden observer in research or clinical settings cannot be used as empirical support for neodissociation theory. Spanos and colleagues conducted a series of hidden observer studies which demonstrated that manifestations of the hidden observer were highly sensitive to the content and the explicitness of instructions the subjects were given regarding the hidden observer phenomenon.[36]

Research has shown that depending on the details of the instructions with which they are created, hidden observers will report more or less pain, will either reverse mathematical figures, or not, and report more or less effort associated with an ideomotor response. Spanos concludes that because of their sensitivity to beliefs and expectations, both preexisting and those arising from situational demands and instructional cues, the phenomenon does not provide support for the existence of spontaneously occurring dissociated aspects of the personality. Such findings led Irving Kirsch and Steven Jay Lynn to dub the hidden observer a "flexible observer." Instead of being the basis for all suggested responses, they view the hidden observer as another expectancy-related product of suggestion.[37] Significant disagreement over how to study the hidden observer phenomenon, and then how to analyze the results, has continued over decades and into the present.[38]

Graham Wagstaff, of the University of Liverpool, is an influential sociocognitive theorist who was strongly influenced by Barber, Sarbin, and Orne. Wagstaff was a founding member of the British Society of Experimental and Clinical Hypnosis, and, beginning in the

1980s, advanced the hypothesis that the term hypnosis refers to a collection of phenomena that can't be accounted for by a single explanation.[39] More than any other sociocognitive theorist, Wagstaff has emphasized the influence of compliance in hypnotic suggestibility.

The particular role of expectancy in the hypnotic subject has become a central focus of sociocognitive theorist Irving Kirsch, who argues that people's expectations of their hypnotic response produce hypnotic experiences through the same mechanism that allows placebos to produce changes in pain, anxiety, and other subjective states, as well as objective, physiological conditions. His "response expectancy theory" predicts that a subject's expectancy can increase the sense of non-volition during their hypnotic experience. When hypnotic inductions are understood to be a systematic manipulation of expectancy, in his view the induction works exactly as placebo drugs do.[40]

Kirsch, who did his doctoral work with Milton Wolpin at the University of Southern California, argues that through the centuries when hypnosis and hypnosis-like techniques have "worked," they have done so regardless of whether the practitioner banged on a gong, flashed a light, magnetized water, counted backwards, or shouted "Sleep!" What they had in common was that they were all labeled as "mesmerism" or "hypnosis." According to Kirsch, under proper conditions most techniques will work as well as any other, because the operative agent is the expectancy of the subject, not the essential power of the technique.

Steven Lynn's "integrative model" is the basis for research that examines the array of situational, personal, and interpersonal factors that a hypnotic subject integrates in a creative problem-solving way during a hypnotic induction.[41]

Lynn did his doctoral work at Indiana University with Kenneth Heller, a clinical psychologist, and Steven J. Sherman, a social psychologist. Lynn's approach places its emphasis on unconscious determinants of hypnotic responsiveness, as well as rapport and relationship factors. Lynn and his colleagues, Judith Rhue at the Ohio College of Osteopathic Medicine, and Joseph Green at Ohio State University (Lima), have argued that features of the hypnotic context discourage awareness and analysis of the personal and situational factors that influence hypnotic responses. For example, typical hypnotic inductions are worded so as to direct attention inward, to reduce vigilance, and to diminish the importance of action on the environment.[42]

Combining aspects of Kirsch's response expectancy theory with Lynn's integrative model, Kirsch and Lynn have collaborated in the development of "response set theory," an approach that looks at the automation of ordinary human activity to investigate the subjective experience of non-volition in hypnotic subjects.[43] Response set theory proposes that most actions, hypnotic or not, ordinary or unusual, planned or unplanned, are initiated automatically at the moment of activation, rather than resulting from a conscious intention. The implication of this hypothesis is that the real illusion is not the subjective experience of involuntary or automatic action that occurs in the hypnotic context; rather it is the experience of volition that we assume characterizes our everyday behavior.[44]

The sociocognitive perspective has been extended to health psychology and dentistry. John Chaves, a long-time colleague of Spanos, investigated the role of suggestions in minimizing catastrophic thinking in response to painful stimuli. As a psychologist who served in administrative positions at Indiana University and Stonybrook University dental schools, Chaves was instrumental in establishing the credibility of hypnosis in the dental profession.

Convergence in the State/Non-State Debate

Despite seemingly incompatible differences in approach to the phenomena associated with hypnosis, the middle ground in the state/non-state debate has also been explored. It has been argued that Hilgard moved toward the center as early as 1969 when he suggested that the term "state" could be productively understood as a descriptive rather than explanatory construct.[45] If the term "altered state of consciousness" is taken to mean that hypnotized individuals "report experiencing subjective alterations,"[46] this presents little problem to most non-state theorists, who have always acknowledged that feelings of relaxation and involuntariness, for example, occur frequently in subjects during hypnosis, though they add the caveat that similar experiences may be reported without a hypnotic induction as well.[47]

Many theorists associated with state theories now accept the "weak" definition of altered state. If it is treated as a metaphor, as Kihlstrom notes, "the question of whether hypnosis is a special state of consciousness disappears as substantive issue."[48] But others have resisted any weakening of the traditional definition. Charles Tart, for instance, another prominent proponent of the altered state position, has been especially critical of weakened versions of the state construct, defining altered states as "major alterations in both the content and pattern of functioning of consciousness."[49]

The altered state controversy continues, despite periodic pronouncements of theoretical convergence.[50] While a number of researchers and clinicians with loyalties to one view or the other are unwilling to allow the debate to be declared "dead,"[51] others make pronouncements of victory: "We can now acknowledge that hypnosis is indeed a 'state' and redirect energies earlier spent on the 'state–nonstate' debate."[52]

Although the state debate clearly has not disappeared, its contours have substantially altered, and the image of two opposing camps is no longer accurate. The field of hypnosis is left with a continuum of varying positions on the issue. At one end are the scholars who hold to a belief in the traditional concept of the hypnotic state in its strongest form, that is to say, a condition that is fundamentally different from normal waking consciousness (but also from other altered states such as daydreaming and relaxation), the presence of which determines whether the hypnotic induction has been successful.

Many followers of Milton Erickson take this view. Erickson believed that there were several specific behavioral markers defining the hypnotic trance state. These included literalness (for instance, answering "no" to the question "Do you mind telling me your name?"), as well as spontaneous catalepsy and amnesia.[53] Erickson used the terms therapeutic trance and clinical hypnosis synonymously, and emphasized the uniqueness of the experience of hypnosis for each person, and the therapist's ability to use "trance" to gain access to and bolster personal resources.

Also at the "state" end of the continuum are psychoanalytic theorists who believe that the defining characteristics of the trance state include easier access to the unconscious, a shift toward primary-process thinking, greater ego-receptivity, and regression of the ego.[54]

The theory of dissociated control, as articulated by Bowers and Woody, has provided another unambiguous state theory.[55] Most recently, new brain imaging technologies that can measure neurophysiological changes during hypnotic procedures seem to be creating a new generation of state theorists.[56]

Other researchers not mentioned earlier in this context who have made important strides in understanding the physiological underpinnings of hypnotic responsiveness include Arreed Barabasz at Washington State University, William Ray at Pennsylvania State University, Vilfredo DePascalis at the University of Rome, Amir Raz at McGill University, David Oakley at University College London, David Spiegel at Stanford University, Helen Joan Crawford at Virginia Polytechnic Institute, Pierre Rainville at the University of Montreal, and Stephen Kosslyn at Harvard University. A number of these researchers have criticized nonstate theorists for exaggerating the influence of expectancies, social demands, and the extent to which hypnotic behaviors are strategic and goal-directed.

The other end of the continuum is populated by those whose approach to the issue tends to fit one of three basic patterns. There are theorists who, like Kihlstrom, use the term state to describe hypnotic phenomena, without claiming that it explains or causes those phenomena.[57] There are others, like McConkey and Sheehan, who value an intellectual relationship to the altered state position, but who do not incorporate an explicit state theory into their models of hypnotic responsiveness.[58] Finally, there are those, like Kirsch, Lynn, and Wagstaff, who reject the state construct entirely as misleading and inaccurate.[59] In the center of the continuum can be found an understanding of trance as an altered state, but a ubiquitous one: "Daily life," wrote Hilgard, "is full of many small dissociations."[60] In this view the trance is not unique to hypnosis, because we dissociate every day in the most ordinary of settings, while we are daydreaming or listening to music.[61] David Spiegel, a prolific researcher and eminent clinician at Stanford University, School of Medicine, proposed that the ability to be absorbed in such experiences and focus attention, along with suggestibility and dissociation, can account for responsiveness to hypnosis.[62]

In contrast, clinicians can be found holding a much wider variety of positions, but which also shift and change. Because modern approaches to the Ericksonian tradition emphasize the interpersonal aspects of hypnosis, for instance, the concept of trance is increasingly perceived by some prominent Ericksonian clinicians as a distraction, with little explanatory value.[63] Other clinical hypnotists remain champions of the validity and salience of the trance state. Differences between laboratory researchers and clinicians became apparent during the late twentieth century, with disagreements flaring on a number of key points, only one of which is the altered state issue.

The Trait Debate

Although the altered state debate has taken up a tremendous amount of research attention during the second half of the twentieth century, it was not the only theoretical issue to drive research agendas and to spark contention. The question of whether hypnotic responsiveness is a trait-like, aptitudinal capacity remains controversial. Contrary to a widespread assumption, however, the theoretical positions do not map to the same lines drawn by the altered state issue. While many Ericksonians view hypnosis as an altered state, they also reject the presumption that hypnotizability is a stable trait. Barber, a non-state theorist, would agree with them, arguing that the hypnotic abilities of supposedly low hypnotizable individuals can be improved if hypnotic techniques are tailored to their particular personality. By counteracting inhibitions that prevent individuals from experiencing hypnosis, their hypnotizability can be "unlocked."[64] Likewise, one of the significant contributions of Spanos' social psychologically oriented work comes from his finding that suggestibility is not an immutable trait, but also can be a learned skill.[65] It is also possible to find non-state theorists who take the other view, or who incorporate aspects of both. As Sarbin initially formulated his social psychological model of hypnosis, he proposed that individual differences in hypnotic responding could be accounted for by looking at differences in the individuals' talent for role-playing.[66]

After Sarbin and Coe introduced the idea that imagining is a skill that people possess to different degrees, Barber extended the variables of absorption and imaginative involvement to serve as possible explanations for differences in hypnotic responsiveness.[67] Elaborating upon these constructs, Barber and Wilson developed their concept of "fantasy proneness," a variable that was later investigated by Lynn, Rhue, and James Council at North Dakota State University. [68]

The trait debate can be understood as breaking down into three general positions. The first is that almost anyone can become responsive to hypnotic suggestion, regardless of any preexisting traits or abilities, as long as appropriate and effective procedures are used. This view is the theoretical basis for clinical techniques in the Ericksonian tradition which place emphasis on complicated and highly individualized inductions. The second position is that although hypnotic responsiveness may reflect some stable traits, having to do with imagination or other cognitive abilities, simply having these skills is not sufficient for subjects to be hypnotically responsive. They must also accurately interpret the suggestions they are given,[69] or be convinced that hypnotic responsiveness falls within their capacity.[70] Research investigating this position has indicated that most, though not all, hypnotic subjects can be trained to respond as well as subjects who are spontaneously high hypnotizables.[71] The minority of subjects who are still hypnotically unresponsive after training are presumed in this view to be outliers, who may be particularly unmotivated for some individual reason, or perhaps do lack an as yet unidentified prerequisite ability. Although most hypnotizability training programs have been developed by those who hold a cognitive-behavioral perspective, at least one program is based in neodissociation theory.[72]

The final position is held by researchers and clinicians who maintain that responses to the most cognitively complex suggestions, for amnesia and for hallucinations, for instance, require a natural aptitude that cannot be successfully taught. Although training for these suggestions may increase compliance, in this view, it cannot enhance suggestibility.[73] These three positions in the trait debate are not completely discrete. Most hypnosis researchers and practitioners will acknowledge that both stable individual differences and contextual variables play a role in hypnotic responsiveness. Differences of opinion on the matter often come down to a matter of emphasis, and some of the most interesting work has been done considering the interaction *between* traits and context.[74]

From State to Trait

The twentieth century was marked by a dramatic increase in experimental exploration designed to test theoretical assertions having to do with the nature of hypnosis. Among many avenues of research, two broad issues attracted particular attention, the first and most important of which had to do with the relationship of hypnosis to altered states of consciousness: the "state debate," and a secondary dialogue which had to do with the qualities associated with the hypnotic subject that might affect hypnotic responsiveness: the "trait debate."

Although the specific issues of the state debate are unique to the late twentieth century, certain aspects of the controversy were visible already in the eighteenth century, when Victor Race first appeared to sleep, but then began to speak to his mesmerist, the Marquis de Puységur, in a voice not quite his own. Puységur's understanding of mesmerism would position the induction of a somnambulistic trance state, rather than the magnetic crisis that Mesmer had invoked, as the central phenomenon that should define whether a subject was actually mesmerized or not.

Through the nineteenth century there were many who were to embrace Puységur's style of mesmerism and those, beginning with Deleuze, Faria, and Bertrand, who moderated claims about the centrality of the trance. In the United States, where the experience of the altered states made possible through mesmerism were frequently seen as an opportunity for spiritual enlightenment and even contact with spirits beyond the grave, others like Sunderland saw parallels between religious ecstatic experiences and mesmeric trances, and looked to the psychological power of suggestion to explain what was going on.

British mesmerists of the nineteenth century were fixated on the trance, regardless of whether they still believed in the magnetic fluid or had been convinced of the power of suggestion, or whether their particular interest in the induction of trance was intended to provide physical relief from pain and illness, psychological healing, or spiritual enlightenment. It was in France at Nancy that the doubts held by Bertrand regarding the necessity of the trance state reappeared in the research of Bernheim and Delboeuf. The theoretical tradition of altered state theorists is more continuous, but it is also more complicated; beyond agreeing that hypnosis involves some kind of other-than-ordinary state of consciousness, opinions about its physiological nature, psychological function, and spiritual potential have dramatically differed.

The contemporary trait debate is a modern engagement with the familiar question of why hypnosis produces the effects that it does on some people and not on others. What is it about certain subjects that make them, depending on the era in which this question is asked, more susceptible or more talented? Just as it is not accurate to say that mesmerism "became" hypnosis, since the techniques overlapped in time and were at times understood to be dramatically different species of procedure, it would also be inaccurate to impose the contemporary debates retrospectively on the controversies of the past.

In the final decades of the twentieth century, the division between state and non-state theorists ceased to define the contemporary field of hypnosis research. This reflected the gracious moves toward convergence made by theorists on both sides; however, the controversy was also overshadowed by the landfall of a more dramatic storm. Some researchers with opposing views in the altered state debate unexpectedly found themselves on the same side of a conflict arising from differing beliefs about the relationship of hypnosis to memory, and the application of those beliefs in a clinical setting.

Notes

1 Hull, *Hypnosis and Suggestibility*, 298.

2 See, for example, Ernest R. Hilgard and Charles Tart, "Responsiveness to Suggestions Following Waking and Imagination Instructions and Following Induction of Hypnosis," *Journal of Abnormal Psychology* 71, no. 3 (1966): 196–208.

3 Robert W. White, "A Preface to a Theory of Hypnotism," *Journal of Abnormal and Social Psychology* 36 (1941): 477–505.

4 White, "A Preface to a Theory of Hypnotism," 483.

5 Edward J. Frischolz, "Remembering Andre," *American Journal of Clinical Hypnosis* 48, no. 1 (2005): 5–28.

6 Ernest R. Hilgard, *Divided Consciousness: Multiple Controls in Human Thought and Action* (New York: Wiley, 1977).

7 Ibid., 228.

8 Ernest R. Hilgard, "A Neodissociation Interpretation of Pain Reduction in Hypnosis," *Psychological Review* 80 (1973): 396–411.

9 Ernest R. Hilgard, "Neodissociation Theory," in S. J. Lynn & J. W. Rhue eds., *Dissociation: Clinical, Theoretical and Research Perspectives* (New York: Guilford Press, 1994): 34.

10 Irving Kirsch and Steven J. Lynn, "Dissociation Theories of Hypnosis," *Psychological Bulletin* 123 (1998): 100–115. Also see, for example, Green,

Page and others, "The 'Hidden Observer' and Ideomotor Responding: A Real-Simulator Comparison," *Contemporary Hypnosis* 22, no. 3 (2005): 123–137.

11 Hilgard, "A Neodissociation Interpretation of Pain Reduction in Hypnosis," 409.

12 Kenneth S. Bowers, "Imagination and Dissociation in Hypnotic Responding," *International Journal of Clinical and Experimental Hypnosis* 10 (1992): 253–275.

13 Irving Kirsch and others, "A Spectral Analysis of Cognitive and Personality Variables in Hypnosis: Empirical Disconfirmation of the Two-Factor Model of Hypnotic Responding," *Journal of Personality and Social Psychology* 69 (1995): 167–175.

14 Kenneth S. Bowers, "Imagination and Dissociation in Hypnotic Responding," 253–275.

15 Erik Z. Woody and Kenneth S. Bowers, "A Frontal Assault on Dissociated Control," In Steven J. Lynn and Judith W. Rhue eds., *Dissociation: Clinical, Theoretical and Research Perspectives* (New York: Guilford Press, 1994): 57.

16 Kenneth S. Bowers, "Imagination and Dissociation in Hypnotic Responding," 267.

17 Mary E. Miller, and Kenneth S. Bowers, "Hypnotic Analgesia: Dissociated Experience or Dissociated Control?" *Journal of Abnormal Psychology* 102 (1992): 29–38; Peter Farvolden and Erik Z. Woody, "Hypnosis, Memory, and Frontal Executive Functioning," *International Journal of Clinical and Experimental Hypnosis* 52, no. 1 (2004): 3–26.

18 John F. Kihlstrom, "Hypnosis: A Sesquicentennial Essay," *International Journal of Clinical and Experimental Hypnosis* 40 (1992): 301–314; John F. Kihlstrom, "Dissociations and Dissociation Theory in Hypnosis: Comment on Kirsch and Lynn (1998)," *Psychological Bulletin* 132, no. 2 (1998): 186–191; John F. Kihlstrom, "Hypnosis and the Psychological Unconscious," in H. J. Friedman ed., *Encyclopedia of Mental Health*, vol. 2 (San Diego: Academic Press, 1998b): 467–477; John F. Kihlstrom, "The Fox, the Hedgehog, and Hypnosis," *International Journal of Clinical and Experimental Hypnosis* 51 (2003): 166–189.

19 Kihlstrom, "Hypnosis," 301–314; Kihlstrom, "Dissociations and Dissociation Theory in Hypnosis," 186–191.

20 Kihlstrom, "The Fox, the Hedgehog, and Hypnosis," 166–189.

21 Kihlstrom and McConkey, "William James and Hypnosis," 174.

22 Martin T. Orne, "The Nature of Hypnosis: Artifact and Essence," *Journal of Abnormal Psychology* 58 (1959): 277–299; Martin T. Orne, "On the Simulating Subject as a Quasi-Control Group in Hypnosis Research: What, Why, and How," in E. Fromm and R. E. Shor eds., *Hypnosis: Developments in Research and New Perspectives*, 2d ed. (New York: Aldine, 1979): 519–601.

23 Peter W. Sheehan, "Hypnosis, Context, and Commitment," 520–541. Kevin M. McConkey "The Construction and Resolution of Experience and Behavior in Hypnosis," in S. J. Lynn & J. W. Rhue eds., *Theories of Hypnosis: Current Models and Perspectives* (New York: Guilford Press, 1991): 542–563.

24 Campbell Perry, "Hypnosis in Australia Forty Years Ago: Recollections of Gordon Hammer, Martin Orne, and Philip Sutcliffe," *Australian Journal of Clinical and Experimental Hypnosis* 29, no. 2 (2001): 83–92.

25 Sheehan, "Hypnosis, Context, and Commitment," 520–541.

26 Orne, "The Nature of Hypnosis: Artifact and Essence," 277–299.

27 Theodore R. Sarbin, "Contributions to Role-Taking Theory: I. Hypnotic Behavior," *Psychological Review* 57 (1950): 225–270.

28 William C. Coe and Theodore R. Sarbin, "Role Theory: Hypnosis from a Dramaturgical and Narrational Perspective," In S. J. Lynn & J. W. Rhue eds., *Theories of Hypnosis: Current Models and Perspectives* (New York: Guilford Press, 1991): 303–323. Theodore R. Sarbin and William C. Coe, *Hypnosis: A Social Psychological Analysis of Influence Communication* (New York: Holt, Rinehart & Winston, 1972): 189.

29 Theodore X. Barber, *Hypnosis: A Scientific Approach* (New York: Van Nostrand Reinhold, 1969): 282.

30 Ibid. See also Theodore X. Barber and David S. Calverley, "The Definition of the Situation as a Variable Affecting "Hypnotic-like" Suggestibility," *Journal of Clinical Psychology* 20 (1964): 438–440; Theodore X. Barber and David S. Calverley, "Toward a Theory of Hypnotic Behavior: Effects on Suggestibility of Defining the Situation as Hypnosis and Defining Response to Suggestions as Easy," *Journal of Abnormal and Social Psychology* 68 (1964): 585–592; Theodore X. Barber, Nicholas P. Spanos, and John F. Chaves, J. F., *Hypnosis, Imagination, and Human Potentialities* (New York: Pergamon Press, 1974): 189.

31 Sheryl C. Wilson and Theodore X. Barber, "Vivid Fantasy and Hallucinatory Abilities in the Life Histories of excellent Hypnotic Subjects ('Somnabules'): Preliminary Report with Female Subjects," in E. Klinger ed., *Imagery*. Vol. 2, *Concepts, Results, and Applications* (New York: Plenum Press, 1981): 133–152; Sheryl C. Wilson and Theodore X. Barber, "The Fantasy-prone Personality: Implications for Understanding Imagery, Hypnosis, and Parapsychological Phenomena," in Anees A. Sheikh ed., *Imagery: Current Theory, Research, and Application* (New York: Wiley, 1983): 340–387.

32 Barber, *Hypnosis*, 282.

33 Theodore X. Barber, "A Comprehensive Three-Dimensional Theory of Hypnosis," in I. Kirsch, A. Capafons, E. Cardeña, & S. Amigó eds., *Clinical Hypnosis and Self-regulation: Cognitive-behavioral Perspectives*

(Washington, DC: American Psychological Association, 1999): 21–48.

34 Nicholas P. Spanos, "Hypnotic Behavior: A Social-Psychological Interpretation of Amnesia, Analgesia, and 'Trance Logic.'" *The Behavioral and Brain Sciences* 9 (1986): 499–502; Nicholas P. Spanos, "A Sociocognitive Approach to Hypnosis," in S. J. Lynn & J. W. Rhue eds., *Theories of Hypnosis: Current Models and Perspectives* (New York: Guilford Press, 1991): 324–361; Nicholas P. Spanos and John F. Chaves, *Hypnosis: The Cognitive-Behavioral Perspective* (Amherst, NY: Prometheus Books, 1989): 511.

35 Nicholas P. Spanos, "Hypnotic Behavior: A Cognitive, Social Psychological Perspective," *Research Communication in Psychology, Psychiatry, & Behavior* 7, no. 2 (1982): 199–213.

36 Nicholas P. Spanos, Maxwell I. Gwynn, and Henderikus J. Stam, "Instructional Demands and Ratings of Overt and Hidden Pain During Hypnotic Analgesia," *Journal of Abnormal Psychology* 92, no. 4 (1983): 479–488; Nicholas P. Spanos and Erin C. Hewitt, "The Hidden Observer in Hypnotic Analgesia: Discovery or Experimental Creation?" *Journal of Personality and Social Psychology* 39 (1980): 1201–1214; Nicholas P. Spanos and Joanne McLean, "Hypnotically Created False Reports Do Not Demonstrate Pseudomemories," *British Journal of Experimental & Clinical Hypnosis* 3, no. 3 (1986): 161–171.

37 Kirsch and Lynn, "Dissociation Theories of Hypnosis," 100–115.

38 See Kihlstrom, "Dissociations and Dissociation Theory in Hypnosis," 186–191; Jean-Roch Laurence, Campbell Perry, and John F. Kihlstrom, "'Hidden Observer' Phenomenon in Hypnosis: An Experimental Creation?" *Journal of Personality and Social Psychology* 44, no. 1 (1983): 163–169; Heather Nogrady and others, "Dissociation, Duality, and Demand Characteristics in Hypnosis," *Journal of Abnormal Psychology* 92, no. 2 (1983): 223–235. For a defense of the "hidden observer," see Spanos, "A Sociocognitive Approach to Hypnosis," 324–361.

39 Graham F. Wagstaff, "Different Approaches to Hypnosis," *Psychology Review* 7 (2001): 2–5.

40 Irving Kirsch, "Clinical Hypnosis as a Nondeceptive Placebo: Empirically Derived Techniques," *American Journal of Clinical Hypnosis* 37, no 2 (1994): 95–106.

41 See Steven J. Lynn and Harry Sivec, "The Hypnotizable Subject as Creative Problem Solving Agent," in E. Fromm and M. Nash eds., *Contemporary Perspectives in Hypnosis Research* (New York: Guilford Press, 1992): 292–333.

42 Lynn, Rhue, and Weekes, "Hypnotic Involuntariness," 169–184.

43 Kirsch and Lynn, "Hypnotic Involuntariness and the Automaticity of Everyday Life," 329–348; Steven J. Lynn and Michael N. Hallquist, "Toward a Scientifically Based Understanding of Milton H. Erickson's

Strategies and Tactics: Hypnosis, Response Sets and Common Factors in Psychotherapy," *Contemporary Hypnosis* 21, no. 2 (2004): 63–78.

44 Irving Kirsch and Steven J. Lynn, "The Automaticity of Behavior in Clinical Psychology," *American Psychologist* 54 (1999): 504–575; Kirsch and Lynn, "Hypnotic Involuntariness and the Automaticity of Everyday Life," 329–348; Steven Jay Lynn, "Automaticity and Hypnosis: A Sociocognitive Account," *International Journal of Clinical and Experimental Hypnosis* 45, no. 3 (1997): 239–250.

45 See John F. Kihlstrom, "Hypnosis," *Annual Review of Psychology* 36 (1985): 405. The original reference can be found at Ernest R. Hilgard, "Altered States of Awareness," *Journal of Nervous and Mental Disease* 149 (1969): 68–79.

46 Campbell Perry, "Theorizing about Hypnosis in either/or Terms," *International Journal of Clinical and Experimental Hypnosis* 50 (1992): 240.

47 Barber, *Hypnosis*, 282.

48 Kilstrom, *Hypnosis*, 405.

49 Charles T. Tart, "Altered States of Consciousness," In R. Harris and R. Lamb eds., *The Encyclopedic Dictionary of Psychology* (Cambridge, MA: MIT Press, 1983): 19.

50 Nicholas P. Spanos and Theodore X. Barber, "Toward a Convergence in Hypnosis Research," *American Psychologist* 29 (1974): 500–511; Hilgard, "A Neodissociation Interpretation of Pain Reduction in Hypnosis," 396–411; Kirsch and Lynn, "The Altered State of Hypnosis," 846–858.

51 See, John F. Chaves, "The State of the 'State' Debate in Hypnosis: A View from the Cognitive-Behavioral Perspective," *International Journal of Clinical and Experimental Hypnosis* 45, no. 3 (1997): 251–265; John F. Kihlstrom, "Convergence in Understanding Hypnosis? Perhaps, but not so Fast," *International Journal of Clinical and Experimental Hypnosis* 45 (1997): 324–332; Sakari Kallio and Antti Revonsuo, "Hypnotic Phenomena and Altered States of Consciousness: A Multilevel Framework of Description and Explanation," *Contemporary Hypnosis* 20, no. 3 (2003): 111–164.

52 John H. Gruzelier, "The State of Hypnosis: Evidence and Applications," *Quarterly Journal of Medicine* 89 (1996): 313–317.

53 Milton H. Erickson, "Hypnosis: A General Review," In E. L. Rossi ed., *The Collected Papers of Milton H. Erickson on Hypnosis*, vol. 3 (New York: Irvington, 1980, original work published in 1941): 13–20.

54 Erika Fromm, "An Ego-Psychological Theory of Hypnosis," In E. Fromm and M. R. Nash eds., *Contemporary Hypnosis Research* (New York: Guilford, 1992): 591; Michael R. Nash, "Hypnosis, Psychopathology, and Psychological Regression," in E. Fromm and M. R. Nash eds., *Contemporary Hypnosis Research* (New York: Guilford, 1992): 591.

55 Woody and Bowers, "A Frontal Assault on Dissociated Control," 52–79.
56 William J. Ray and Desmond Oathies, "Brain Imaging Techniques," *International Journal of Clinical and Experimental Hypnosis* 51, no. 2 (2003): 97–104; Kallio and Revonsuo, "Hypnotic Phenomena and Altered States of Consciousness," 111–164.
57 Kihlstrom, "Hypnosis," 385–418.
58 McConkey "The Construction and Resolution of Experience and Behavior in Hypnosis," 542–563; Sheehan, "Hypnosis, Context, and Commitment," 520–541.
59 Coe and Sarbin, "Role Theory: Hypnosis from a Dramaturgical and Narrational Perspective," 303–323; Michael Dixon and Jean-Roch Laurence, "Two Hundred Years of Hypnosis Research: Questions Resolved? Questions Unanswered!," in E. Fromm and M. Nash Eds., *Contemporary Hypnosis Research* (New York: Guilford, 1992): 34–66; Irving Kirsch, "The Social Learning Theory of Hypnosis," In S. J. Lynn and J. W. Rhue eds., *Theories of Hypnosis: Current Models and Perspectives* (New York: Guilford Press, 1991): 439–466; Steven J. Lynn and Judith W. Rhue, "An Integrative Model of Hypnosis," in S. J. Lynn and J. W. Rhue, eds., *Theories of Hypnosis: Current Models and Perspectives* (New York: Guilford Press, 1991): 397–438.
60 Ernest R. Hilgard, "A Neodissociation Interpretation of Pain Reduction in Hypnosis," 406.
61 See, for example, David B. Cheek and Leslie M. LeCron, *Clinical Hypnotherapy* (New York: Grune & Stratton, 1968): 245; Ronald A. Havens and Catherine Walters, *Hypnotherapy Scripts: A Neo-Ericksonian Approach to Persuasive Healing* (Philadelphia: Brunner/Mazel, 1989): 196.
62 Herbert Spiegel and David Spiegel, *Trance and Treatment: Clinical Uses of Hypnosis* (New York: Basic Books, 1978): 382.
63 Jeffery K. Zeig and Peter J. Rennick, "Ericksonian Hypnotherapy: A Communications Approach to Hypnosis," in S. J. Lynn and J. W. Rhue eds., *Theories of Hypnosis: Current Models and Perspectives* (New York: Guilford Press, 1991): 275–300.
64 Joseph Barber, "The Locksmith Model: Accessing Hypnotic Responsiveness," in S. J. Lynn and J. W. Rhue eds., *Theories of Hypnosis: Current Models and Perspectives* (New York: Guilford Press, 1991): 241–274.
65 Donald R. Gorassini and Nicholas P. Spanos, "The Carleton Skill Training Program for Modifying Hypnotic Suggestibility: Original Version and Variations," in I. Kirsch and others eds., *Clinical Hypnosis and Self-Regulation: Cognitive-Behavioral Perspectives* (Washington, DC: American Psychological Association, 1999): 141–177.
66 Sarbin, "Contributions to Role-Taking Theory," 225–270.

67 Barber, Spanos, and Chaves, *Hypnosis, Imagination, and Human Potentialities*, 189.

68 Wilson and Barber, "The Fantasy-Prone Personality," 340–387; Steven J. Lynn and Judith W. Rhue, "Fantasy Proneness: Hypnosis, Developmental Antecedents, and Psychopathology," *American Psychologist* 43, no. 1 (1988): 35–44.

69 Donald R. Gorassini and Nicholas P. Spanos, "A Social-Cognitive Skills Approach to the Successful Modification of Hypnotic Susceptibility," *Journal of Personality and Social Psychology* 50 (1986): 1004–1012.

70 Cynthia Wickless and Irving Kirsch, "Effects of Verbal and Experiential Expectancy Manipulations on Hypnotic Susceptibility," *Journal of Personality and Social Psychology* 57, no. 5 (1989): 762–768.

71 See for review, Spanos, "A Sociocognitive Approach to Hypnosis," 324–361.

72 Arreed Barabasz and Marianne Barabasz, "Effects of Restricted Environmental Stimulation: Enhancement of Hypnotizability for Experimental and Chronic Pain Control," *International Journal of Clinical and Experimental Hypnosis* 37, no. 3 (1989): 217–231.

73 Brad L. Bates, "Compliance and the Carleton Skill Training Program," *British Journal of Experimental and Clinical Hypnosis* 7, no. 3 (1990): 159–164; Kenneth S. Bowers and Thomas M. Davidson, "A Neodissociative Critique of Spanos's Social-Psychological Model of Hypnosis," in S. J. Lynn and J. W. Rhue eds., *Theories of Hypnosis: Current Models and Perspectives* (New York: Guilford Press, 1991): 105–143.

74 Spanos, "A Sociocognitive Approach to Hypnosis," 329–330; Dixon and Laurence, "Two Hundred Years of Hypnosis Research," 57; Lynn and Rhue, "An Integrative Model of Hypnosis," 397–438; Nadon, Laurence, and Perry, "The Two Disciplines of Scientific Hypnosis," 485–519.

CHAPTER EIGHT

Memory and Identity

The memory controversies of the late twentieth century began with high profile child abuse investigations during the 1980s and into the 1990s. The use of hypnosis to recover repressed traumatic memories was increasingly questioned as it became implicated in the creation of "false memories."[1] At the same time sensationalized news accounts began to emerge of hypnotists generating multiple personalities in their vulnerable, dissociative clients.

Some researchers and practitioners argued that hypnosis used inappropriately can indeed facilitate the creation of confabulated memories and dissociated personalities, and should be used for the purposes of memory retrieval and to explore dissociations in identity with care, if at all. But other clinicians found substantial value in the use of hypnosis for the retrieval of repressed, traumatic memories, and in the psychiatric diagnoses of multiple personality disorder, rejecting charges that they were somehow complicit in its iatrogenic creation.

Contentious and at times acrimonious debate over these issues took place at professional meetings, and played out in a flood of published books and articles. What was never in contention was the presence of hypnosis in some of the clinical settings where memories were being recovered and personalities discovered, but only the interpretation of its role there. Was hypnosis being used appropriately, as a constructive therapeutic tool, or had it become the unfortunate engine for the production of false memories and multiple personalities?

There is no controversy over the phenomenon of people remembering events that they have not thought about since they first occurred, even years before. The question is whether the experience of forgetting and remembering is reflective of some cognitive mechanism of repression or dissociation.

Repression of Traumatic Memory

When Freud and Breuer floated the idea that traumatic memories could be repressed and forgotten, it was not met with much enthusiasm. The hypnotic techniques they first employed in the treatment of Bertha Pappenheim made liberal use of directed suggestion. At the end of the nineteenth century, the psychological world was hypnosis-savvy, and there was legitimate concern that Freud's techniques were likely to create, more than to uncover, the forgotten traumatic experiences in his patients that he theorized were there.[2] Although Freud was to eschew hypnosis by that name, he retained the use of suggestive techniques as part of the development of psychoanalysis. The community of nineteenth century hypnosis researchers and practitioners was well acquainted with the apparent power of suggestion to permanently alter memory, and to create what came to be termed "pseudo-memories."[3]

Much has been made during the last decades of the twentieth century of Freud's motives for his "abandonment" of his seduction theory, when he replaced the idea that hysterical patients were repressing memories of having been sexually abused as children with a different conviction, that they were repressing fantasies about early sexual seductions.[4] That debate aside, regardless of the etiology of the traumatic amnesia, Freud's understanding of the mechanism of repression remained the same. He maintained that it resulted from a situation where the "ego was confronted by an experience, an idea, a feeling, arousing an affect so painful that the person resolved to forget it, since he had no confidence in his power to resolve the incompatibility between the unbearable idea and his ego by the processes of thought."[5] Contradicting his own phrase, "resolved to forget," the key aspect of Freud's conceptualization of repression was that the experience of forgetting was an unconscious reaction, rather than a conscious act.[6]

The treatments that Freud developed for the obsessional neurosis and hysteria that he believed to be the result of traumatic forgetting involved processes of therapeutic remembering and abreaction, the emotionally reliving of the lost memories.

The presumption that mental healing would follow the recovery of repressed traumatic memory was to become the central tenet of psychoanalysis. Both sides of the equation: that it is common for childhood victims of abuse to forget the traumatic memories, and that healing follows upon their recall, were also key when modern therapists began to practice the recovery of memory during the late 1970s and the 1980s.[7]

The empirical question of whether traumatic memories can be forgotten for many years and then therapeutically recovered with accurate detail became the subject of widespread research attention beginning at that time. The accumulation of anecdotal reports from clinicians supported claims for the existence of this type of repression.[8] A case described in 1979, in which a woman with presenting symptoms of insomnia and poor self-esteem came to remember that she had been sexually assaulted by her father, was paradigmatic, and as the frequency of such cases increased, the idea of "recovered memory" became an increasingly compelling one in clinical settings.[9]

Memory researchers found the evidence to be significantly less compelling. Theorists noted that distressing experiences, because of their emotional content, should be easier to recall.[10] One review of 60 years of laboratory research concluded that there was no empirical support for a mechanism of traumatic childhood amnesia.[11] But analysis of the available data remained contentious. In one review of 25 studies, conclusive evidence for repression was found.[12] Reviewing the same cases the following year, another researcher saw substantial ambiguity in the data, pointing out, for instance, that failure to report abuse did not constitute evidence that it had been repressed.[13]

The reliability of "failure to report" as an indicator of actual forgetting was tested in a study of documented child sexual abuse, in which the victims were repeatedly interviewed more than a decade after the abuse occurred. Of the 175 subjects in the study, 18.9% did not report the abuse during the first phone call, a number that dropped to 15% during the second phone call, and to 8% by the third contact, an in-person interview. The study concluded that factors other than repression can explain nonreporting of traumatic events, and that some of these may be social and relational in nature.[14]

Much of the research on childhood amnesia has centered on the role of hypnosis and other suggestive techniques in clinical settings where memory retrieval became valued as a central therapeutic task. A survey done in the United States in 1995 found that 29–34% of psychologists sampled reported using hypnosis to aid the recall of sexual abuse. The prevalence of the task and the assumptions upon which it was based drew increasing scrutiny from memory researchers. There is an uncontroversial consensus among cognitive scientists that memory, even everyday memory of nontraumatic events, is a fallible construction. Ironically, despite their intrinsic inaccuracy, people still apparently can feel certain about, and will express confidence in, the details of memories, even when it can be established empirically that they never actually took place.[15]

Elizabeth Loftus was one of the first memory researchers to demonstrate that complex memories can be formed through suggestion, both direct and subtle. A series of studies she directed in the early 1990s attracted significant attention in the popular media and cast her into the national spotlight, where she became a controversial figure, admired by some and pilloried by others. In one study, Loftus and her colleagues caused experimental subjects to integrate an entirely fabricated event into their personal histories. Older siblings of subjects were recruited as participants in the research, and were directed to provide to the subject a few details about a false event that supposedly occurred in childhood. In subsequent interviews held over several days, some of the subjects claimed to remember the fictitious event, even providing substantial detail beyond what their siblings had suggested to them.[16]

Similar experimental research conducted in other laboratories has shown that false events will be embraced by a significant minority of subjects. College students, for instance, in numbers ranging from 20% to 50%, will report experiencing being lost in a shopping mall,[17] being hospitalized overnight, accidentally spilling a bowl of punch at a wedding reception, and evacuating a grocery store when its sprinkler system activated;[18] being attacked by an animal, experiencing a serious indoor accident, a serious outdoor accident, a serious medical procedure, and being injured by another child;[19] being bullied as a child;[20] and taking a ride in a hot air balloon.[21]

There is no consensus over the question of whether hypnotic techniques are riskier than non-hypnotic techniques that are also intended to encourage recall of traumatic memories; however, because it is the most frequently employed memory recovery technique, hypnosis became the target of a significant proportion of research on the issue of recovered memory.

Hypnosis and Memory

A dramatic discrepancy between the views of clinicians and memory researchers continued through the 1990s, while hypnosis continued to be widely advocated as a technique for the recovery of forgotten memories of traumatic experiences.[22] A significant body of research that looked at memory accuracy was amassed during the period. In his 1994 review of 34 studies, Matthew Erdelyi concluded that hypnotic recollections seem to be no more accurate than non-hypnotic recollections. The reason that they appear to be so is that hypnosis is correlated with a significant increase in the sheer volume of both accurate and inaccurate recollections.[23]

The risk of false memories seems to be associated with the common hypnotic technique of age regression.[24] In a 1997 study, participants were age-regressed to the age of 5, with the suggestion that they were playing with either a "Cabbage Patch" or a "He-Man" doll, although these particular toys had not been available until two or three years later than the target time of the age regression. Only half the subjects received their age-regression instructions in a hypnotic context, while the others did not. The study found that while none of the non-hypnotized subjects rated the memory as real, or were confident that the event had occurred at the age to which they had been regressed, 20% of the hypnotized subjects did so.[25] Interestingly, what hypnotized individuals are, if not more accurate, is somewhat more *confident* about the dependability of their recall accuracy than non-hypnotized individuals.[26]

Those who support therapeutic techniques of memory retrieval argue that the results of research conducted in laboratory settings on nontraumatic memory cannot be used to refute memory processes in individuals whose actual experiences were significantly more distressing.[27] Attempts were made to address this objection, for instance, in seven studies that compared hypnotic versus non-hypnotic memory in the face of relatively emotionally arousing stimuli (including film depictions of shop accidents, fatal stabbings, a mock assassination, an actual murder videotaped serendipitously). The researchers involved in these studies came to the same conclusion: hypnosis does not improve the recall of emotionally arousing events, nor does a higher level of emotional arousal lead to greater accuracy.[28]

Although multiple studies have demonstrated that hypnosis produces more false information proportional to accurate information than do non-hypnotic methods of encouraging recall,[29] the difference narrows or vanishes as the suggestive elements of non-hypnotic procedures, such as guided imagery, increase.[30] Sociocognitive psychologists argue that the dynamics that encourage the creation of false memories, including, for example, expectations, attitudes, and the plausibility of the event in question, are also likely to operate in both hypnotic and non-hypnotic contexts.[31]

Seeking a practical resolution to the disparate views of clinicians and researchers, beginning in the 1990s, professional societies, including divisions and task forces of the American Psychological Association and the Canadian Psychiatric Association, increasingly have recommended against the use of hypnosis for memory retrieval.[32] The American Medical Association has suggested that hypnosis be used only for investigative purposes in forensic contexts.[33] The issue, however, remains unresolved. Some workers in the field maintain that hypnosis may be useful in recovering memories when leading questions and suggestive procedures are not inserted into hypnotic interrogations or psychotherapy.

Dissociation and Traumatic Memory

The influence of the Freudian concept of repression on the memory debates at the turn of the twentieth century originates in the theoretical victory that took place a hundred years earlier. Freud's concept of repression was representative of a particular view of human consciousness, "unconscious cerebration," which postulated that cognitive actions could take place without consciousness. The competing idea, associated with the work of Janet, James, and Prince, was that the unconscious was actually co-conscious, separated from ordinary consciousness through a barrier of amnesia, but operating simultaneously. Janet's approach to dissociation, which he termed "disaggregation," can be understood as a horizontal splitting of different parts of consciousness, whereas Freud's concept of repression imagined a vertical split, with ordinary consciousness above and the unconscious below. In Janet's view, under certain, usually pathological, conditions, the mechanism of splitting could result in "double consciousness," and manifest itself within a clinical context as multiple personality disorder. For James and Prince, the potential multiplicity of selves reflected a more general, and not necessarily pathological aspect of human consciousness.

The dissociative view of repressed memory thus differs from the Freudian idea of repression in its particular conviction that a traumatic memory can become isolated from ordinary consciousness, and yet continue in a parallel stream. It is this model of traumatic memory, Janet's view of dissociation, rather than Freud's concept of repression, that provides the theoretical foundation for the modern "posttraumatic model" of severe dissociative disorders. Proponents of the posttraumatic model believe that the human mind can create multiple personalities as a response to the childhood experience of severe physical or sexual abuse, a dissociative means of coping with intense emotional pain.[34]

What the nineteenth century researchers knew as multiple personality disorder (MPD) was renamed in the 1990s as dissociative identity disorder (DID). It is listed in the DSM-IV as one of several dissociative disorders, including depersonalization disorder, dissociative fugue, and dissociative amnesia.[35] The symptoms of these disorders manifest as dramatic disturbances in memory, identity, and consciousness. Dissociative identity disorder, in particular, is recognized to be occurring in individuals who present two or more distinct personalities, or alternative "personality states," which exhibit behavior markedly different from, and even opposite to, the primary or "host" personality.

Following the cases reported in detail by Janet and Prince at the turn of the twentieth century, the next instance to attract considerable attention from both the public and the medical community was the case of Chris Sizemore. The story of her life became the basis of the book, and later the Hollywood film, *The Three Faces of Eve*.[36] In therapy, Sizemore eventually revealed three personalities, "Eve White," "Eve Black," and a third personality named Jane. Consistent with the prevalent understanding of symptoms of multiple personality disorder, two of these personalities exhibited diametrically opposed behaviors: Eve White was demure, while Eve Black was seductive.

In 1970 there were only 79 well-documented cases of MPD in the literature worldwide. The number of cases of reported MPD began to rise during the 1970s, and by 1986 had increased to nearly 6,000. By the end of the twentieth century the number of reported cases of DID, although difficult to accurately determine, has been estimated at 40,000. Those who support the posttraumatic model account for the increase in reported cases as a direct and positive consequence of heightened awareness of the disorder by clinicians.[37] To others, the apparent "epidemic" called into question the validity of the disorder, as well as the techniques employed to diagnose it.

Challenges to the Posttraumatic Model

The controversy over dissociative identity disorder's scientific status is often stated as an existential question: is multiplicity real or not?[38] Others argue that the question of the "existence" of DID is a pseudocontroversy.[39] There is no doubt that individuals experience the symptoms of having multiple identities. The question is why. Those who support the posttraumatic model believe it is a spontaneous occurrence, an intrapsychic disorder resulting from childhood trauma; others argue from a sociocultural perspective that the diagnosis is a cultural construction and that the symptoms manifest in response to the influence of the media, suggestive therapist cueing, and broader sociocultural beliefs and expectations.[40] Few theorists contend that the disorder is "fake" in the sense that those who are diagnosed with the condition are intentionally producing their symptoms. Outside of criminal settings, where cases of deliberate malingering have been documented,[41] there is substantial agreement from all sides that such deception is exceedingly rare.

Proponents of the sociocultural view of DID often point to the release of the bestselling book *Sybil* as having played a substantial role in shaping conceptions of multiple personality disorder during the 1970s.[42] The book tells the story of a young woman who gradually discovered that she was inhabited by 16 separate personalities, who each split off from her primary personality as a defense against experiences of extreme abuse by her mother.

In 1977 a made-for-television film version of the story was released starring Sally Fields in an Emmy-award-winning performance. The story placed the powerful image of multiplicity into public consciousness, contributing to the shared belief that hypnosis has the power to reveal the disorder in disturbed individuals with childhood histories of abuse. According to Spanos, the character of Sybil "became a model of the MPD survivor that greatly influenced the expectations of therapists and patients alike."[43] In the decades following *Sybil*, television coverage of MPD/DID dramatically increased, with a notable spike following the revelations by television star Roseanne Barr that she suffered from the disorder.[44]

Commentators on the phenomenon note other changes in the larger patterns of the disorder. Prior to the 1970s, most cases of MPD were characterized by the appearance of one or two additional personalities. Those who suffer from contemporary DID exhibit many more.[45] In 1989 the mean number of personalities was 16, the same number that Sybil had.[46] More significantly for critics, although few individuals with multiple personality disorder prior to *Sybil* connected their disorder to a history of child abuse, this connection was made in a substantial proportion of cases that followed in its wake.[47]

In articulating the sociocultural approach, Spanos theorized that individuals with DID are engaged in a form of role-playing, not unlike what happens to actors when they "lose themselves" in a part. Spanos did not mean to imply by this that they are intentionally play-acting or engaging in conscious deception. Role-playing studies designed by Spanos and other sociocognitive researchers did not attempt to create DID in subjects, but to determine how hard it would be to get subjects to produce DID-like behaviors. What these studies consistently found was that subjects were so familiar with what DID was supposed to look and sound like, that even without explicit suggestions, and only incomplete prompts and cues, subjects easily exhibited key features of the disorder.[48]

In contrast to the belief of those who take the posttraumatic view, that the dramatic rise in DID cases over recent decades reflects greater awareness on the part of clinicians, the opposing view is that DID most often develops iatrogenically within a particularly suggestive social context. This has been described as a kind of autocatalytic feedback loop, which got set in motion when

DID became familiar to both psychotherapists and the general public.[49] Increased media attention heightened public knowledge and therapeutic expectations regarding the features of DID, which led to a greater number of cases of DID, which in turn increased public knowledge and therapeutic expectations, which gave rise to an even greater number of cases, which in turn gave rise to a still greater number of cases.

The same mechanism is hypothesized to be at work in creating a constellation of historical conditions that are all characterized by identity distortions, including, for example, demonic possession, spirit channeling, and speaking in tongues.[50] The particular manifestations are tuned to cultural expectations, which can produce dramatically different behaviors through time, and across cultures. Despite these enormous differences, common underlying features have suggested to sociocognitive theorists that there is also a common etiology.[51] While Spanos placed more emphasis on social role expectations and iatrogenic influences than on individual difference variables,[52] others maintain that there may be individual differences that would make certain individuals more susceptible to suggestive influences of all varieties, cultural or therapeutic.[53]

Until fairly recently DID was a condition known only in North America,[54] but it has begun to appear in Europe and particularly in the Netherlands.[55] It has been suggested that the increase in reported cases reflects the increased media and professional attention the disorder has received as a result of the writings of Dutch researcher Bessel Van der Kolk and his colleagues.[56] These connections are difficult to establish. Some of the most persuasive evidence of the power of cultural transmission comes from cross-cultural comparisons. Although the disorder is rarely reported in India, for instance, when it does appear, the transition period as the individual shifts between alter personalities is typically preceded by sleep. This reflects the common media portrayals of DID in India. In the United States this phenomenon is not typically observed, nor reported in the media.[57]

Hypnosis and Dissociation of Identity

The woman known as "Sybil" and her therapist, Cornelia Wilbur, are both now deceased, so it is impossible to know the truth about what went on between them during their sessions. A psychiatrist who had direct knowledge of the case recently alleged that Sybil's dissociative symptoms were the product of therapeutic suggestion. Herbert Spiegel, who served as a backup therapist for Sybil, has clamed that Wilbur frequently encouraged Sybil to display different personalities in therapy, by calling her personalities by different names and communicating with them individually. Spiegel also has alleged that Wilbur, along with Flora Schreiber, the author of *Sybil*, crafted the character to have MPD in order to sell it to the publisher.[58]

Whether these allegations are true or not, hypnosis was a central feature in the relationship between Sybil and her therapist. Whether it was a tool for the discovery of personalities that were already there, or the method of their creation, hypnosis was a key feature in the Sybil case, and in many other reported cases of MPD/DID. Hypnosis has been the mainstream treatment of choice in therapeutic settings, used to discover, call out, and communicate with alters, as well as to foster apparent recall of traumatic memories implicated in the appearance of dissociated personalities.[59]

The diagnosis of DID presumes the validity of the dissociative view of memory, particularly the idea that memories that have split off from ordinary consciousness in childhood can be recalled in adulthood without distortion. Recently it has been suggested that fragments of memory, including sensory images, can be retrieved and woven together to produce a coherent and accurate narrative memory of a traumatic event.[60] Other memory researchers are skeptical of whether sensory impressions that were not initially encoded into a narrative could be retrieved at all, much less accurately interpreted.[61] They cite research findings that one of the common contributing factors to the creation of false memories is the therapeutic reconstruction of past events from feelings, intuition, and fragments of memory.[62] These processes are highlighted in the use of hypnosis to communicate with alters who presumably are the repositories of these fragments. While the primary personality has amnesia for traumatic childhood events, the alters hold the key to discovering what really happened.

The hypnotic suggestions used for these purposes resemble those that have been used in research to evaluate the hypothesized "hidden observer" phenomenon of neodissociation theory. Results of laboratory studies on hidden observers have been used to evaluate the hypothesized mechanisms of DID. In a hidden observer study, temporary amnesia is produced by hypnotic suggestion: "you will forget what just happened," followed by a reversal cue: "now you can remember everything." According to neodissociation theory, the temporarily forgotten material is isolated in a dissociated stream of consciousness, until the retrieval cue makes it accessible to a parallel, non-dissociated stream of consciousness. Spanos was successful in producing two hidden observers in eight highly hypnotizable subjects, one ostensibly associated with the right hemisphere of their brain, and one with the left.[63] After memorizing a list of words, some concrete and some abstract, they received an amnesia suggestion to forget them. Half of the subjects had been told that abstract words get stored in the right hemisphere of their brain, and that concrete words were stored in their left. The other half of the participants were told the opposite. Depending on the instructions they had received, when the hypnotist contacted the hidden observer associated with the right hemisphere or left hemisphere, individuals recalled the words, abstract or concrete, they believed were stored there. In other words, the division of consciousness appears to have been produced by the hidden observer instructions, not as a result of the suggested amnesia. The study is understood to be disconfirming the hypothesis that amnesia spontaneously produces a division of consciousness, while lending support to the idea that such divisions can be produced by suggestion.[64] Reflecting on DID, what this view proposes is that alter personalities can be produced, through suggestion, that will have only partial access to memories and other cognitive functions.

Studies of the hidden observer phenomenon, understood through the lens of the sociocognitive perspective as a "flexible observer," suggest that manifestations of symptoms of DID following hypnotic suggestions are not the product of an amnesic barrier separating consciousness into two simultaneous streams. It has also been suggested that a single, undivided stream of consciousness changes in a manner consistent with instructional cues.[65]

Critics of the use of hypnosis in the diagnosis and treatment of DID point to several sources of indirect evidence to bolster their cautions. They point out that, for example, psychotherapists who employ hypnosis tend to have more patients diagnosed with DID than those who do not use hypnosis.[66] Secondly, the majority of

DID cases appear to be clustered within the practices of a relatively small number of professionals, particularly those who are specialists in the disorder. And finally, hypnosis is correlated with increased reporting of sexual and physical abuse: patients with DID who had not been hypnotized reported significantly less abuse than those who had been hypnotized.[67]

The sociocognitive view of DID does not discount the subjective experience of dissociating patients, or the suffering their symptoms may cause them, as critics of this view sometimes charge. They do, however, reject the idea that DID arises spontaneously, as a result of a hardwired mechanism. They argue that alters are products of imagination, constructed from cultural material combined with suggestions received in a therapeutic context. Still, the question of whether DID may arise in certain instances independent of any suggestive influences has not been resolved on an empirical basis.

In seeking to understand the dynamics at work when hypnosis is used to explore dissociated memory, researchers have turned particular attention to "age-regression," a common technique used by hypnotists to take their patients "back in time." Cognitive research has demonstrated that adults regressed to childhood continue to function cognitively and developmentally as adults, even when they report the subjective feeling of being a child.[68] The implication of this research is that the experiences of "age-regression" should not be interpreted literally, as accurate reflections of childhood feelings or behaviors, regardless of the subjective conviction that they are.

Multiple studies of related issues have focused their attention on the relationship of hypnosis to the recovered memories of extremely implausible events, like satanic ritual abuse, alien abduction, and past-life regression. Reports of satanic ritual abuse recalled through psychotherapy began to surface with increasing frequency beginning in the 1980s.[69] American law enforcement agencies, including the FBI, spent years conducting formal investigations into allegations of lurid and appalling child abuse, including, for instance, frequent accounts of sexual torture, and baby breeding for human sacrifice, but were unable to uncover any physical evidence to support the accounts.[70] Sociohistorical analysis of the accounts also questioned the literal veracity of the reports,[71] as did researchers who found that the reports were clustered within the practices of a relatively small group of therapists.[72]

Similar conclusions were drawn from investigations into recovered memories of abduction by aliens.[73]

Finally, researchers have turned a skeptical eye to the practice of "past-life regression" as a form of therapy, which is based on the assumption that current psychological and physical symptoms are related to traumas that occurred in previous lives.[74] If the information recovered from past lives were empirically reliable, that would constitute strong evidence for the existence of the soul and the reality of reincarnation, not to mention the accuracy of recovered memory techniques. Despite anecdotal accounts of astonishing accuracy, the available research has demonstrated that the information about the past recalled by regressed individuals is almost "invariably incorrect."[75] Additionally, the remembered lives appeared to reflect prehypnotic suggestions regarding the content of those lives, particularly the gender, culture, and race of the person whose life the subject would recall, or the frequency of child abuse during the historical period likely to be visited. Spanos concluded his investigation of the matter by declaring past-life experiences to be elaborate imaginative fantasies constructed from cultural narratives in combination with hypnotic cues.[76] Those who support the reality of past-life age-regression are not persuaded by these arguments, and continue their work outside the medical mainstream.

From Memory to Identity

Although the memory debates of the late twentieth century may seem to us to be particularly modern, the issues are, in fact, more than a century old. The therapeutic creation of pseudomemories was familiar to Bernheim who, during the 1880s, used hypnosis deliberately to create memories in his patients. He referred to these as "retroactive hallucinations."[77] He was able to demonstrate their power by observing the conviction of those who insisted the false memories were real. After suggesting to one of his patients, for example, that she had been the victim of a rape, she expressed willingness to report the crime.[78]

Janet employed hypnosis to uncover traumatic memories in his subjects, but also to replace the traumatic images with less disturbing, false ones.[79] In one of his more famous cases Janet treated a young woman named Justine who was troubled by images of naked corpses. It turned out that as a child she had helped her mother, who was a nurse, treat patients who were dying of cholera. Using hypnosis, Janet was able to clothe the bodies, and to reanimate them. Justine's hysterical symptoms ceased after she was successful in "recalling" a Chinese general comically dancing. Beyond transforming real memories to make them less disturbing, he also created completely false memories in some of his clients, which, when they were accepted as "real," seemed to have the power to diminish the intrusion of the original, factually accurate images.

The nineteenth century fascination with multiple personality disorder also included an awareness of the imaginative component that was involved. Flournoy's work with medium Helene Smith, who claimed to be communicating with Martians, was not based on any unconditional belief in the objective reality of what his dissociated patients experienced. He was convinced, however, that human beings are capable of dramatic dissociations of personality. He wanted to understand how these dissociations occurred, and why they so often produced such creative narratives that proved so convincing to those who experienced them. Flournoy's approach is remarkably similar to the modern sociocognitive view that pseudomemories, altered personalities, and past-life experiences are "believed-in imaginings."[80]

The issue, then as now, is a familiar one running all through the history of hypnosis: how to determine which of the phenomena associated with hypnosis are essential, and which are epiphenomenal products of suggestion. Certainly the content that is produced during a mesmeric or hypnotic session has dramatically changed in response to the expectations of the era in which they took place. Mesmer expected his patients to have crises, and they did; Puységur expected his patients to go into a trance state, and they did. Fluidists expected their patients to experience a tangible force moving between them, and they experienced it; animists expected their patients to feel nothing, and they felt nothing. The expectable experiences for hypnotic subjects – spontaneous amnesia and the appearance of catalepsy – came to be replaced by the "discovery" of dissociated personalities and the retrieval of forgotten memories through a literal reexperience of the past.

Disagreements continue between researchers and clinicians about the balance of danger and utility in the use of hypnosis in dealing with memory and dissociation. Psychodynamic therapists, for example, still maintain that hypnosis has a positive role to play in the retrieval of unconscious material, and in exploring personality.[81] Despite disagreements, there is a widespread consensus position, accepted by both researchers and clinicians alike, that hypnotically induced recollections of the past are not necessarily more accurate than non-hypnotic recall, and that hypnosis can sometimes foster inaccuracies in memory.[82]

Hypnosis research blossomed in the second half of the twentieth century, as multiple laboratories were able to grapple with traditional questions and with new issues and controversies, providing more substantial and reliable data. Hypnosis research was also directed toward the needs of clinical practitioners, providing more effective evaluation of techniques and uses of hypnosis than had ever been available before. By acknowledging the limitations and potential misuses of hypnosis, researchers and clinicians were able to maintain the professional integrity of hypnosis and increase its standing as a mainstream therapeutic practice, even as it emerged from the tempest.

Notes

1 See Steven J. Lynn and Kevin M. McConkey, *Truth in Memory* (New York: Guilford Press, 1998): 508.

2 Russell A. Powell and Douglas P. Boer, "Did Freud Mislead Patients to Confabulate Memories of Abuse?" *Psychological Reports* 74, no. 3 (1994): 1283–1298.

3 Jean-Roch Laurence and Campbell Perry, "Forensic Hypnosis in the Late Nineteenth Century," *International Journal of Clinical and Experimental Hypnosis* 31, no. 4 (1983): 266–283.

4 For an excellent discussion of this controversy, see Richard J. McNally, *Remembering Trauma* (Cambridge, MA: Belknap Press/Harvard University Press, 2003).

5 Sigmund Freud, "The Neuro-Psychoses of Defense," in *The Standard Edition of the Complete Psychological Works of Sigmund Freud*, vol. 3 (Early Psychoanalytic Publications, 1894): 61.

6 McNally, *Remembering Trauma*, 420. See also David S. Holmes, "Investigations of Repression: Differential Recall of Material Experimentally

or Naturally Associated with Ego Threat," *Psychological Bulletin* 81, no. 10 (1974): 632–653.

7 Frederick C. Crews ed., *Unauthorized Freud: Doubters Confront a Legend* (New York: Viking, 1998): 301.

8 Daniel L. Schacter and John F. Kihlstrom, "Functional Amnesia," *Handbook of Neuropsychology* 3 (1989): 209–231.

9 Elanor Schuker, "Psychodynamics and Treatment of Sexual Assault Victims," *Journal of American Academy of Psychoanalysis and Dynamic Psychiatry* 7, no. 4 (1979): 553–573. See also, for instance, Patricia P. Rieker and Elaine Carmen, "The Victim to Patient Process: The Disconfirmation and Transformation of Abuse," *American Journal of Orthopsychiatry* 56, no. 3 (1986): 360–370.

10 Katherine K. Shobe and John F. Kihlstrom, "Is Traumatic Memory Special?" *Current Directions in Psychological Science* 6, no. 3 (1997): 70–74.

11 Holmes, "Investigations of Repression: Differential Recall of Material Experimentally or Naturally Associated with Ego Threat," 632–653.

12 Alan W. Scheflin and Daniel Brown, "Repressed Memory or Dissociative Amnesia: What the Science Says," *Journal of Psychiatry and Law* 24, no. 2 (1996): 143–188.

13 August Piper, Jr., "What Science Says—and Doesn't Say—About Repressed Memories: A Critique of Scheflin and Brown," *Journal of Psychiatry and Law* 25, no. 4 (1997): 614–639.

14 Gail S. Goodman and others, "A Prospective Study of Memory for Child Sexual Abuse: New Findings Relevant to the Repressed-Memory Controversy," *Psychological Science* 14, no. 2 (2003): 113–118.

15 Jean-Roch Laurence and Campbell Perry, "Hypnotically Created Memory among Highly Hypnotizable Subjects," 523–524; Kevin M. McConkey, Amanda J. Barnier, and Peter W. Sheehan, "Hypnosis and Pseudomemory: Understanding the Findings and Their Implications," in S. J. Lynn and K. M. McConkey eds., *Truth in Memory* (New York: Guilford Press, 1998): 508.

16 Elizabeth F. Loftus, "The Reality of Repressed Memories," *American Psychologist* 48, no. 5 (1993): 518–537; Elizabeth F. Loftus and Katherine Ketcham, *The Myth of Repressed Memory* (New York: St. Martin's Press, 1994) 290; Elizabeth F. Loftus and Jacqueline E. Pickrell, "The Formation of False Memories," *Psychiatric Annals* 25, no. 12 (1995): 720–725.

17 Ibid.

18 Ira E. Hyman, Troy H. Husband, and F. James Billings, "False Memories of Childhood Experiences," *Applied Cognitive Psychology* 9, no. 3 (1995): 181–197.

19 Stephen Porter, John C. Yuille, and Darrin R. Lehman, "The Nature of Real, Implanted, and Fabricated Childhood Emotional Events:

Implications for the Recovered Memory Debate," *Law and Human Behavior* 23 (1999): 517–537.

20 Guilliana A. L. Mazzoni, Elizabeth F. Loftus, Aaron Seitz, and Steven J. Lynn, "Changing Beliefs and Memories Through Dream Interpretation," *Applied Cognitive Psychology* 13, no. 2 (1999): 125–144.

21 Kimberley A. Wade, Maryanne Garry, J. Don Read, and Stephen Lindsay, "A Picture is worth a Thousand Lies: Using False Photographs to Create False Childhood Memories," *Psychonomic Bulletin and Review* 9, no. 3 (2002): 597–603.

22 Daniel Brown, Alan W. Scheflin, and D. Corydon Hammond, *Memory, Trauma Treatment, and the Law* (New York: W. W. Norton & Co, 1998): 786; D. Corydon Hammond and others, *Clinical Hypnosis and Memory: Guidelines for Clinicians and for Forensic Hypnosis* (Des Plaines: American Society of Clinical Hypnosis Press, 1995): 73.

23 For a review of 34 studies see, Matthew H. Erdelyi, "Hypnotic Hypermnesia: The Empty Set of Hypermnesia," *International Journal of Clinical and Experimental Hypnosis* 42 (1994): 379–390. For a review of 24 studies see, Nancy M. Steblay and Robert K. Bothwell, "Evidence for Hypnotically Refreshed Testimony: The View from the Laboratory," *Law and Human Behavior* 18 (1994): 635–651. Wayne G. Whitehouse and others, "Hypnotic Hypermnesia: Enhanced Memory Accessibility or Report Bias?" *Journal of Abnormal Psychology* 97, no. 3 (1988): 289–295.

24 Michael R. Nash and others, "Accuracy of Recall by Hypnotically Age-Regressed Subjects," *Journal of Abnormal Psychology* 95, no. 3 (1986): 298–300.

25 Harry J. Sivec, Steven J. Lynn, and Peter T. Malinoski, "Hypnosis in the Cabbage Patch: Age Regression with Verifiable Events" (Unpublished Manuscript, State University of New York at Binghamton, 1997).

26 Steblay and Bothwell, "Evidence for Hypnotically Refreshed Testimony: The View from the Laboratory," 635–651. See also Steven J. Lynn and others, "Memory in the Hall of Mirrors: The Experience of 'Retractors' in Psychotherapy," *Psychological Inquiry* 8, no. 4 (1997): 307–312.

27 Daniel Brown, Alan Sheflin, and Cory Hammond, *Memory, Trauma, Treatment and the Law* (New York: Norton, 1998).

28 See also Steven J. Lynn and others, "Recalling the Unrecallable: Should Hypnosis be Used to Recover Memories in Psychotherapy?" *Current Directions in Psychological Science* 6, no. 3 (1997): 79–83.

29 Steblay and Bothwell, "Evidence for Hypnotically Refreshed Testimony: The View from the Laboratory," 635–651.

30 Alan Scoboria, Giuliana Mazzoni, Irving Kirsch, and Leonard S. Milling, "Immediate and Persisting Effects of Misleading Questions

and Hypnosis on Memory Reports," *Journal of Experimental Psychology: Applied* 8, no. 1 (2002): 26–32.

31 Steven J. Lynn, Bryan Myers, and Peter Malinoski, "Hypnosis, Pseudomemories, and Clinical Guidelines: A Sociocognitive Perspective," *NATO ASI Series: Series A: Life Sciences*, vol. 291, (New York: Plenum Press, 1997): 660; Lynn and others, "Recalling the Unrecallable, 79–83.

32 See American Psychological Association, Division 17 Committee on Women, "Psychotherapy Guidelines For Working with Clients who may have an Abuse or Trauma History" (American Psychological Association Trauma and Gender Issues Committee, 1995); American Psychological Association, "Working Group on Investigation of Memories of Childhood Abuse: Final Report" (American Psychological Association, 1996); Canadian Psychiatric Association, "Position Statement: Adult Recovered Memories of Childhood Sexual Abuse," *Canadian Journal of Psychiatry* 41 (1996): 305–306.

33 See American Medical Association Council on Scientific Affairs, "Memories of Childhood Abuse" (Council on Scientific Affairs Report, 1994): 5-A-94.

34 See, for example, David H. Gleaves, "The Sociocognitive Model of Dissociative Identity Disorder: A Reexamination of the Evidence," *Psychological Bulletin* 120, no. 1 (1996): 42–59; David H. Gleaves, Mary C. May, and Etzel Cardeña, "An Examination of the Diagnostic Validity of Dissociative Identity Disorder," *Clinical Psychology Review* 21, no. 4 (2001): 577–608; Colin A. Ross, *Dissociative Identity Disorder: Diagnosis, Clinical Features, and Treatment of Multiple Personality*, 2d ed. (Hoboken: John Wiley & Sons Inc., 1997): 452.

35 American Psychiatric Association (APA), *Diagnostic and Statistical Manual of Mental Disorders*, 4th ed. (Washington, DC: American Psychiatric Publishing Inc., 1994): 886.

36 Corbett H. Thigpen and Hervey M. Cleckley, *The Three Faces of Eve* (New York: McGraw-Hill, 1957): 308.

37 Gleaves, "The Sociocognitive Model of Dissociative Identity Disorder," 42–59.

38 See, for example, Hean M. Arrigo and Kathy Pezdek, "Textbook Models of Multiple Personality: Source, Bias, and Social Consequences," in S. J. Lynn and K. M. McConkey eds., *Truth in Memory* (New York: Guilford, 1998): 508; Gary E. Dunn and others, "Belief in the Existence of Multiple Personality Disorder among Psychologists and Psychiatrists," *Journal of Clinical Psychology* 50, no. 3 (1994): 454–457; François M. Mai, "Psychiatrists' Attitudes to Multiple Personality Disorder: A Questionnaire Study," *The Canadian Journal of Psychiatry* 40, no. 3 (1995): 154–157; Ian Hacking, *Rewriting the Soul:*

Multiple Personality and the Sciences of Memory (Princeton, NJ: Princeton University Press, 1995): 336.

39 Scott O. Lilienfeld and others, "Dissociative Identity Disorder and the Sociocognitive Model: Recalling the Lessons of the Past," *Psychological Bulletin* 125, no. 5 (1999): 507–523.

40 Lilienfeld and others, "Dissociative Identity Disorder and the Sociocognitive Model," 507–523; Steven J. Lynn and Judith Pintar, "A Social Narrative Model of Dissociative Identity Disorder," *Australian Journal of Clinical and Experimental Hypnosis* 25, no. 1 (1997): 1–7.

41 For example, Kenneth Bianchi, one of the Hillside Stranger murderers, is widely believed to have faked DID in order to escape criminal responsibility. See Martin T. Orne, David F. Dinges, and Emily C. Orne, "On the Differential Diagnosis of Multiple Personality in the Forensic Context," *International Journal of Clinical and Experimental Hypnosis* 32 (1984): 118–169.

42 Flora R. Schreiber, *Sybil* (Henry Regency Company, 1973): 359.

43 Spanos, *Multiple Identities and False Memories*, 267.

44 Ibid., 371; Elaine Showalter, *Hystories: Hysterical Epidemics and Modern Culture* (New York: Columbia University Press, 1997): 244; Jeanne A. Heaton and Nona L. Wilson, "Memory, Media, and the Creation of Mass Confusion," in Steven J. Lynn, and Kevin McConkey (eds.) *Truth in Memory* (London: The Guilford Press, 1998).

45 Carol S. North and others, "Multiple Personalities, Multiple Disorders: Psychiatric Classification and Media Influence," *Oxford Monographs on Psychiatry* 1 (New York: Oxford University Press, 1993): 278.

46 Colin A. Ross, G. Ron Norton, and Kay Wozney, "Multiple Personality Disorder: An Analysis of 236 Cases," *The Canadian Journal of Psychiatry* 34, no. 5 (1989): 413–418. See also Joan Acocella, *Creating Hysteria: Women and Multiple Personality Disorder* (San Francisco: Jossey-Bass, 1999): 214.

47 Spanos, *Multiple Identities and False Memories*, 371.

48 Spanos, *Multiple Identities and False Memories*, 371.

49 See for examples, Michael Shermer, *Why People Believe Weird Things: Pseudoscience, Superstition, and Other Confusions of Our Time* (New York: W. H. Freeman/Times Books/Henry Holt & Co, 1997): 306.

50 See Spanos, *Multiple Identities and False Memories*, 371.

51 Lilienfeld and others, "Dissociative Identity Disorder and the Sociocognitive Model," 507–523. See also Hacking, *Rewriting the Soul*, 336.

52 See, for example, Spanos, "Multiple Identity Enactments and Multiple Personality Disorder," 143–165; Spanos, *Multiple Identities and False Memories*, 371.

53 Steven J. Lynn, Judith W. Rhue, and Joseph P. Green, "Multiple Personality and Fantasy Proneness: Is There an Association or

Dissociation?" *British Journal of Experimental and Clinical Hypnosis* 5, no. 3 (1988): 138–142; Auke Tellegen and Gilbert Atkinson, "Openness to Absorbing and Self-Altering Experiences ('Absorption'), A Trait Related to Hypnotic Susceptibility," *Journal of Abnormal Psychology* 83, no. 3 (1974): 268–277.

54 For data suggesting considerably greater acceptance of DID in North American countries compared with non-North American English-speaking countries, see also John Hochman and Harrison G. Pope, Jr., "Debating Dissociative Diagnoses," *American Journal of Psychiatry* 154, no. 6 (1997): 887–888.

55 Gleaves, "The Sociocognitive Model of Dissociative Identity Disorder," 42–59. See also Herman N. Sno and Henk F. A. Schalken, "Dissociative Identity Disorder: Diagnosis and Treatment in the Netherlands," *European Psychiatry* 14, no. 5 (1999): 270–277.

56 See, for example, Onno van der Hart, "Multiple Personality Disorder in Europe: Impressions," *Dissociation: Progress in the Dissociative Disorders* 6, no. 2–3 (1993): 102–118; Bessel A. van der Kolk, Onno van der Hart, and Charles R. Marmar, "Dissociation and Information Processing in Posttraumatic Stress Disorder," in B. A. van der Kolk, A. C. McFarlane, and L. Weisaeth eds., *Traumatic Stress: The Effects of Overwhelming Experience on Mind, Body, and Society* (New York: Guilford Press, 1996): 303–327.

57 North and others, "Multiple Personalities, Multiple Disorders," 278.

58 See Acocella, *Creating Hysteria*, 214.

59 See, for example, Ross, *Dissociative Identity Disorder*, 452; Spanos, "Multiple Identity Enactments and Multiple Personality Disorder," 143–165; Spanos, *Multiple Identities and False Memories*, 371.

60 Van der Kolk, van der Hart, and Marmar, "Dissociation and Information Processing in Posttraumatic Stress Disorder," 303–327.

61 Mitchell L. Eisen and Steven J. Lynn, "Dissociation, Memory and Suggestibility in Adults and Children," *Applied Cognitive Psychology* 15, no. 7 (2001): S49–S73.

62 For a review see, Loftus, "The Reality of Repressed Memories," 518–537. Also see Elizabeth F. Loftus, "Make-believe Memories," *American Psychologist* 58, no. 11 (2003): 867–873.

63 Nicholas P. Spanos, H. Lorraine Radtke, and Lorne D. Bertrand, "Hypnotic Amnesia as a Strategic Enactment: Breaching Amnesia in Highly Susceptible Subjects," *Journal of Personality and Social Psychology* 47, no. 5 (1984): 1155–1169.

64 Kirsch and Lynn, "Dissociation Theories of Hypnosis," 100–115.

65 Ibid.

66 Russell A. Powell and Travis L. Gee, "The Effects of Hypnosis on Dissociative Identity Disorder: A Reexamination of the Evidence," *The Canadian Journal of Psychiatry* 44, no. 9 (1999): 914–916.

67 Colin A. Ross and G. Ron Norton, "Effects of Hypnosis on the Features of Multiple Personality Disorder," *American Journal of Clinical Hypnosis* 32, no. 2 (1989): 99–106.

68 Michael Nash, "What, if Anything, is Regressed About Hypnotic Age Regression? A Review of the Empirical Literature," *Psychological Bulletin* 102, no. 1 (1987): 42–52.

69 Jianjian Quin and others, "Repressed Memories of Ritualistic and Religion-Related Child Abuse," in S. J. Lynn and K. M. McConkey eds., *Truth in Memory* (New York: Guilford, 1998): 260–283; Sherrill A. Mulhern, "Ritual Abuse: Defining a Syndrome versus Defending a Belief," *Journal of Psychology and Theology* 20, no. 3 (1992): 230–232.

70 Kenneth V. Lanning and Ann W. Burgess, "Child Pornography and Sex Rings," in D. Zillmann and J. Bryant eds., *Pornography: Research Advances and Policy Considerations. Communication* (Hillsdale, NJ: Lawrence Erlbaum Associates, Inc., 1989): 235–255.

71 Mulhern, "Ritual Abuse," 230–232.

72 Quin and others, "Repressed Memories of Ritualistic and Religion-Related Child Abuse," 260–283.

73 Nicholas P. Spanos, Cheryl A. Burgess, and Melissa F. Burgess, "Past-life Identities, UFO Abductions, and Satanic Ritual Abuse: The Social Construction of Memories," *International Journal of Clinical and Experimental Hypnosis* 42, no. 4 (1994): 433–446.

74 See, Antonia Mills and Steven J. Lynn, "Past-life Experiences," in E. Cardeña, S. J. Lynn, and S. Krippner eds., *Varieties of Anomalous Experience: Examining the Scientific Evidence* (Washington, DC: American Psychological Association, 2000): 283–313.

75 Nicholas P. Spanos and others, "Secondary Identity Enactments during Hypnotic Past-Life Regression: A Sociocognitive Perspective," *Journal of Personality and Social Psychology* 61, no. 2 (1991): 137.

76 Spanos, *Multiple Identities and False Memories*, 371.

77 Hippolyte Bernheim, *Hypnosis and Suggestion in Psychotherapy* (New York: Aronson, 1973, original work published 1888).

78 Hippolyte Bernheim, *Suggestive Therapeutics: A Treatise on the Nature and Uses of Hypnotism* (New York: Putnam, 1889); Gerald M. Rosen, Marc Sageman, and Elizabeth Loftus, "A Historical Note on False Traumatic Memories," *Journal of Clinical Psychology* 60, no. 1 (2003): 137–139.

79 Pierre Janet, "Histoire d'une idée fixe," *Revue Philosophique* 37, no. 1 (1894) 121–168.

80 Coe and Sarbin, "Role Theory: Hypnosis from a Dramaturgical and Narrational Perspective," 303–323.

81 Erika Fromm and Michael R. Nash, "Psychoanalysis and Hypnosis," Mental Health Library Series, Monograph 5 (Madison, CT: International Universities Press, Inc., 1997): 312; M. T. Orne, D. F.

Dinges, and P. B. Bloom, "Hypnosis," in H. I. Kaplan and B. J. Sadock eds., *Comprehensive Textbook of Psychiatry VI,* 6th ed. (Baltimore: Williams and Wilkins, 1995): 1807–1821.

82 American Psychological Association, *Criteria For Guideline Development and Review* (Washington, DC: Author, 1995); Maryanne Garry and Devon L. L. Polaschek, "Imagination and Memory," *Current Directions in Psychological Science* 9, no. 1 (2000): 6–10.

CHAPTER NINE

Present and Future

Practitioners of mesmerism and, later, hypnosis produced a steady stream of case reports and anecdotal observations over 300 years, suggesting that their practices were effective in the treatment of countless physical and psychological complaints. It was not until the 1980s, however, that well-controlled studies evaluated the use of hypnosis in the treatment of medical conditions, and began to testify to the merits of hypnosis-based interventions.

By the end of the twentieth century there was a substantial body of empirical evidence supporting the use of hypnosis for multiple medical purposes, from pain management to dentistry. Hypnosis came to be seen as a promising addition to the treatment of obesity, smoking cessation, eating disorders, anxiety, and post-traumatic conditions as well. These applications of hypnosis in medicine, dentistry, and psychotherapy are now mainstream and pose little in the way of controversy, though a complete understanding of the processes underlying its effectiveness remains elusive. The relationship of hypnosis to the placebo effect suggests new avenues for research into the relationship between body and mind, as they are intricately entwined in the processes of illness, health, and healing.

As the twentieth century ended, consensus had been achieved by theoreticians on a range of issues, particularly those addressing the myths of hypnosis that have been circulating in theory, practice, and popular culture since mesmerism began, and are still widely disseminated in books and films. Yet, despite the existence of this set of facts accepted by hypnosis practitioners, researchers, and theorists (if not by the general public), there is no final resolution of many of the larger issues. Recently, for instance, research in neurobiology has opened up the state debate once again, while the controversies of the late twentieth century fall out of concern amid shifting funding priorities.

The lack of final resolution on some of the central questions about the nature of hypnosis has proved, ironically, to be a positive force in the field, since it energizes theoretically relevant research. It is likely to continue to do so as the study and practice of hypnosis unfold and transform in the twenty-first century.

Medical Applications of Hypnosis

The clinical use of mesmerism and hypnosis to provide relief from both chronic and acute pain has been its most consistent practical application across the centuries. One of the central preoccupations of the British mesmerists of the nineteenth century was pain reduction during surgical procedures. Following the focused work of Elliotson, Esdaile, and Braid, however, interest waned, and the more psychologically oriented theories of hypnosis shifted toward mental, rather than physical distress. The twentieth century saw a return of attention to pain, although its study had moved from the clinic to the laboratory. Systematic experimental research began taking place in the United States during the 1930s when Robert Sears published the results of his work on hypnotically induced pain analgesia in 1932, followed by a study on tactile anesthesia by Frank Pattie in 1937.[1]

As further studies provided empirical evidence that hypnotic suggestion could powerfully alter subjects' perceptions of pain,[2] attention to the phenomenon increased markedly in the 1950s and 60s.[3] Now, half a century later, it appears that hypnosis may provide substantial pain relief for 75% of the population.[4] Patients who are highly and moderately suggestible experience the greatest effect, but even low suggestible people report pain relief as well. Based on a review of clinical trials, it appears that hypnosis is an effective treatment not only for chronic pain,[5] including cancer[6] and headache,[7] but also for acute pain associated with labor during childbirth,[8] burns,[9] and surgical procedures,[10] in both medical and dental settings.[11] Patients who receive hypnotic suggestions for pain relief have been found, across several studies, to require less pain medication,[12] and pregnant women who are trained in hypnotic techniques appear to have easier and shorter deliveries.[13] The weight of empirical evidence has helped hypnosis to become a mainstream treatment for pain reduction.[14]

Hypnosis has also been found effective, with varying degrees of reliability, in a wide variety of medical conditions as diverse as asthma, warts, and irritable bowel syndrome (IBS). The use of hypnosis in the treatment of IBS has been supported by several important studies that have demonstrated that its use not only decreases the use of medication and the need for medical consultation, but also reduces depression and improves overall quality of life. These results have been shown to be stable over time.[15]

Studies examining the use of hypnosis in preparing surgical patients have also produced impressive results.[16] A review of 20 research reports, all dealing with the use of hypnosis in the context of surgical procedures, found that 89% of the patients who received hypnotic suggestions had experiences significantly more successful than the control group who had not.[17] Hypnosis has proved to have multiple uses in the surgical context, including the control of postoperative nausea and pain among patients who received general anesthesia; these include children being treated for cancer[18] and bone-marrow transplant patients receiving chemotherapy.[19]

The prevalence and efficacy of the use of hypnosis in dentistry has also been evaluated through systematic research. More than a quarter of dental schools in North America and Canada now offer courses in clinical hypnosis.[20] Hypnotic suggestion has proved to have multiple uses in coordination with dental procedures, helping patients to relax, release anxieties and phobias, as well as improving tolerance for the installation of orthodontic or prosthetic appliances. The use of hypnosis appears to reduce patients' need for chemical anesthetics and sedation, and has other purely physiological benefits as well, in controlling salivary flow and bleeding.[21]

The most mainstream application of hypnosis is its application as an aid in smoking cessation. Evidence supporting its efficacy has been collected for more than 40 years. More recently, a meta-analysis of 633 studies of smoking cessation, including 48 studies that assessed the use of "hypnosis," concluded that hypnosis was more successful than any of the comparison treatments, with a success rate of 36%.[22] Evidence also suggests that hypnotic approaches are more effective than no treatment.[23] The efficacy of hypnosis for "quitting smoking" is more widely apparent to the public at large, a result, perhaps, of the significant research attention it has received since the late 1970s. Less apparent to the public, interest in the use of hypnotic suggestions to control eating disorders also grew significantly during the same period, as empirical evidence mounted that hypnosis was an effective supplement to therapeutic procedures. Positive results were found with the use of suggestions for enjoyment of eating and increased hunger.[24] Other studies found that hypnosis could increase treatment compliance when used with behavior modification programs.[25] More recent research and clinical case reports have produced a body of evidence suggesting that hypnosis is a useful clinical tool for the treatment of both anorexia and bulimia.[26] Still, it is not altogether clear whether hypnosis produces treatment gains above and beyond alternative treatment approaches and what is offered by relaxation and guided imagery.

Psychotherapeutic Applications of Hypnosis

The mainstream position that hypnosis now enjoys in the psychotherapeutic world reflects changes in the institutions of medical insurance and health care occurring at the end of the twentieth century that particularly benefited brief therapies. As a result, the surge of interest in behavioral and cognitive-behavioral interventions provided increased opportunities for the practice of techniques, like hypnosis, that focus on symptom reduction. In addition, the increasing influence of professional hypnosis societies and sympathetic interest groups made training in the techniques of hypnosis widely available to individuals across professions. The Society for Clinical and Experimental Hypnosis was initiated as early as 1949. Milton Erickson was to become the founding president of the American Society for Clinical Hypnosis, founded in 1957. Conflict between the two organizations led to the initiation, in 1958, of the International Society for Clinical and Experimental Hypnosis, organized around National Divisions with members from 30 different nations.[27] In the same year, hypnosis was recognized by the American Medical Association's Council on Mental Health, which began to offer professional training to practitioners. In 1968, the Society of Psychological Hypnosis, Division 30, was set up within the American Psychological Association.[28] Most recently, in 2007 the British Society of Clinical and Academic Hypnosis was formed to incorporate the British Society of Medical and Dental Hypnosis, which began in 1952, and the British Society of Experimental and Clinical Hypnosis, founded in 1977.

Health psychologists made important contributions to the surge of interest in integrating hypnosis into behavioral and cognitive-behavioral interventions that focus on symptom reduction. Some of the clinicians and researchers (not mentioned earlier in this context) who played an influential role in this movement include David Patterson and Mark Jensen at the University of Washington, Guy Montgomery at Mount Sinai Hospital (New York), Peter Whorwell at South Manchester University Hospitals (UK), D. Corydon Hammond at the University of Utah, Joseph Green at Ohio State University (Lima), Cornelia Pinnell at Argosy University, Donna Copeland at the M.D. Anderson Cancer Center, Len Milling at Hartford University, Nicholas Covino at the Massachusetts School of Professional Psychology, and Elvira Lang at Harvard University Medical School.

The enthusiastic resurgence of hypnosis as a psychotherapeutic tool during the late twentieth century owes a great deal to the work of seasoned clinicians who disseminated knowledge about hypnosis to a broad national and international audience. Some of the first therapists to be inspired by Erickson were Jay Haley, who published Erickson's case studies illustrating brief and strategic interventions tailor-made to each patient, and Ernest Rossi, who compiled and analyzed Erickson's papers and cases, revealing the subtleties of Erickson's approach. Erickson's techniques were also promoted by Jeffrey Zeig through the establishment of the Milton H. Erickson foundation in Phoenix, Arizona, which sponsored workshops and international conferences to promote Erickson's contributions to mental health professionals. In addition to Zeig, other students of Erickson or therapists whose clinical publications were directly influenced by him included independent practitioners Stephen Gilligan, Richard Bandler, Robert Dilts, John Grinder, Stephen Lankton, Michael Yapko, and William Matthews at the University of Massachusetts.

Other clinicians, as well as researchers who studied clinically relevant topics and problems, also contributed immensely to collective scientific knowledge, and to the waxing of interest in the therapeutic applications of hypnosis. Some of these individuals (not mentioned earlier in this context) include Herbert Spiegel at Columbia University and his son David Spiegel at Stanford University, Arreed and Marianne Barabasz at Washington State University, Auke Tellegen at the University of Minnesota, James Council at North Dakota State University, Emily Orne, Martin Orne, and Peter Bloom at the University of Pennsylvania, John and Helen Watkins at the University of Montana, Dierdre Barrett and Daniel Brown at Harvard Medical School, Fred H. Frankel of Beth Israel Hospital and Harvard Medical School, Edward Frischholz at Loyola University (Chicago), Lynne Hornyak (independent practice), Edmund Thomas Dowd at Kent State University, Stephen Kahn at the Illinois School of Professional Psychology, Claire Frederick at Tufts University Medical School, Melvin Gravitz at George Mason University, Don Gibbons (independent practice), and William Morgan at the University of Wisconsin.

Researchers and clinicians made important applied and theoretical contributions on the international scene as well. Some of these individuals (not mentioned earlier in this context) include Michael Heap at the University of Sheffield, Brian Fellows at the University of Portsmouth, Eva Banyai at Etvos Lorand University in Budapest, Daniel David at Babes Bolyai University in Romania, Jerzy Siuta at Jagiellonian University in Poland, Camillo Loriedo at the University of Rome, Antonio Capafons and Salvador Amigo at the University of Valencia, Richard van Dyke at the Free University of Amsterdam, Walter Bongartz at the University of Konstanz, Burkhard Peter at the University of Munich, Philip Spinhoven at Leiden University, and Etzel Cardeña at the University of Lund. Cardeña formerly taught in the United States and collaborated with David Spiegel and Steven Lynn, as well as with Stanley Krippner at the Saybrook Institute, who shared Cardeña's interest in understanding hypnosis through the lens of cross-cultural studies.

Rigorous, systematic research taking place at the end of the twentieth century, evaluating theoretical and clinical innovations, has been a significant contributing factor to the increasing use of hypnosis as a psychotherapeutic tool during that period. In 1985, Theodore Barber laid out the ways in which administering suggestions in a hypnotic context can improve therapeutic outcomes. He argued that hypnosis can generate positive treatment motivation and expectancies that serve as self-fulfilling prophesies; that it can enhance patients' confidence in their therapist, by capitalizing on patients' beliefs that therapists who use hypnosis are more highly trained, skilled, and knowledgeable; and finally that hypnosis gives a therapist the means to speak directly to a patient in a powerfully meaningful way that is not possible in ordinary conversation. Barber's general assessment was supported, 10 years later, by a meta-analysis which indicated that using hypnosis as an adjunctive procedure enhances the effectiveness of cognitive-behavioral therapy.[29]

Cognitive-behavioral approaches to the psychotherapeutic treatment of anxiety disorders have been among the most widely studied.[30] Research appears to support the contention that hypnosis can effectively supplement the cognitive-behavioral approach. A study conducted in 1997 evaluated the use of hypnotic induction and suggestions in the treatment of public-speaking anxiety. The study compared the cognitive-behavioral treatment, involving cognitive restructuring and "real-life" exposure to public speaking, to a similar treatment that replaced the use of relaxation with a hypnotic induction. Participants in the study rated their anxiety after giving an impromptu speech. Only the group that had been treated with hypnosis differed from the control group, which had received no treatment at all on behavioral and subjective measures of anxiety during the speech. Their anxiety also dissipated more quickly than it did for participants in the other groups.[31]

The use of hypnosis in the treatment of a variety of posttraumatic conditions, brought about by a wide range of circumstances including combat, sexual assault, anesthesia failure, and transportation accidents, has been documented in anecdotal reports for the past 200 years.[32] More recently, empirical evidence exists to support the contention that hypnosis can be an effective technique in the treatment of stress disorders.[33] Those who suffer from posttraumatic conditions score more highly on tests of hypnotic suggestibility than other mental health patient populations,[34] which may give them an advantage in benefiting from hypnotic procedures.[35]

The use of hypnosis in coordination with psychotherapy in the treatment of depression has not been extensively researched. There is, however, indirect evidence that supports its potential. The placebo response seems to have a particularly strong role in success in the treatment of depression. One review of published clinical trials found that, regardless of the type of antidepressants prescribed, inert placebos duplicated 75% of their effects.[36] There is evidence that overestimation of the potency of antidepressants, and an underestimation of placebo effects, in industry research reports means that this number could prove to be much higher.[37] Since conditions that are responsive to placebo treatment appear to be responsive to hypnosis as well, it follows that hypnosis may prove to be an effective treatment option for depression.

Making constructive use of the "placebo effect" poses an interesting ethical dilemma for psychotherapists. Irving Kirsch has pointed out that since the development of trust between therapist and client is an important contributor to positive outcomes in psychotherapy, employing a technique that is, essentially, deception is significantly problematic. Hypnosis resolves this dilemma in an elegant way. It can take advantage of the "placebo effect" by enhancing patients' expectancies for positive outcomes, but it can do so without deception. It follows that attempting to alter expectations for the experiencing of symptoms may be a useful technique for reducing the experience of those symptoms.[38]

There is evidence that hypnosis is useful to mediate and minimize "anxiety expectancy," the fear of having an uncomfortable physiological stress reaction.[39] For the treatment of depression, for example, Michael Yapko has developed a systematic application of hypnosis specifically designed to build positive expectancies in clients. He has found some of his depressed clients to have a rigid view of their lives and the assumption that negative circumstances cannot be changed.[40] He uses hypnotic suggestion to help clients expect that making changes will lead to positive benefits in the future.[41]

The fact that physical ailments that are susceptible to placebo treatment may be more likely to be affected by hypnotic intervention suggests that clinical investigation into the power of expectancies is likely to continue to be a constructive area of research. The wide successes of hypnosis in treatment in both medical and psychotherapeutic contexts underscore the connection of mind to body, and body to mind.

Unanswered Questions in the Trait Debate

In tandem with the general agreement within the mainstream medical and psychotherapeutic community about the efficacy of hypnosis in the treatment of a wide variety of ailments, there has also emerged consensus among theoreticians on a wide range of previously controversial issues. Many of these understandings were achieved to respond to persistent myths of hypnosis that have been circulating in theory, practice, and popular culture for hundreds of years.

It is widely accepted by theoreticians and practitioners, for example, that the ability to experience hypnotic phenomena does not indicate gullibility or weakness,[42] that hypnosis is not related to sleep,[43] that hypnotic responsiveness depends more on the efforts and abilities of the subject than on the skill of the hypnotist,[44] that hypnotized subjects don't lose the ability to control their behavior and can't be made to act against their will,[45] that spontaneous posthypnotic amnesia is relatively rare,[46] that people respond to suggestions when they are not hypnotized,[47] that hypnosis does not increase the accuracy of memory,[48] nor does it foster a literal reexperiencing of childhood events.[49]

Despite the consensus that has been achieved on these assertions, there has been no resolution of the larger and more contentious issues, including both questions about hypnotic responsiveness, related to the "Trait" debates, and the physiological correlates of hypnosis, related to the "state" debate. These will continue to be among the key areas of interest, disagreement, research, and controversy in the future, though the specific research tasks may be significantly redefined.

The trait issue has the most immediate importance for clinical hypnotists, whose interest is in enhancing suggestibility as a strategy for improving hypnotic responsiveness, and thus therapeutic effectiveness. Research has demonstrated that hypnotic induction increases suggestibility, but for most subjects the increase is relatively small. For example, someone who responded to six out of twelve suggestions without a hypnotic induction will typically respond to seven or eight after being hypnotized. The correlation between suggestibility in hypnotic and non-hypnotic contexts is so strong that it has been argued that it is imaginative suggestibility that is actually being measured in many studies of hypnotizability.[50]

Although there has been no recent survey to determine how many therapists routinely test the hypnotizability of their patients, in 1989 only 54% reported that they did so, and it is unlikely that the number would have changed much since then. Some clinicians view the assessment of hypnotizability as a potentially "misleading, intrusive, and transference-contaminating obstacle to the therapeutic work ahead."[51] Others simply question the point of measuring hypnotizability scores when they are not predictive of positive treatment outcome.[52]

For most therapeutic tasks involving hypnosis, high hypnotizability is not a prerequisite, but proponents of suggestibility testing argue that it is not irrelevant to outcome. Although the correlations between hypnotizability and treatment outcome are mixed, some effect has been measured in the use of hypnosis for smoking cessation, obesity, warts, anxiety, somatization, conversion disorders, and asthma.[53] One study that looked at the use of hypnosis in the treatment of conversion disorder found that hypnotizability predicted outcome more accurately than expectancies.[54]

The most dependable finding in this regard is the well-documented link between high and medium hypnotizability scores and responsiveness to analgesia suggestions. Intriguingly, some people who do not experience pain reduction in response to analgesia suggestions in a hypnotic context do achieve some relief from the same suggestions presented without the hypnotic language. It can be as difficult to untangle stable traits from learnable skills as it is to distinguish effects of hypnosis from the effects of subjects' expectations about hypnosis.

A range of questions still remain regarding hypnotic responsiveness. Researchers have not yet identified specific personality variables that can reliably predict who will test high on measures of hypnotizability, and who will not.[55] Research is also ongoing on the question of whether or not hypnotizability is a stable or modifiable trait. If an effective method for training hypnotizability were discovered, it would have important clinical implications for the treatment of pain, and other disorders and conditions that have proved responsive to hypnotic suggestion. Also, concerns have been expressed that laboratory gains in hypnotizability reflect compliance rather than genuine changes in abilities to experience and respond to hypnosis. Hypnotizability has been shown to be modifiable in the laboratory, but it remains to be seen whether patient training protocols will lead to significantly better clinical outcomes outside it. This research will inform the theoretical issues by contributing to the search for an understanding of the "trait-like" properties of hypnosis.[56]

Significant disagreement remains on the role of cognitive-behavioral variables, like belief and expectations, and psychodynamic ones (primary process, and access to emotions), not only on hypnotizability, but on the less common and more spectacular (and controversial) responses observed in hypnotic subjects, such as age-regression, the appearance of pseudomemories, amnesia, and analgesia. One possibility is that expectancy operates as a kind of final mediator in a complicated chain of events that produces what we understand as "response to suggestion."[57]

The power of expectancies to shape hypnotic response has long been observed. Martin Orne demonstrated in a 1957 study that spontaneous arm catalepsy will occur more frequently among people who expect it to occur.[58] The implication is that expectancies don't just determine whether or not hypnotic responses occur, but also influence what the nature of those responses is going to be. Only people who expect to be amnesiac following hypnosis actually do experience "spontaneous" amnesia. Likewise, what subjects are told about their ability to resist suggestions appears to directly influence their ability to resist them.[59] If they're told they can, they do; if they're told they can't, they demonstrate a greater inability to resist. Expectations can be shaped both by shared cultural beliefs and assumptions, as well as by the more immediate suggestions (direct, or implied) delivered by the therapist.

Researchers claim expectancy as one of the few stable factors to correlate with hypnotizability, although studies have produced different results as to the power of the effect. Most show moderate correlations between expectancy and suggestibility; however, under certain conditions significantly higher correlations have been reported.[60] Other studies have shown that subjects' level of responsiveness is highly sensitive to experimenter manipulations of their expectations about their own level of suggestibility.[61] For example, in one study, while the experimenters administered the suggestion that the room in which the participants were sitting was getting redder and redder, they also surreptitiously added red-tinted light to the room. The participants were then tested for hypnotic suggestibility, with startling result: while the control group scored in the normal distribution of suggestibility, 73% of those who had their expectancy manipulated in the red room scored in the high range for suggestibility, and no one scored in the low range.[62]

Although the correlation obtained in this study is strongly suggestive of a causal relationship between expectancy and suggestibility, not all the variance has been explained. The remaining variance could be due to measurement error, but it could also reflect any number of variables, including some unmeasured talent or an unidentified personality trait. In addition to manipulating expectancy, suggestibility modification techniques including encouraging imagination, enhancing rapport, and suggesting specific cognitive strategies that may help them to experience the suggested events have all been studied.[63]

There is no easy or straightforward resolution of the question of whether there is some stable trait that can predict hypnotic responsiveness. In recent years, theorists have called for an inquiry that considers multiple, interacting factors that might influence hypnotic responses, both behavioral and subjective, and this is the likely direction for future research.[64]

Unanswered Questions in the State Debate

Like the trait debate, the state debate continues, with new angles and issues emerging, into the twenty-first century. The hunt for proof that hypnosis involves a discrete altered state has been enlivened in recent years by increasingly sophisticated brain imaging technologies.[65] There is actually little debate over whether or not hypnotic suggestions can affect brain functioning. Neurophysiological studies of hypnosis have pointed to the anterior cingulate area of the brain as involved in some alterations of consciousness experienced during hypnosis.[66] To some researchers, findings like these provide evidence that hypnosis is a discrete state of consciousness.[67]

Non-state theorists readily acknowledge that hypnotic suggestion can bring about the experience of an altered state, and that it follows that corresponding neurophysiological changes should be measurable. They point out, however, that merely documenting physiological changes is insufficient to demonstrate causality between the altered state and other hypnotic responses.[68] Specifically they argue that unless physiological markers of response to the suggestion to enter trance are detectable without any further suggestions (what has been termed "neutral hypnosis") *and* also that these markers are found to be necessary prerequisites for response to at least some suggestions, then the evidence does not support an altered state hypothesis.[69] To satisfy non-state theorists, proponents of the altered state view would have to show that something beyond responsivity to suggestions, beliefs, expectations, motivation, and imaginative abilities accounts for the physiological changes.[70]

Neurophysiological research is one of the most intriguing areas of hypnosis-related inquiry, and whether or not it leads to a resolution of the altered state debate, it will continue to add to our knowledge of the workings of human consciousness and perhaps will provide evidence that challenges the sociocognitive perspective.[71]

The Executive Committee of the APA Division of Psychological Hypnosis revised their definition of hypnosis in 2004 to include clinical techniques of self-hypnosis and to acknowledge the continuing coexistence of competing theories regarding the reality of altered states: "Many believe that hypnotic responses and experiences are characteristic of a hypnotic state. While some think that it is not necessary to use the word 'hypnosis' as part of the hypnotic induction, others view it as essential."[72]

This definition embraces the contradictions surrounding the practice of hypnosis, reflecting the pragmatic view that has been a recurring strength of the field through all its tangled history. Hypnotic techniques may vary. The convictions of practitioners about the nature of hypnosis may vary. Even the relationship between the hypnotist and the subject can vary, since the apparent efficacy of self-hypnosis indicates that the physical presence of a hypnotist may not be necessary at all.

It's not that modern practitioners no longer care which phenomena are essential to hypnosis. They have just learned a key lesson that the history of hypnosis has demonstrated time and again: hypnosis still seems to "work" even if the most existential questions about why it works remain unresolved.

From the Present to the Future

Considering its winding and complicated history, it is difficult to predict with any accuracy where hypnosis research and practice will really find itself in the future. It is possible, however, to note trends in clinical practice and research interest that allow a glimpse into what may lie ahead.

The American Psychological Association Division of Psychological Hypnosis conducted a poll of hypnosis experts that included clinicians, researchers, editorial board members, and officers of professional associations. They were asked to give their opinions on substantive and specific research areas within the field of hypnosis, and to evaluate the importance of each area to the common knowledge base of hypnosis research, its clinical utility, and its potential fundability. The poll was conducted twice, in 1997 and again in 2004–2005.[73]

A comparison of the two polls gives insight into the changing interests and priorities from the end of the twentieth century to the beginning of the twenty-first. The most dramatic change was the shift in importance of eyewitness memory and the hypnotic production of pseudomemories. In research importance, these dropped from 2nd and 3rd in ranking down to 16th and 17th, with a similar drop in the evaluation of their clinical utility. Associated with these two areas, the poll also captured a shift away from research interest and clinical utility of dissociative processes, as well as imagination and fantasy.

Although the areas of neuroscience and psychophysiological processes were ranked very high in fundability in both polls, its research importance jumped upward from 13th to 3rd in rankings between 1997 and 2005. Research on the relationship between hypnotic and non-hypnotic processes also increased, from 25th to 5th in rank.

The issue that remained the area of most consistent interest was the use of hypnosis for pain control. In research importance this was ranked 1st in both polls, by both clinicians and academics. Cancer, self-hypnosis, surgical interventions, as well as the treatment of mental health conditions were also areas that retained their high levels of significance. Though anxiety disorders, post-traumatic stress disorder (PTSD), child problems, and eating disorders were all ranked highly for clinical utility, anxiety and PTSD stood out for their research importance and fundability as well.

Taken as a whole, the poll demonstrates that behavioral medicine and health psychology are at the forefront of both experimental and clinical hypnosis. The complicated interdependent relationship between the workings of the mind and body are what mesmerism and hypnosis throughout their long history have always spoken to, even before there was a scientific vocabulary adequate to capture what they were trying to say. That vocabulary exists now. There is every reason to expect that explorations into hypnosis will illuminate the mind–body connection in significant ways in the future.

The poll also underscores the resolution, for the present, of the controversies surrounding pseudomemory and dissociative identity disorder that occurred at the end of the twentieth century. No one who was participating in the false memory debates would have believed it would leave the spotlight so thoroughly within the first few years of the twenty-first century. Of course, when the explosive interest in the appearance of multiple personality disorder in hypnotic subjects that took place at the end of the nineteenth century was over, no one was likely then to have predicted it would reappear again so soon. It did so, in part, in response to popular interest in, and intense media coverage of, clinical events.

In popular culture, everything seems to come around again. An eBay search on the term "magnetic healing" produces several hundred products touting the healing properties of electromagnetism, including what is advertised as the "Mens 2-Tone Magnetic Golf Healing Bracelet." The persistence of discredited scientific ideas in popular culture is a phenomenon that is easy to lampoon.

History tells us that the entanglement of culture and science is more intimate than many scientists would be comfortable admitting, but the relationship in the development of mesmerism and hypnosis has had significant positive as well as negative consequences.

It is widely recognized that funding for scientific research follows cultural, social, and political trends; what is less acknowledged is that scientific breakthroughs owe much to the inspiration they gain from popular culture. The flow of ideas and enthusiasm goes both ways. Many major figures in the history of hypnosis, from Alexander Bertrand to James Braid to Sigmund Freud, saw the process for the first time being performed on stage, as entertainment. Though many nineteenth century medical practitioners of hypnosis would deride the activities of stage performances and dismiss the activities of lay practitioners as counterproductive to scientific progress, from a retrospective historical perspective this seems disingenuous.

Without Charles Lafontaine, James Braid might never have coined the term hypnosis; without Trilby and Sybil, the twentieth century enthusiasm for hypnosis might never have taken place. Popular understandings and representations of hypnosis developed alongside the theories and practices of important historical figures, a testament to the complicated, problematic, and productive relationship between scientific inquiry and the social world in which it is necessarily embedded.

Notes

1 Robert R. Sears, "Experimental Study of Hypnotic Anesthesia," *Journal of Experimental Psychology* 15 (1932): 1–22; Pattie, "The Genuineness of Hypnotically Produced Anesthesia of the Skin," 435–443.

2 Ralph. R. Brown and Victor. H. Vogel, "Psycho-Physiological Reactions Following Painful Stimuli under Hypnotic Analgesia Contrasted with Gas Anesthesia and Novocain Block," *Journal of Applied Psychology* 22, no. 4 (1938): 408–420; Louis J. West, Karleen C. Niell, and James D. Hardy, "Effects of Hypnotic Suggestion on Pain Perception and Galvanic Skin Response," *Archives of Neurology and Psychiatry* 68 (1952): 549–560.

3 Theodore X. Barber, "The Effects of Hypnosis on Pain," *Psychosomatic Medicine* 25, no. 4 (1963): 303–333; Theodore X. Barber and Karl W. Hahn, Jr., "Physiological and Subjective Responses to Pain Producing Stimulation under Hypnotically-Suggested and Waking-Imagined

'Analgesia,'" *Journal of Abnormal and Social Psychology* 65, no. 6 (1962): 411–418; Ronald E. Shor, "Physiological Effects of Painful Stimulation during Hypnotic Analgesia under Conditions Designed to Minimize Anxiety," *International Journal of Clinical and Experimental Hypnosis* 10, no. 3 (1962): 183–202; John P. Sutcliffe, "'Credulous' and 'Skeptical' Views of Hypnotic Phenomena: Experiments on Esthesia, Hallucination, and Delusion," *Journal of Abnormal and Social Psychology* 62, no. 2 (1961): 189–200.

4 Guy H. Montgomery, Katherine N. DuHamel, and William H. Redd, "A Meta-analysis of Hypnotically Induced Analgesia: How Effective is Hypnosis?" *International Jounral of Clinical and Experimental Hypnosis* 48, no. 2 (2000): 138–153.

5 David R. Patterson and Mark P. Jensen, "Hypnosis and Clinical Pain," *Psychological Bulletin* 129, no. 4 (2003): 495–521.

6 David Spiegel and Joan R. Bloom, "Group Therapy and Hypnosis Reduce Metastatic Breast Carcinoma Pain," *Psychosomatic Medicine* 45, no. 4 (1983): 333–339.

7 Theodore Andreychuk and Christian Skriver, "Hypnosis and Biofeedback in the Treatment of Migraine Headache," *International Journal of Clinical and Experimental Hypnosis* 23, no. 3 (1975): 172–183; Phillip Spinhoven and others, "Autogenic Training and Self-Hypnosis in the Control of Tension Headache," *General Hospital Psychiatry* 14, no. 6 (1992): 408–415.

8 Teresa M. Harmon, Michael T. Hynan, Timothy E. Tyre, "Improved Obstetric Outcomes using Hypnotic Analgesia and Skill Mastery Combined with Childbirth Education," *Journal of Consulting and Clinical Psychology* 58, no. 5 (1990): 525–530.

9 David R. Patterson, Kent A. Questad, and Barbara J. de Lateur, "Hypnotherapy as an Adjunct to Narcotic Analgesia for the Treatment of Pain for Burn Debridement," *American Journal of Clinical Hypnosis* 31, no. 3 (1989): 156–163; David R. Patterson and others, "Hypnosis for the Treatment of Burn Pain," *Journal of Consulting and Clinical Psychology* 60, no. 5 (1992): 713–717; John R. Wakeman and Jerold Z. Kaplan, "An Experimental Study of Hypnosis in Painful Burns," *American Journal of Clinical Hypnosis* 21, no. 1 (1978): 3–12; Bernadette R. Wright and Peter D. Drummond, "Rapid Induction Analgesia for the Alleviation of Procedural Pain during Burn Care," *Burns* 26, no. 3 (2000): 275–282.

10 Elvira V. Lang and others, "Adjunctive Non-Pharmacologic Analgesia for Invasive Medical Procedures: A Randomized Trial," *Lancet* 355 (2000): 1486–1490.

11 See Cornelia M. Pinnell and Nicholas A. Covino, "Empirical Findings on the Use of Hypnosis in Medicine: A Critical Review," *International Journal of Clinical and Experimental Hypnosis* 48, no. 2 (2000): 170–194.

12 See Montgomery, DuHamel, and Redd, "A Meta-analysis of Hypnotically Induced Analgesia: How Effective is Hypnosis?", 138–153; Patterson and Jensen, "Hypnosis and Clinical Pain," 495–521; Guy Montgomery, Daniel David, Gary Winkel, Jeffrey H. Silverstein, and Dana H. Bovbjerg, "The Effectiveness of Anjunctive Hypnosis with Surgical Patients: A Meta-analysis," *Anesthesia and Analgesia* 94 (2002): 1639–1645; Karen Syrjala, Claudette Cummings, and Gary W. Donaldson, "Hypnosis or Cognitive Behavioral Training for the Reduction of Pain and Nausea during Cancer Treatment," Pain 48 (1992): 137–146.

13 Harmon, Hynan, and Tyre, "Improved Obstetric Outcomes using Hypnotic Analgesia and Skill Mastery Combined with Childbirth Education," 525–530.

14 Montgomery, DuHamel, and Redd, "A Meta-analysis of Hypnotically Induced Analgesia,"138–153.

15 Wendy Gonsalkorale, Lesley Houghton, and Peter Whorwell, "Hypnotherapy in Irritable Bowel Syndrome: A Large-Scale Audit of a Clinical Service with Examination of Factors Influencing Responsiveness," *American Journal of Gastroenterology* 97, no. 4 (1997): 954–961; Arreed Barabasz and Marianne Barabasz, "Effects of Tailored and Manualized Hypnotic Inductions for Complicated Irritable Bowel Syndrome Patients," *International Journal of Clinical and Experimental* Hypnosis 54, no. 1 (2006): 100–112; Olafur Palsson, Marsha Turner, and William Whitehead, "Hypnosis Home Treatment for Irritable Bowel Syndrome: A Pilot Study," *International Journal of Clinical and Experimental Hypnosis* 54, no 1 (2006): 85–99.

16 Sally A. Lambert, "The Effects of Hypnosis/Guided Imagery on the Postoperative Course of Children," *Journal of Developmental and Behavioral Pediatrics* 17, no. 5 (1996): 307–310.

17 Guy H. Montgomery and others, "The Effectiveness of Adjunctive Hypnosis with Surgical Patients: A Meta-analysis," *Anesthesia and Analgesia* 94, no. 6 (2002): 1639–1645.

18 Dale S. Jacknow, Jeanne M. Tschann, Michael P. Link, and W. Thomas Boyce, "Hypnosis in the Prevention of Chemotherapy-Related Nausea and Vomiting in Children: A Prospective Study," *Journal of Developmental and Behavioral Pediatrics* 15, no. 4 (1994): 258–264; Lonnie K. Zeltzer, Michael J. Dolgin, Samuel LeBaron, and Christine LeBaron, "A Randomized, Controlled Study of Behavioral Intervention for Chemotherapy Distress in Children with Cancer," *Pediatrics* 88, no. 1 (1991): 34–42.

19 Syrjala, Cummings, and Donaldson, "Hypnosis or Cognitive Behavioral Training for the Reduction of Pain and Nausea during Cancer Treatment," 137–146.

20 J. Henry Clarke, "Teaching Clinical Hypnosis in U.S. and Canadian Dental Schools," *American Journal of Clinical Hypnosis* 39 (1996): 89–92.

21 John F. Chaves, "Hypnosis in Dentistry: Historical Overview and Critical Appraisal," *Hypnosis International Monographs* 3 (1997b): 5–23.
22 Chockalingam Viswesvaran and Frank. L. Schmidt, "A Meta-analytic Comparison of the Effectiveness of Smoking Cessation Methods," *Journal of Applied Psychology* 77, no. 4 (1992): 554–561.
23 Joseph Green and Steven J. Lynn, "Hypnosis and Suggestion-based Approaches to Smoking Cessation: An examination of the evidence," *International Journal of Clinical and Experimental Hypnosis* 48 (2000): 195–224.
24 Harold B. Crasilneck and James Hall, *Clinical Hypnosis: Principles and Applications* (New York: Grune & Stratton, 1975): 13–35.
25 William S. Kroger and William D. Fezler, *Hypnosis and Behavior Modification: Imagery Conditioning* (Oxford, England: J. B. Lippincott, 1976): 426; William S. Kroger, *Clinical and Experimental Hypnosis in Medicine, Dentistry, and psychology* 2d ed. (Oxford, England: J. B. Lippincott, 1977): 406; Spiegel and Spiegel, *Trance and Treatment,* 382.
26 Steven Lynn, Irving Kirsch, Maryellen Crowley, and Anna Campion, "Eating Disorders and Obesity," in Steven Lynn and Irving Kirsch eds., *Essentials of Clinical Hypnosis* (Washington, DC: American Psychological Association, 2006).
27 For the full story, see John G. Watkins, "Organization and Functioning of ISCEH, the International Society for Clinical and Experimental Hypnosis, *International Journal of Clinical and Experimental Hypnosis* 43, no. 3 (1995): 332–341.
28 See Society of Psychological Hypnosis Division 30 of the American Psychological Association website: www.apa.org/divisions/div30.
29 Irving Kirsch, Guy Montgomery, and Guy Sapirstein, "Hypnosis as an Adjunct to Cognitive-Behavioral Psychotherapy: A Meta-analysis," *Journal of Consulting and Clinical Psychology* 63, no. 2 (1995): 214–220.
30 David H. Barlow, *Anxiety and Its Disorders. The Nature and Treatment of Anxiety and Panic* (New York: Guilford, 2002): 704; Dianne L. Chambless and Thomas H. Ollendick, "Empirically Supported Psychological Interventions: Controversies and Evidence," *Annual Review of Psychology* 52 (2001): 685–716; Brett J. Deacon and Jonathan S. Abromowitz, "Cognitive and Behavioral Treatments for Anxiety Disorders: A Review of Meta-analytic Findings," *Journal of Clinical Psychology* 60 (2004): 429–441.
31 Nancy E. Schoenberger and others, "Hypnotic Enhancement of a Cognitive Behavioral Treatment for Public Speaking Anxiety," *Behavior Therapy* 28, no. 1 (1997): 127–140.
32 Joost Vijselaar and Onno Van der Hart, "The First Report of Hypnotic Treatment of Traumatic Grief: A Brief Communication," *International Journal of Clinical and Experimental Hypnosis* 40, no. 1 (1992): 1–6. See also Etzel Cardeña, "Hypnosis in the Treatment of Trauma: A Promising, but not Fully Supported, Efficacious Intervention,"

International Journal of Clinical and Experimental Hypnosis 48, no. 2 (2000): 225–238.

33 Etzel Cardeña and others, "Hypnosis," in E. B. Foa, T. M. Keane, and J. Matthew eds., *Effective Treatments for PTSD: Practice Guidelines from the International Society for Traumatic Stress Studies* (New York: Guilford Press, 2000): 270.

34 David Spiegel, Thurman Hunt, and Harvey E. Dondershine, "Dissociation and Hypnotizability in Posttraumatic Stress Disorder," *American Journal of Psychiatry* 145, no. 3 (1988): 301–305; Randall K. Stutman and Eugene L. Bliss, "Posttraumatic Stress Disorder, Hypnotizability, and Imagery," *American Journal of Psychiatry* 142, no. 6 (1985): 741–743.

35 See Cardeña, "Hypnosis in the Treatment of Trauma," 225–238; Etzel Cardeña and others, "Hypnosis," 350–353.

36 Irving Kirsch and Guy Sapirstein, "Listening to Prozac but Hearing Placebo: A Meta-analysis of Antidepressant Medication," *Prevention and Treatment* 1, no. 2 (1998).

37 Irving Kirsch and others, "The Emperor's New Drugs: An Analysis of Antidepressant Medication Data Submitted to the U.S. Food and Drug Administration," *Prevention and Treatment* 5, no. 1 (2002).

38 See Kirsch, "Clinical Hypnosis as a Nondeceptive Placebo," 95–106.

39 Steven J. Lynn and Irving Kirsch, *Essentials of Clinical Hypnosis: An Evidence-Based Approach* (Washington, DC: American Psychological Association, 2006): 271.

40 Michael D. Yapko, *Treating Depression with Hypnosis:* Integrating Cognitive-Behavioral and Strategic Approaches (Philadelphia: Brunner-Routledge, 2001). *Brief Therapy Approaches to Treating Anxiety and Depression* (New York: Brunner/Mazel, 1989).

41 Michael D. Yapko, "Hypnosis and Depression," in J. W. Rhue, S. J. Lynn, and I. Kirsch eds., *Handbook of Clinical Hypnosis* (Washington, DC: American Psychological Association, 1993): 345.

42 Theodore X. Barber, *Hypnosis: A Scientific Approach,* 282.

43 William E. Edmonston, Jr., "Anesis," in S. J. Lynn and J. W. Rhue eds., *Theories of Hypnosis: Current Models and Perspectives* (New York: Guilford Press, 1991): 197–237.

44 Lynn, Neufeld, and Maré, "Direct versus Indirect Suggestions," 124–152.

45 Steven J. Lynn, Judith W. Rhue, and John R. Weekes, "Hypnotic Involuntariness: A Social Cognitive Analysis," *Psychological Review* 97, no. 2 (1990): 169–184.

46 Michael J. Simon and Herman C. Salzberg, "The Effect of Manipulated Expectancies on Posthypnotic Amnesia," *International Journal of Clinical and Experimental Hypnosis* 33, no. 1 (1985): 40–51.

47 Ernest R. Hilgard, *Hypnotic Susceptibility,* 434.

48 Pettinati, *Hypnosis and Memory,* 301.

49 Nash, "What, if Anything, is Regressed About Hypnotic Age Regression?" 42–52.

50 Irving Kirsch and Wayne Braffman, "Imaginative Suggestibility and Hypnotizability," *Current Directions in Psychological Science* 10, no. 2 (2001): 57–61.
51 Michael J. Diamond, "Is Hypnotherapy Art or Science," *American Journal of Clinical Hypnosis* 32, no. 1 (1989): 12.
52 Joseph Barber, "Predicting the Efficacy of Hypnotic Treatment," *American Journal of Clinical Hypnosis* 32, no. 1 (1989): 10–11.
53 Steven J. Lynn, Kelley Shindler, and Eric Meyer, "Hypnotic Suggestibility, Psychopathology, and Treatment Outcome," *Sleep and Hypnosis* 5, no. 1 (2003): 2–10.
54 Franny C. Moene and others, "A Randomized Controlled Clinical Trial of a Hypnosis-Based Treatment for Patients with Conversion Disorder, Motor Type," *International Journal of Clinical and Experimental Hypnosis* 51, no. 1 (2003): 29–50.
55 Joseph C. Johnston and others, "The Effects of Manipulated Expectancies on Behavioural and Subjective Indices of Hypnotisability," *Australian Journal of Clinical and Experimental Hypnosis* 17, no. 2 (1989): 121–130; Kirsch, "The Social Learning Theory of Hypnosis," 439–466; Irving Kirsch and James R. Council, "Situational and Personality Correlates of Hypnotic Responsiveness," in E. Fromm and M. R. Nash eds., *Contemporary Hypnosis Research* (New York: Guilford Press, 1992): 267–291; James R. Council, Irving Kirsch, and Laurin P. Hafner, "Expectancy versus Absorption in the Predication of Hypnotic Responding," *Journal of Personality and Social Psychology* 50, no. 1 (1986): 182–189.
56 Steven J. Lynn and Judith W. Rhue, *Theories of Hypnosis: Current Models and Perspectives* (New York: Guilford Press, 1991): 634.
57 James R. Council and Irving Kirsch, "Response Expectancy as a Determinant of Hypnotic Behavior," in N. P. Spanos and J. F. Chaves eds., *Hypnosis the Cognitive-Behavioral Perspective* (Amherst, NY: Prometheus Books, 1989): 360–379; Kirsch, "The Social Learning Theory of Hypnosis," 439–466.
58 Orne, "The Nature of Hypnosis," 277–299.
59 Jon Young and Leslie M. Cooper, "Hypnotic Recall Amnesia as a Function of Manipulated Expectancy," *Proceedings of the Annual Convention of the American Psychological Association* 7 (1972): 857–858. See also, David C. Henry, "Subjects' Expectancies and Subjective Experience of Hypnosis," *Dissertation Abstracts International* 46 (1985): 2063.
60 Kirsch and Council, "Situational and Personality Correlates of Hypnotic Responsiveness," 267–291; Kirsch and others, "A Spectral Analysis of Cognitive and Personality Variables in Hypnosis," 167–175.
61 Irving Kirsch, James R. Council, and Charles Mobayed, "Imagery and Response Expectancy as Determinants of Hypnotic Behavior," *British Journal of Experimental and Clinical Hypnosis* 4, no. 1 (1987): 25–31.
62 Wickless and Kirsch, "Effects of Verbal and Experiential Expectancy Manipulations on Hypnotic Susceptibility," 762–768.

63 See, Jeffrey D. Gfeller, "Enhancing Hypnotizability and Treatment Responsiveness," in J. W. Rhue, S. J. Lynn, and I. Kirsch eds., *Handbook of Clinical Hypnosis* (Washington, DC: American Psychological Association, 1993): 235–249.

64 See, for example, Lynn and Rhue, *Theories of Hypnosis*, 634; Spanos, "A Sociocognitive Approach to Hypnosis," 324–361.

65 Ray and Oathies, "Brain Imaging Techniques," 97–104.

66 See Harutomo Hasegawa and Graham A. Jamieson, "Conceptual Issues in Hypnosis Research: Explanations, Definitions and the State/Non-State Debate," *Contemporary Hypnosis* 19, no. 3 (2002): 103–117; Marie-Elisabeth Faymonville and others, "Neural Mechanisms of Antinociceptive Effects of Hypnosis," *Anesthesiology* 92 (2000): 1257–1265; Juri D. Kropotov, Helen J. Crawford, and Yuri I. Polyakov, "Somatosensory Event-Related Potential Changes to Painful Stimuli during Hypnotic Analgesia: Anterior Cingulated Cortex and Anterior Temporal Cortex Intracranial Recordings," *International Journal of Psychophysiology* 27, no. 1 (1997): 1–8; Pierre Rainville and others, "Pain Affect Encoded in Human Anterior Cingulated but not Somatosensory Cortex," *Science* 277, no. 5328 (1997): 968–971; Henry Szechtman and others, "Where the Imaginal Appears Real: A Positron Emission Tomography Study of Auditory Hallucinations," *Proceedings of the National Academy of Sciences* 95 (1998): 1956–1960.

67 Kallio and Revonsuo, "Hypnotic Phenomena and Altered States of Consciousness," 111–164.

68 Hasegawa and Jamieson, "Conceptual Issues in Hypnosis Research," 113.

69 Steven Lynn, Irving Kirsch, Joshua Knox, and Scott Lilienfeld, "Hypnosis and Neuroscience: Implications for the Altered State Debate," in Graham Jamieson ed., *Hypnosis and Conscious States: The Cognitive-Neuroscience Perspective* (New York: Oxford University Press, 2006).

70 Graham F. Wagstaff, "The Semantics and Physiology of Hypnosis as an Altered State: Towards a Definition of Hypnosis," *Contemporary Hypnosis* 15, no. 3 (1998): 149–165; Graham F. Wagstaff, "The Hypnotic State: Semantics and Pragmatics," *Contemporary Hypnosis* 15, no. 3 (1998): 182–188; Theodore R. Sarbin and Robert W. Slagle, "Hypnosis and Psychophysiology Outcomes," in E. Fromm and R. E. Shor eds., *Developments in Research and New Perspectives* (New York: Aldine, 1979), 273–303.

71 See Hasegawa and Jamieson, "Conceptual Issues in Hypnosis Research," 103–117.

72 American Psychological Association, Division 30, "Hypnosis: A definition," *Psychological Hypnosis: A Bulletin of Division 30* 13 (2004, Winter/Spring).

73 Steven Lynn, Jane Stafford and Abigail Matthews, "The Present and Future State of Hypnosis: A Delphi Poll" (Unpublished, 2005).

References

Acocella, Joan. (1999). *Creating Hysteria: Women and Multiple Personality Disorder*. San Francisco: Jossey-Bass.

Albanese, Catherine L. (1992). On the Matter of Spirit: Andrew Jackson Davis and the Marriage of God and Nature. *Journal of the American Academy of Religion*, 60, no. 1, 1–17.

American Medical Association Council on Scientific Affairs. (1994). *Memories of Childhood Abuse*. AMA, 5-A-94.

American Psychological Association. (1995). *Criteria for Guideline Development and Review*. Washington, DC: APA.

American Psychological Association. (1996). *Working Group on Investigation of Memories of Childhood Abuse: Final Report*. Washington, DC: APA.

American Psychological Association, Division 17 Trauma and Gender Issues Committee. (1995). *Psychotherapy Guidelines for Working with Clients Who may have an Abuse or Trauma History*. Washington, DC: APA.

American Psychological Association, Division 30. (2004). Hypnosis: A Definition. *Psychological Hypnosis: A Bulletin of Division 30, no.* 13.

American Psychiatric Association. (1994). *Diagnostic and Statistical Manual of Mental Disorders*. 4th ed. Washington, DC: American Psychiatric Publishing Inc.

Andreychuk, Theodore, and Christian Skriver. (1975). Hypnosis and Biofeedback in the Treatment of Migraine Headache. *International Journal of Clinical and Experimental Hypnosis* 23, no. 3, 172–183.

Arrigo, Helen M., and Kathy Pezdek. (1998). Textbook Models of Multiple Personality: Source, Bias, and Social Consequences. In S. J. Lynn and K. M. McConkey eds. *Truth in Memory*. New York: Guilford Press.

Bale, Robert F., David H. P. Maybury-Lewis, Brendan A. Maher, and Sheldon H. White. (2002). FAS Memorial Minute: Robert Winthrop White. *Harvard University Gazette*, May 23.

Barabasz, Arreed, and Marianne Barabasz. (1989). Effects of Restricted Environmental Stimulation: Enhancement of Hypnotizability for

Experimental and Chronic Pain Control. *International Journal of Clinical and Experimental Hypnosis* 37, no. 3, 217–231.

Barabasz, Arreed, and Marianne Barabasz. (2006). Effects of Tailored and Manualized Hypnotic Inductions for Complicated Irritable Bowel Syndrome Patients. *International Journal of Clinical and Experimental Hypnosis* 54, no. 1, 100–112.

Barber, Joseph. Predicting the Efficacy of Hypnotic Treatment. (1989). *American Journal of Clinical Hypnosis* 32, no. 1, 10–11.

Barber, Joseph. (1991). The Locksmith Model: Accessing Hypnotic Responsiveness. In S. J. Lynn and J. W. Rhue eds. *Theories of Hypnosis: Current Models and Perspectives*. New York: Guilford Press, 241–274.

Barber, Theodore X. (1963). The Effects of Hypnosis on Pain. *Psychosomatic Medicine* 25, no. 4, 303–333.

Barber, Theodore X. (1969). *Hypnosis: A Scientific Approach*. New York: Van Nostrand Reinhold.

Barber, Theodore X. (1999). A Comprehensive Three-Dimensional Theory of Hypnosis. In Irving Kirsch, Antonio Capafons, Etzel Cardeña, and Salvador Amigó eds. *Clinical Hypnosis and Self-regulation: Cognitive-Behavioral Perspectives*. Washington, DC: American Psychological Association, 21–48.

Barber Theodore X., and David S. Calverley. (1964). The Definition of the Situation as a Variable Affecting "Hypnotic-like" Suggestibility. *Journal of Clinical Psychology* 20, 438–440.

Barber Theodore X., and David S. Calverley. (1964). Toward a Theory of Hypnotic Behavior: Effects on Suggestibility of Defining the Situation as Hypnosis and Defining Response to Suggestions as Easy. *Journal of Abnormal and Social Psychology* 68, 585–592.

Barber, Theodore X., and Karl W. Hahn, Jr. (1962). Physiological and Subjective Responses to Pain Producing Stimulation under Hypnotically-Suggested and Waking-Imagined 'Analgesia'. *Journal of Abnormal and Social Psychology* 65, no. 6, 411–418.

Barber, Theodore X., Nicholas P. Spanos, and John F. Chaves. (1974). *Hypnosis, Imagination, and Human Potentialities*. New York: Pergamon Press.

Barlow, David H. (2002). *Anxiety and Its Disorders. The Nature and Treatment of Anxiety and Panic*. New York: Guilford Press.

Bates, Brad L. (1990). Compliance and the Carleton Skill Training Program. *British Journal of Experimental and Clinical Hypnosis* 7, no. 3, 159–164.

Bernheim, Hippolyte. (1973). *Hypnosis and Suggestion in Psychotherapy*. New York: Aronson, original work published 1888.

Bernheim, Hippolyte. (1889). *Suggestive Therapeutics: A Treatise on the Nature and Uses of Hypnotism*. New York: Putnam.

Bernheim, Hippolyte. (1897). *L'hypnotisme et la suggestion*. Paris: O. Doin.

Bertrand, Alexandre J. F. (1823). *Traité du somnambulisme et des différentes modifications qu'il présente*. Paris: Dentu.

Bertrand, Alexandre J. F. (1826). *Du magnétisme animal en France, et des jugements qu'en ont portés les sociétiés savants*. Paris: J. B. Bailliere.

Binet, Alfred. (1896). *Alterations of Personality: On Double Consciousness*. London: Chapman and Hall.

Binet, Alfred, and Charles Féré. (1888). *Hypnotism*. New York: D. Appleton.

Blumenthal, Arthur L. (1991). The Intrepid Joseph Jastrow. In *Pioneers in Psychology*. Edited by Gregory A. Kimble, Michael Wertheimer, and Charlotte White. Washington, DC: American Psychological Association & Lawrence Erlbaum Associates, 75–87.

Borch-Jacobsen, Mikkel. (1996). *Remembering Anna O*. New York: Routledge.

Bowers, Kenneth S., and Thomas M. Davidson. (1991). A Neodissociative Critique of Spanos's Social-Psychological Model of Hypnosis. In S. J. Lynn and J. W. Rhue eds. *Theories of Hypnosis: Current Models and Perspectives*. New York: Guilford Press, 105–143.

Bowers, Kenneth S. (1992). Imagination and Dissociation in Hypnotic Responding. *International Journal of Clinical and Experimental Hypnosis* 40, 253–275.

Braid, James. (1842). *Satanic Agency and Mesmerism Reviewed, in a Letter to the Rev. H. McNeile, A.M. of Liverpool, in Reply to a Sermon Preached by Him in St. Jude's Church, Liverpool, on Sunday, April 10th, 1842*. Manchester: Sims and Dinham, Galt and Anderson.

Braid, James. (1843). *Neurypnology; or the Rationale of Nervous Sleep Considered in Relation with Animal Magnetism. Illustrated by Numerous Cases of Its Successful Application in the Relief and Cure of Disease*. London: John Churchill.

Braid, James. (1843). Hypnotic Therapeutics, Illustrated by Cases. With an Appendix on Table-Moving and Spirit-Rapping. *Monthly Journal of Medical Science* 17, 3–44.

Braid, James. (1845). Mr. Braid on Hypnotism: To the Editor of *The Lancet*. *The Lancet*, May.

Braid, James. (1851). *Electro-Biological Phenomena Considered Physiologically and Psychologically*. Edinburgh: Sutherland and Knox.

Braude, Ann (1989). *Radical Spirits: Spiritualism and Women's Rights in Nineteenth Century America*. Boston: Beacon Press.

Brown, Daniel, Alan W. Scheflin, and D. Corydon Hammond. (1998). *Memory, Trauma Treatment, and the Law*. New York: W. W. Norton & Co.

Brown, Edward M., Pierre Janet, and Félida Artificielle. (2003). Multiple Personality in a Nineteenth Century Guise. *Journal of the History of the Behavioral Sciences* 39, 279–288.

Brown, Ralph R., and Victor H. Vogel. (1938). Psycho-Physiological Reactions Following Painful Stimuli under Hypnotic Analgesia

Contrasted with Gas Anesthesia and Novocain Block. *Journal of Applied Psychology* 22, no. 4, 408–420.

Bruce, H. Addington. (1908). *The Riddle of Personality*. New York: Moffat, Yard & Company.

Bruce, H. Addington. (1909). Mental Healing of To-day. *Outlook* XCIII (September 4th), 32.

Bruce, H. Addington. (1911). *Scientific Mental Healing*. Boston: Little, Brown & Co.

Buchanan, Joseph R. (1850). Spirituality—Recent Occurrences. In *Buchanan's Journal of Man*. New York.

Buchanan, Joseph R. (1854). *Outlines of Lectures on the Neurological System of Anthropology as Discovered, Demonstrated and Taught in 1841 and 1842*. Cincinnati: *Journal of Man*.

Buranelli, Vincent. (1975). *The Wizard from Vienna*. New York: Coward, McCann & Geoghegan.

Bush, George. (1830). *The Life of Mohammad*. New York: J. & J. Harper.

Bush, George. (1847). *Mesmer and Swedenborg; Or, the Relation of the Development of Mesmerism to the Doctrines and Disclosures of Swedenborg*. New York: John Allen.

Caplan, Eric. (1998). *Mind Games: American Culture and the Birth of Psychotherapy*. Berkeley, University of California Press.

Caldwell, Charles. (1842). *Facts in Mesmerism: And Thoughts on Its Causes and Uses*. Louisville: Prentice and Weissinger.

Canadian Psychiatric Association. (1996). Position Statement: Adult Recovered Memories of Childhood Sexual Abuse. *Canadian Journal of Psychiatry* 41, 305–306.

Cardeña, Etzel. (2000). Hypnosis in the Treatment of Trauma: A Promising, but not Fully Supported, Efficacious Intervention. *International Journal of Clinical and Experimental Hypnosis* 48, no. 2, 225–238.

Cardeña, Etzel, Jose Maldonado, Onno van der Hart, and David Spiegel. (2000). Hypnosis. In Edna B. Foa, Terence. M. Keane, and Matthew J. Friedman eds. *Effective Treatments for PTSD: Practice Guidelines from the International Society for Traumatic Stress Studies*. New York: Guilford Press.

Chambless, Dianne L., and Thomas H. Ollendick. (2001). Empirically Supported Psychological Interventions: Controversies and Evidence. *Annual Review of Psychology* 52, 685–716.

Chastenet de Puységur, Amand M. J. (1784). *Détails des cures opérées à Buzancy par le magnétisme animal*. Paris.

Chastenet de Puységur, Amand M. J. (1809). *Mémoires pour servir à l'histoire et à l'éstablissement du magnétisme animal*. 2d ed. Paris: Cellot.

Chastenet de Puységur, Amand M.J. (1811). *Recherches, expériences et observations physiologique sur l'homme dans l'état de somnambulisme naturel, et dans le somnambulisme provoqué par l'acte magnétique.* Paris: Dentu.

Chastenet de Puységur, Amand M. J. (1813). *Appel aux savans observateurs du dix-neuvième siècle, de la décision portée pa leur prédécesseurs contre le magnétisme animal, et fin de la traitement du jeune Hébert.* Paris: Dentu.

Chaves, John F. (1997). The State of the 'State' Debate in Hypnosis: A View from the Cognitive-Behavioral Perspective. *International Journal of Clinical and Experimental Hypnosis* 45, no. 3, 251–265.

Chaves, John F. (1997). Hypnosis in Dentistry: Historical Overview and Critical Appraisal. *Hypnosis International Monographs* 3, 5–23.

Clarke, J. Henry. (1997). Teaching Clinical Hypnosis in U.S. and Canadian Dental Schools. *American Journal of Clinical Hypnosis* 39 (1996), 89–92.

Cheek, David B., and Leslie M. LeCron. (1968). *Clinical Hypnotherapy.* New York: Grune & Stratton.

Coe, William C., and Theodore R. Sarbin. (1991). Role Theory: Hypnosis from a Dramaturgical and Narrational Perspective. In S. J. Lynn & J. W. Rhue eds. *Theories of Hypnosis: Current Models and Perspectives.* New York: Guilford Press, 303–323.

Colquhoun, John Campbell. (1836). *Isis Revelata: An Inquiry into the Origins, Progress and Present State of Animal Magnetism.* 2d ed. 2 vols. Edinburgh: Maclachlan and Stewart.

Commun, Joseph. (1828). On the Cause of Freshwater Springs, Fountains, etc. … *American Journal of Science* 14, 174–176.

Comte, August. (1855). *The Positive Philosophy of Auguste Comte.* Translated by Harriet Martineau. New York: Calvin Blanchard.

Condon, Richard. (1959). *The Manchurian Candidate.* New York: McGraw Hill.

Coué, Emile. (1922). *Self-mastery through Conscious Autosuggestion.* New York: American Library Service.

Council, James R., Irving Kirsch, and Laurin P. Hafner. (1986). Expectancy versus Absorption in the Predication of Hypnotic Responding. *Journal of Personality and Social Psychology* 50, no. 1, 182–189.

Council, James R., and Irving Kirsch. (1989). Response Expectancy as a Determinant of Hypnotic Behavior. In N. P. Spanos and J. F. Chaves eds. *Hypnosis the Cognitive-Behavioral Perspective.* Amherst, NY: Prometheus Books, 360–379.

Crabtree, Adam. (1993). *From Mesmer to Freud: Magnetic Sleep and the Roots of Psychological Healing.* New Haven, CT: Yale University Press.

Crasilneck, Harold B., and James Hall. (1975). *Clinical Hypnosis: Principles and Applications.* New York: Grune & Stratton.

Crews, Frederick C. ed. (1998). *Unauthorized Freud: Doubters Confront a Legend.* New York: Viking.

Cunningham, Raymond J. (1962). The Emmanuel Movement: A Variety of American Religious Experience. *American Quarterly* 14, no. 1, 48–63.

Darnton, Robert. (1968). *Mesmerism and the End of the Enlightenment in France*. Cambridge, MA: Harvard University Press.

Daudet, Léon A. (1894). *Les Morticoles*. Paris: Bibliotèque-Charpentier.

Daudet, Léon A. (1925). *Memoirs of Leon Daudet*. Translated by Arthur Kingsland Griggs. New York: Dial Press.

Davies, John D. (1955). Phrenology, Fad and Science: A Nineteenth Century American Crusade. New Haven, CT: Yale University Press.

Davis, Andrew Jackson (1859). *The Magic Staff: An Autobiography of Andrew Jackson Davis*. New York: J. S. Brown & Co.

Deacon, Brett J., and Jonathan S. Abromowitz. (2004). Cognitive and Behavioral Treatments for Anxiety Disorders: A Review of Meta-analytic Findings. *Journal of Clinical Psychology* 60, 429–441.

Delboeuf, Joseph. (1886). La mémoire chez les hypnotisés. *Revue philosophique* 21.

Delboeuf, Joseph. (1889). *Le magnétisme animal: à propos d'une visite à l'école de Nancy*. Paris: F. Alcan.

Delboeuf, Joseph. (1891–2). Comme quoi il n'y a pas d'hypnotisme. *Revue de l'hypnotisme* 6, 129–135.

Deleuze. Joseph P. F. (1813). *Histoire Critique de Magnétisme Animal*. 2 vols. Paris: Mame.

Deleuze. Joseph P. F. (1837). *Practical Instruction in Animal Magnetism*. Translated by Thomas C. Hartshorn. Providence: B. Cranston.

Deleuze, Joseph. P. F. (1846). *Practical Instruction in Animal Magnetism*. Translated by Thomas C. Hartshorn. Revised Edition. New York: D. Appleton and Co.

Dessoir, Max. (1890). *Das-Doppel-Ich*. Leipzig: Gunther.

Diamond, Michael J. (1989). Is Hypnotherapy Art or Science? *American Journal of Clinical Hypnosis* 32, no. 1, 11–12.

Dixon, Michael, and Jean-Roch Laurence. (1992). Two Hundred Years of Hypnosis Research: Questions Resolved? Questions Unanswered! In Erika Fromm and Michael R. Nash eds. *Contemporary Hypnosis Research*. New York: Guilford Press, 34–66.

Dresser, Annetta G. (1895). *The Philosophy of P. P. Quimby*. Boston: George H. Ellis.

Dresser, Horatio, ed. (1921). *The Quimby Manuscripts: Showing the Discovery of Spiritual Healing and the Origin of Christian Science*. New York: Thomas Y. Crowell.

Du Maurier, George. (1982). *Svengali: George du Maurier's Trilby*. Edited by Peter Alexander. London: W. H. Allen.

Du Maurier, George. (1992). *Trilby*. New York: J. M. Dent.

Dunn, Gary E., Anthony M. Paolo, Joseph J. Ryan, and Jay N. van Fleet. (1994). Belief in the Existence of Multiple Personality Disorder among Psychologists and Psychiatrists. *Journal of Clinical Psychology* 50, no. 3, 454–457.

Edmonston, William E. Jr. (1991). Anesis. In S. J. Lynn and J. W. Rhue eds. *Theories of Hypnosis: Current Models and Perspectives*. New York: Guilford Press, 197–237.

Edmonston, William E. (2000). Frank A. Pattie, PhD: In Memoriam. *American Journal of Clinical Hypnosis* 43, no. 2, 105–106.

Eisen, Mitchell L., and Steven J. Lynn. (2001). Dissociation, Memory and Suggestibility in Adults and Children. *Applied Cognitive Psychology* 15, no. 7, 49–73.

Ellenberger, Henri. (1970). *The Discovery of the Unconscious*. New York: Basic Books.

Elliotson, John. (1843). *Numerous Cases of Surgical Operations without Pain in the Mesmeric State with Remarks upon the Opposition of Many Members of the Royal Medical and Chirurgical Society and Others to the Reception of the Inestimable Blessings of Mesmerism*. London: H. Bailliere.

Elliotson, John. (1846). Accounts of More Painless Surgical Operations, Communicated by Dr. Elliotson. *The Zoist*, 3, 196–197.

Erdelyi, Matthew H. (1994). Hypnotic Hypermnesia: The Empty Set of Hypermnesia. *International Journal of Clinical and Experimental Hypnosis* 42, 379–390.

Erickson, Milton H. (1964). Initial Experiments Investigating the Nature of Hypnosis. *The American Journal of Clinical Hypnosis* 7, 152–162.

Erickson, Milton H. (1967). Further Experimental Investigation of Hypnosis: Hypnotic and Nonhypnotic Realities. *The American Journal of Clinical Hypnosis* 10, 87–135.

Erickson, Milton H. (1980). Hypnosis: A General Review. In *The Collected Papers of Milton H. Erickson on Hypnosis*. Vol. 3. Edited by Ernest L. Rossi. New York: Irvington, 13–20.

Erickson, Milton H. (1980). Respiratory Rhythm in Trance Induction: The Role of Minimal Sensory Cues in Normal and Trance Behavior. In *The Nature of Hypnosis and Suggestion: The Collected Papers of Milton H Erickson on Hypnosis*. Vol. 1. Edited by Ernest L. Rossi. New York: Irvington Publishers, 360–365.

Esdaile, James. (1846). *Mesmerism in India and its Practical Applications in Surgery and Medicine*. London: Longman, Brown, Green, and Longmans.

Estabrooks, George H. (1928). That Question of Racial Inferiority. *American Anthropologist* 30, 470–475.

Estabrooks, George H. (1943). *Hypnotism*. New York: E.P. Dutton.

Estabrooks, George H. (1971). Hypnosis Comes of Age. *Science Digest*, April, 44–50.

Faria, José-Custodio. (1906). *De la cause du sommeil lucide ou étude de la nature de l'homme*. Paris: H. Jouve.

Farvolden, Peter, and Erik Z. Woody. (2004). Hypnosis, Memory, and Frontal Executive Functioning. *International Journal of Clinical and Experimental Hypnosis* 52, no. 1, 3–26.

Faymonville, Marie-Elisabeth, Steven Laureys, Christian Degueldre, Guy DelFiore, Andre Luxen, Georges Franck, Maurice Lame, and Pierre Maquet. (2000). Neural Mechanisms of Antinociceptive Effects of Hypnosis. *Anesthesiology* 92, 1257–1265.

Flournoy, Theodore. (1900). *From India to the Planet Mars: A Study of a Case of Somnambulism.* Translated by Daniel B. Vermilye. New York: Harper & Brothers.

Freud, Sigmund, and Josef Breuer. (1893). Üeber den psychischen Mechanismus hysterische Phänomene. *Neurologische Centralblatt* 12, 4–10, 43–47.

Freud, Sigmund. (1894). The Neuro-Psychoses of Defense. In *The Standard Edition of the Complete Psychological Works of Sigmund Freud.* Vol. 3, *Early Psychoanalytic Publications.* London: The Hogarth Press.

Freud, Sigmund. (2001). On Psychotherapy. Originally published 1905. In *The Standard Edition of the Complete Psychological Works of Sigmund Freud.* Vol. VII (1901–1905), *A Case of Hysteria, Three Essays on Sexuality and Other Works.* London: Random House, 255–268.

Frischolz, Edward J. (2005). Remembering Andre. *American Journal of Clinical Hypnosis* 48, no. 1, 5–28.

Fromm, Erika. (1992). An Ego-Psychological Theory of Hypnosis. In Erika Fromm and Michael R. Nash eds. *Contemporary Hypnosis Research.* New York: Guilford Press.

Fromm, Erika, and Michael R. Nash. (1997). *Psychoanalysis and Hypnosis.* Mental Health Library Series, Monograph 5. Madison, CT: International Universities Press, Inc.

Fuller, Robert C. (1982). *Mesmerism and the American Cure of Souls.* Philadelphia: University of Pennsylvania Press.

Gallo, David A., and Stanley Finger. (2000). The Power of a Musical Instrument: Franklin, the Mozarts, Mesmer, and the Glass Armonica. *History of Psychology* 3, no. 4, 326–343.

Garry, Maryanne, and Devon L. Polaschek. (2000). Imagination and Memory. *Current Directions in Psychological Science* 9, no. 1, 6–10.

Gaskell, Elizabeth. (1857). *The Life of Charlotte Brontë.* Vol. 1. New York: D. Appleton.

Gauld, Alan. (1992). *A History of Hypnotism.* Cambridge, MA: Cambridge University Press.

Gauld, Alan. (2006). Joseph Delboeuf 1831–1896: A Forerunner of Modern Ideas on Hypnosis. *Contemporary Hypnosis* 14, no. 4, 216–225.

Genter, Robert. (2006). "Hypnotizzy" in the Cold War: The American Fascination with Hypnotism in the 1950s. *Journal of American and Comparative Cultures* 29, no. 2, 154–169.

Gfeller, Jeffrey D. (1993). Enhancing Hypnotizability and Treatment Responsiveness. In J. W. Rhue, S. J. Lynn, and I. Kirsch eds. *Handbook of*

Clinical Hypnosis. Washington, DC: American Psychological Association, 235–249.

Gifford, Sandford. (1997). *The Emmanuel Movement The Origins of Group Treatment and the Assault on Lay Psychotherapy*. Boston: Harvard University Press.

Gilman, Sander. (1982). *Seeing the Insane*. New York: J. Wiley.

Gleaves, David H. (1996). The Sociocognitive Model of Dissociative Identity Disorder: A Reexamination of the Evidence. *Psychological Bulletin* 120, no. 1, 42–59.

Gleaves, David H., Mary C. May, and Etzel Cardeña. (2001). An Examination of the Diagnostic Validity of Dissociative Identity Disorder. *Clinical Psychology Review* 21, no. 4, 577–608.

Goldsmith, Ronald. (1979). *The Life and Work of Théodore Flournoy*. Ph.D. thesis, Michigan State University.

Goodman, Gail S., Simona Ghetti, Jodi Quas, Robin S. Edelstein, Kristen Weede Alexander, Allison D. Redlich, Ingrid M. Cordon, and David P. H. Jones. (2003). A Prospective Study of Memory for Child Sexual Abuse: New Findings Relevant to the Repressed-Memory Controversy. *Psychologcial Science* 14, no. 2, 113–118.

Gonsalkorale, Wendy, Lesley Houghton, and Peter Whorwell. (1997). Hypnotherapy in Irritable Bowel Syndrome: A Large-Scale Audit of a Clinical Service with Examination of Factors Influencing Responsiveness. *American Journal of Gastroenterology* 97, no. 4, 954–961.

Gorassini, Donald R., and Nicholas P. Spanos. (1986). A Social-Cognitive Skills Approach to the Successful Modification of Hypnotic Susceptibility. *Journal of Personality and Social Psychology* 50, 1004–1012.

Gorassini, Donald R., and Nicholas P. Spanos. (1999). The Carleton Skill Training Program for Modifying Hypnotic Suggestibility: Original Version and Variations. In Irving Kirsch, Antonio Capafons, Etzel Cardeña, and Salvador Amigo, eds. *Clinical Hypnosis and Self-regulation: Cognitive-behavioral Perspectives*. Washington, DC: American Psychological Association, 141–177.

Gravitz, Melvin A. (1993). Etienne Félix d'Hénin de Cuvillers: A Founder of Hypnosis. *American Journal of Clinical Hypnosis* 36, no. 1, 7–11.

Gravitz, Melvin A. (1994). First Use of Self-Hypnosis: Mesmer Mesmerizes Mesmer. *American Journal of Clinical Hypnosis* 37, 49–52.

Gravitz, Melvin A. (1997). Mesmerism and Masonry: Early Historical Interactions. *American Journal of Clinical Hypnosis* 39, no. 4, 266–270.

Green, Joseph. (2000). Hypnosis and Suggestion-based Approaches to Smoking Cessation: An Examination of the Evidence. *International Journal of Clinical and Experimental Hypnosis* 48, 195–224.

Green, Joseph P., Rodger Page, George Handley, and Rue Rasekhy. (2005). The "Hidden Observer" and Ideomotor Responding: A Real-Simulator Comparison. *Contemporary Hypnosis* 22, no. 3, 123–137.

Grimes, James Stanley. (1850). *Etherology, and the Phreno-philosophy of Mesmerism and Magic Eloquence: Including a New Philosophy of Sleep and of Consciousness*. 2d ed. Edited by W. G. Le Duc. Boston: Munroe.

Grimes, James Stanley. (1875). *The Mysteries of the Head and the Heart Explained*. Chicago: Sumner and Co.

Gruzelier, John H. (1996). The State of Hypnosis: Evidence and Applications. *Quarterly Journal of Medicine* 89, 313–317.

Hacking, Ian. (1988). Telepathy: Origins of Randomization in Experimental Design. *Isis* 79, no. 3, 427–451.

Hacking, Ian. (1995). *Rewriting the Soul: Multiple Personality and the Sciences of Memory*. Princeton, NJ: Princeton University Press.

Hammond, D. Corydon, Richard Garver, Charles B. Mutter, Harold B. Crasilneck, Edward Frischholz, and Melvin A. Gravitz. (1995). *Clinical Hypnosis and Memory: Guidelines for Clinicians and for Forensic Hypnosis*. Des Plaines: American Society of Clinical Hypnosis Press.

Hansen, Uffe. (1991). *Hypnotisoren Carl Hansen og Sigmund Freud*. Copenhagen: Akademisk Forlag.

Harmon, Teresa M., Michael T. Hynan, and Timothy E. Tyre. (1990). Improved Obstetric Outcomes using Hypnotic Analgesia and Skill Mastery Combined with Childbirth Education. *Journal of Consulting and Clinical Psychology* 58, no. 5, 525–530.

Hasegawa, Harutomo, and Graham A. Jamieson. (2002). Conceptual Issues in Hypnosis Research: Explanations, Definitions and the State/Non-State Debate. *Contemporary Hypnosis* 19, no. 3, 103–117.

Havens, Ronald A., and Catherine Walters. (1989). *Hypnotherapy Scripts: A Neo-Ericksonian Approach to Persuasive Healing*. Philadelphia: Brunner/Mazel.

Hawthorne, Nathaniel. (1851). *The House of Seven Gables*. Boston: Ticknor, Reed & Fields.

Hawthorne, Nathaniel. (1852). *The Blithedale Romance*. Boston: Ticknor, Reed & Fields.

Heaton, Jeanne A., and Nona L. Wilson. (1998). Memory, Media, and the Creation of Mass Confusion. In Steven J. Lynn, and Kevin McConkey eds. *Truth in Memory*. London: The Guilford Press.

Henry, David C. (1985). Subjects' Expectancies and Subjective Experience of Hypnosis. *Dissertation Abstracts International* 46.

Hilgard, Ernest R. (1965). *Hypnotic Susceptibility*. New York: Harcourt, Brace & World.

Hilgard, Ernest R. (1969). Altered States of Awareness. *Journal of Nervous and Mental Disease* 149, 68–79.

Hilgard, Ernest R. (1973). A Neodissociation Interpretation of Pain Reduction in Hypnosis. *Psychological Review* 80, 396–411.

Hilgard, Ernest R. (1977). *Divided Consciousness: Multiple Controls in Human Thought and Action*. New York: Wiley.

Hilgard, Ernest R. (1987). *Psychology in America: A Historical Survey*. Forth Worth, TX: Harcourt Brace Jovanovich.

Hilgard, Ernest R. (1994). Neodissociation Theory. In S. J. Lynn & J. W. Rhue eds. *Dissociation: Clinical, Theoretical and Research Perspectives*. New York: Guilford Press, 32–51.

Hilgard, Ernest R., and Charles Tart. (1966). Responsiveness to Suggestions Following Waking and Imagination Instructions and Following Induction of Hypnosis. *Journal of Abnormal Psychology* 71, no. 3, 196–208.

Hilton, Claire. (2006). Mill Hill Emergency Hospital, 1939–1945. *Psychiatric Bulletin* 30, no. 3, 106–108.

Hochman, John, and Harrison G. Pope, Jr. (1997). Debating Dissociative Diagnoses. *American Journal of Psychiatry* 154, no. 6, 887–888.

Holmes, David S. (1974). Investigations of Repression: Differential Recall of Material Experimentally or Naturally Associated with Ego Threat. *Psychological Bulletin* 81, no. 10, 632–653.

Hudson, Thomas. (1898). *The Law of Psychic Phenomena*. Chicago: A. C. McClurg.

Hull, Clark L. (1929). Hypnotism in Scientific Perspective. *The Scientific Monthly* 29, no. 2, 154–162.

Hull, Clark L. (1933). *Hypnosis and Suggestibility: An Experimental Approach*. New York: Appleton-Century-Crofts, x.

Hull, Clark L. (1944). Joseph Jastrow, 1863–1944. *The American Journal of Psychology* 57, no. 4, 581–585.

Hyman, Ira E., Troy H. Husband, and F. James Billings. (1995). False Memories of Childhood Experiences. *Applied Cognitive Psychology* 9, no. 3, 181–197.

International Journal of Clinical and Experimental Hypnosis 50, no. 4 (2002). The 50th Anniversary Special Issue: Mesmer, Franklin, and the Royal Commission.

Jacknow, Dale S., Jeanne M. Tschann, Michael P. Link, and W. Thomas Boyce. (1994). Hypnosis in the Prevention of Chemotherapy-Related Nausea and Vomiting in Children: A Prospective Study. *Journal of Developmental and Behavioral Pediatrics* 15, no. 4, 258–264.

James, William. (1890). *Principles of Psychology*. 2 vols. London: Macmillan.

James, William. (1902). *The Varieties of Religious Experience: A Study in Human Nature*. New York: Longmans, Green & Co.

Janet, Pierre. (1889). *L'automatisme psychologique: essai de psychologie expérimentale sur les formes inférieures de l'activité humaine*. Paris: F. Alcan.

Janet, Pierre. (1894). Histoire d'une idée fixe. *Revue Philosophique* 37, no. 1, 121–168.

Janet, Pierre. (1925). *Psychological Healing*. London: George Allen & Unwin.

Jastrow, Joseph J. (1907). *The Subconscious*. New York: Houghton Mifflin.

Jastrow, Joseph J. (1901). *Fact and Fable in Psychology*. New York: Houghton Mifflin.

Jastrow, Joseph J. (1961). Joseph Jastrow. In *A History of Psychology in Autobiography*. Vol. 1. Edited by Carl Murchison. New York: Russell & Russell, 135–162.

Jenkins, Emily. (1998). Trilby: Fads, Photographers, and 'Over-Perfect Feet.' *Book History* 1, 221–267.

Johnston, Joseph C., Judi Chajkowaski, Susan DuBreuil, and Nicholas P. Spanos. (1989). The Effects of Manipulated Expectancies on Behavioural and Subjective Indices of Hypnotisability. *Australian Journal of Clinical and Experimental Hypnosis* 17, no. 2, 121–130.

Kallio, Sakari, and Antti Revonsuo. (2003). Hypnotic Phenomena and Altered States of Consciousness: A Multilevel Framework of Description and Explanation. *Contemporary Hypnosis* 20, no. 3, 111–164.

Kaplan, Fred. (1974). "Mesmeric Mania": The Early Victorians and Animal Magnetism. *Journal of the History of Ideas* 35, no. 4, 691–702.

Kaplan, Fred. (1975). *Dickens and Mesmerism: The Hidden Springs of Fiction*. Princeton, NJ: Princeton University Press.

Kaufman, Ralph M., and Lindsay Beaton. (1947). A Psychiatric Treatment Program in Combat. *Bulletin of the Menninger Clinic* 11, no. 1, 411–421.

Kenyon, Frederic G. ed. (1897). *The Letters of Elizabeth Barrett Browning*. New York: Macmillan.

Kerner, Justinus. (1856). *Franz Anton Mesmer, der Entdecker des thierischen Magnetismus*. Frankfurt am Main: Literarische Anstalt.

Kihlstrom, John F. (1985). Hypnosis. *Annual Review of Psychology* 36, 385–418.

Kihlstrom, John F. (1987). The Two Svengalis: Making the Myth of Hypnosis. *Australian Journal of Clinical & Experimental Hypnosis*. 15, no 2, 69–81.

Kihlstrom, John F. (1992). Hypnosis: A Sesquicentennial Essay. *International Journal of Clinical and Experimental Hypnosis* 40, 301–314.

Kihlstrom, John F. (1997). Convergence in Understanding Hypnosis? Perhaps, but not so Fast. *International Journal of Clinical and Experimental Hypnosis* 45, 324–332.

Kihlstrom, John F. (1998). Dissociations and Dissociation Theory in Hypnosis: Comment on Kirsch and Lynn. *Psychological Bulletin* 132, no. 2, 186–191.

Kihlstrom, John F. (1998). Hypnosis and the Psychological Unconscious. In H. J. Friedman ed. *Encyclopedia of Mental Health*. Vol. 2. San Diego: Academic Press, 467–477.

Kihlstrom, John F. (2003). The Fox, the Hedgehog, and Hypnosis. *International Journal of Clinical and Experimental Hypnosis* 51, 166–189.

Kihlstrom, John F., and Kevin M. McConkey. (1990). William James and Hypnosis: A Centennial Reflection. *Psychological Science* 1, no. 3, 174–178.

Kirsch, Irving. (1991). The Social Learning Theory of Hypnosis. In Steven J. Lynn and Judith W. Rhue eds. *Theories of Hypnosis: Current Models and Perspectives*. New York: Guilford Press, 439–466.

Kirsch, Irving. (1994). Clinical Hypnosis as a Nondeceptive Placebo: Empirically Derived Techniques. *American Journal of Clinical Hypnosis* 37, no. 2, 95–106.

Kirsch, Irving, and Wayne Braffman. (2001). Imaginative Suggestibility and Hypnotizability. *Current Directions in Psychological Science* 10, no. 2, 57–61.

Kirsch, Irving, and James R. Council. (1992). Situational and Personality Correlates of Hypnotic Responsiveness. In Erika Fromm and Michael R. Nash eds. *Contemporary Hypnosis Research*. New York: Guilford Press, 267–291.

Kirsch, Irving, James R. Council, and Charles Mobayed. (1987). Imagery and Response Expectancy as Determinants of Hypnotic Behavior. *British Journal of Experimental and Clinical Hypnosis* 4, no. 1, 25–31.

Kirsch, Irving, and Steven J. Lynn. (1995). The Altered State of Hypnosis: Changes in the Theoretical Landscape. *American Psychologist* 50, 846–858.

Kirsch, Irving, and Steven Jay Lynn. (1997). Hypnotic Involuntariness and the Automaticity of Everyday Life. *American Journal of Clinical Hypnosis* 40, 329–348.

Kirsch, Irving, and Steven J. Lynn. (1998). Dissociation Theories of Hypnosis. *Psychological Bulletin* 123, no. 1, 100–115.

Kirsch, Irving, and Steven J. Lynn. (1999). The Automaticity of Behavior in Clinical Psychology. *American Psychologist* 54, 504–575.

Kirsch, Irving, Guy Montgomery, and Guy Sapirstein. (1995). Hypnosis as an Adjunct to Cognitive-Behavioral Psychotherapy: A Meta-analysis. *Journal of Consulting and Clinical Psychology* 63, no. 2, 214–220.

Kirsch, Irving, Thomas J. Moore, Alan Scoboria, and Sarah S. Nicholls. (2002). The Emperor's New Drugs: An Analysis of Antidepressant Medication Data Submitted to the U.S. Food and Drug Administration. *Prevention and Treatment* 5, no. 1: n.p.

Kirsch, Irving, and Guy Sapirstein. (1998). Listening to Prozac but Hearing Placebo: A Meta-analysis of Antidepressant Medication. *Prevention and Treatment* 1, no. 2: n.p.

Kirsch, Irving, Christopher E. Silva, Gail Comey, and Steven Reed. (1995). A Spectral Analysis of Cognitive and Personality Variables in Hypnosis: Empirical Disconfirmation of the Two-Factor Model of Hypnotic Responding. *Journal of Personality and Social Psychology* 69, 167–175.

Kroger, William S., and William D. Fezler. (1976). *Hypnosis and Behavior Modification: Imagery Conditioning*. Oxford: J. B. Lippincott.

Kroger, William S. (1977). *Clinical and Experimental Hypnosis in Medicine, Dentistry, and psychology*. 2d ed. Oxford: J. B. Lippincott.

Kropotov, Juri D., Helen J. Crawford, and Yuri I. Polyakov. (1997). Somatosensory Event-Related Potential Changes to Painful Stimuli during Hypnotic Analgesia: Anterior Cingulated Cortex and Anterior Temporal Cortex Intracranial Recordings. *International Journal of Psychophysiology* 27, no. 1, 1–8.

Lafontaine, Charles. (1866). *Mémoires d'un Magnétiseur, par Ch. Lafontaine, suivis de l'examen phrénologique de l'auteur par le Docteur Castle*. Vol. 1. Paris.

Lambert, Sally A. (1996). The Effects of Hypnosis/Guided Imagery on the Postoperative Course of Children. *Journal of Developmental and Behavioral Pediatrics* 17, no. 5, 307–310.

Lang, Elvira V., Greg Benotsch, Lauri Fick, Susan Lugendorff, Michael Berbaum, and Kevin Berman. (2000). Adjunctive Non-Pharmacologic Analgesia for Invasive Medical Procedures: A Randomized Trial. *Lancet* 355, 1486–1490.

Lanning, Kenneth V., and Ann W. Burgess. (1989). Child Pornography and Sex Rings. In D. Zillmann and J. Bryant eds. *Pornography: Research Advances and Policy Considerations. Communication*. Hillsdale, NJ: Lawrence Erlbaum Associates, 235–255.

Laurence, Jean-Roch, and Campbell Perry. (1983). Forensic Hypnosis in the Late Nineteenth Century. *International Journal of Clinical and Experimental Hypnosis* 31, no. 4, 266–283.

Laurence, Jean-Roch, Campbell Perry, and John F. Kihlstrom. (1983). "Hidden Observer" Phenomenon in Hypnosis: An Experimental Creation? *Journal of Personality and Social Psychology* 44, no. 1, 163–169.

Laurence, Jean-Roch, and Campbell Perry. (1983). Hypnotically Created Memory among Highly Hypnotizable Subjects. *Science* 222, 523–524.

Lilienfeld, Scott O., Steven J. Lynn, Irving Kirsch, John C. Chaves, Theodore Sarbin, George Ganaway, and Russell Powell. (1999). Dissociative Identity Disorder and the Sociocognitive Model: Recalling the Lessons of the Past. *Psychological Bulletin* 125, no. 5, 507–523.

Loftus, Elizabeth F. (1993). The Reality of Repressed Memories. *American Psychologist* 48, no. 5, 518–537.

Loftus, Elizabeth F., and Katherine Ketcham. (1994). *The Myth of Repressed Memory*. New York: St. Martin's Press.

Loftus, Elizabeth F. (2003). Make-believe Memories. *American Psychologist* 58, no. 11, 867–873.

Loftus, Elizabeth F., and Jacqueline E. Pickrell. (1995). The Formation of False Memories. *Psychiatric Annals* 25, no. 12, 720–725.

Lynn, Steven Jay. (1997). Automaticity and Hypnosis: A Sociocognitive Account. *International Journal of Clinical and Experimental Hypnosis* 45, no. 3, 239–250.

Lynn, Steven J., and Michael N. Hallquist. (2004). Toward a Scientifically Based Understanding of Milton H. Erickson's Strategies and Tactics: Hypnosis, Response Sets and Common Factors in Psychotherapy. *Contemporary Hypnosis* 21, no. 2, 63–78.

Lynn, Steven J., and Irving Kirsch. (2006). *Essentials of Clinical Hypnosis: An Evidence-based Approach*. Washington, DC: American Psychological Association, 271.

Lynn, Steven J., Irving Kirsch, Maryellen Crowley, and Anna Campion. (2006). Eating Disorders and Obesity. In Steven Lynn and Irving Kirsch eds. *Essentials of Clinical Hypnosis*. Washington, DC: American Psychological Association.

Lynn, Steven, Irving Kirsch, Joshua Knox, and Scott Lilienfeld. (2006). Hypnosis and Neuroscience: Implications for the Altered State Debate. In Graham Jamieson ed. *Hypnosis and conscious states: The cognitive-neuroscience perspective*. New York: Oxford University Press.

Lynn, Steven J., Timothy Lock, Bryan Myers, and David Payne. (1997). Recalling the Unrecallable: Should Hypnosis be Used to Recover Memories in Psychotherapy? *Current Directions in Psychological Science* 6, no. 3, 79–83.

Lynn, Steven J., and Kevin M. McConkey. (1998). *Truth in Memory*. New York: Guilford Press.

Lynn, Steven J., Bryan Myers, and Peter Malinoski. (1997). Hypnosis, Pseudomemories, and Clinical Guidelines: A Sociocognitive Perspective. *NATO ASI Series: Series A: Life Sciences*. Vol. 291. New York: Plenum Press.

Lynn, Steven J., Victor Neufeld, and Cornelia Maré, (1993). Direct versus Indirect Suggestions: A Conceptual and Methodological Review. *International Journal of Clinical and Experimental Hypnosis* 41, no. 2, 124–152.

Lynn, Steven J., and Judith Pintar. (1997). A Social Narrative Model of Dissociative Identity Disorder. *Australian Journal of Clinical and Experimental Hypnosis* 25, no. 1, 1–7.

Lynn, Steven J., and Judith W. Rhue. (1988). Fantasy Proneness: Hypnosis, Developmental Antecedents, and Psychopathology. *American Psychologist* 43, no. 1, 35–44.

Lynn, Steven J., and Judith W. Rhue. (1991). *Theories of Hypnosis: Current Models and Perspectives*. New York: Guilford Press.

Lynn, Steven J., and Judith W. Rhue. (1991). An Integrative Model of Hypnosis. In S. J. Lynn and J. W. Rhue, eds. *Theories of hypnosis: Current Models and Perspectives*. New York: Guilford Press, 397–438.

Lynn, Steven J., Judith W. Rhue, and Joseph P. Green. (1988). Multiple Personality and Fantasy Proneness: Is There an Association or Dissociation? *British Journal of Experimental and Clinical Hypnosis* 5, no. 3, 138–142.

Lynn, Steven J., Judith W. Rhue, and John R. Weekes. (1990). Hypnotic Involuntariness: A Social Cognitive Analysis. *Psychological Review* 97, no. 2, 169–184.

Lynn, Steven J., Kelley Shindler, and Eric Meyer. (2003). Hypnotic Suggestibility, Psychopathology, and Treatment Outcome. *Sleep and Hypnosis* 5, no. 1, 2–10.

Lynn, Steven J., and Harry Sivec. (1992). The Hypnotizable Subject as Creative Problem Solving Agent. In Erika Fromm and Michael R. Nash eds. *Contemporary Perspectives in Hypnosis Research*. New York: Guilford Press, 292–333.

Lynn, Steven J., Jane Stafford, and Abigail Matthews. (2005). *The Present and Future State of Hypnosis: A Delphi Poll*. Unpublished.

Lynn, Steven J., Jane Stafford, Peter Malinoski, and Judith Pintar. (1997). Memory in the Hall of Mirrors: The Experience of "Retractors" in Psychotherapy. *Psychological Inquiry* 8, no. 4, 307–312.

Mai, François M. (1995). Psychiatrists' Attitudes to Multiple Personality Disorder: A Questionnaire Study. *The Canadian Journal of Psychiatry* 40, no. 3, 154–157.

Martineau, Harriet. (1879). *Autobiography, with Memorials*. Vol. 2. Edited by Maria Weston Chapman. 4th ed. Boston: Houghton, Osgood and Co.

Martineau, Harriet. (1844). *Life in the Sickroom: Essays by an Invalid*. London: E. Moxon.

Mazzoni, Guilliana A. L., Elizabeth F. Loftus, Aaron Seitz, and Steven J. Lynn. (1999). Changing Beliefs and Memories Through Dream Interpretation. *Applied Cognitive Psychology* 13, no. 2, 125–144.

McConkey, Kevin M. (1991). The Construction and Resolution of Experience and Behavior in Hypnosis. In S. J. Lynn & J. W. Rhue eds. *Theories of Hypnosis: Current Models and Perspectives*. New York: Guilford Press, 542–563.

McConkey, Kevin M. Amanda J. Barnier, and Peter W. Sheehan. (1998). Hypnosis and Pseudomemory: Understanding the Findings and Their Implications. In S. J. Lynn and K. M. McConkey eds. *Truth in Memory*. New York: Guilford Press, 508.

McDougall, William. (1961). William McDougall. In *A History of Psychology in Autobiography*. Vol. 1. Edited by Carl Murchison. New York: Russell & Russell, 191–223.

McNally, Richard J. (2003). *Remembering Trauma*. Cambridge, MA: Belknap Press/Harvard University Press.

Meerlo, Joost A. M. (1956). *The Rape of the Mind: The Psychology of Thought Control, Menticide, and Brainwashing*. New York: World Publishing Co.

Mesmer, Franz A. (1980). *Mesmerism: A Translation of the Original Scientific and Medical Writings of F. A. Mesmer*. Translated by George Bloch. Los Altos, CA: William Kaufmann.

Micale, Mark. (1985). The Salpêtrière in the Age of Charcot: An Institutional Perspective on Medical History in the Late Nineteenth Century. *Journal of Contemporary History* 20, no. 4, 703–731.

Micale, Mark. (1995). *Approaching Hysteria.* Princeton, NJ: Princeton University Press.

Midelfort, H. C. Erik. (2005). *Johann Joseph Gassner and the Demons of Eighteenth-Century Germany.* New Haven, CT: Yale University Press.

Miller, Mary E., and Kenneth S. Bowers. (1992). Hypnotic Analgesia: Dissociated Experience or Dissociated Control? *Journal of Abnormal Psychology* 102, 29–38.

Mills, Antonia, and Steven J. Lynn. (2000). Past-life Experiences. In E. Cardeña, S. J. Lynn, and S. Krippner eds. *Varieties of Anomalous Experience: Examining the Scientific Evidence.* Washington, DC: American Psychological Association, 283–313.

Moene, Franny C., Philip Spinhoven, Kees A. L. Hoogduin, and Richard Van Dyck. (2003). A Randomized Controlled Clinical Trial of a Hypnosis-based Treatment for Patients with Conversion Disorder, Motor Type. *International Journal of Clinical and Experimental Hypnosis* 51, no. 1, 29–50.

Moore, R. Laurence. (1977). *In Search of White Crows: Spiritualism, Parapsychology, and American Culture.* New York: Oxford University Press.

Montgomery, Guy, Daniel David, Gary Winkel, Jeffrey H. Silverstein, and Dana H. Bovbjerg. (2002). The Effectiveness of Anjunctive Hypnosis with Surgical Patients: A Meta-analysis. *Anesthesia and Analgesia* 94, 1639–1645.

Montgomery, Guy H., Katherine N. DuHamel, and William H. Redd. (2000). A Meta-analysis of Hypnotically Induced Analgesia: How Effective Is Hypnosis? *International Journal of Clinical and Experimental Hypnosis* 48, no. 2, 138–153.

Mims, Sue Harper. (1902). Jesus in Christian Science. *The Christian Science Journal* October.

Moll, Albert. (1889). *Der Hypnotismus.* Berlin: Fischer.

Mulhern, Sherrill A. (1992). Ritual abuse: Defining a Syndrome Versus Defending a Belief. *Journal of Psychology and Theology* 20, no. 3, 230–232.

Munthe, Axel. (2004). *The Story of San Michele.* London: John Murray.

Murray, Henry A. (1938). *Explorations in Personality: A Clinical Study of Fifty Men in College.* New York: Oxford University Press.

Murray, Henry A. (1956). Morton Prince: Sketch of his Life and Work. *Journal of Abnormal and Social Psychology 52*, 291–295.

Murray, Henry A. (1985). "Dr. Henry A. Murray Replies (Letter to the Editor)," *Second Century Radcliffe News* 6, no. 1, 2.

Myers, Frederic W. H. (1903). *Human Personality and its Survival of Bodily Death.* New York: Longmans, Green & Co.

Nash, Michael. (1987). What, if Anything, is Regressed About Hypnotic Age Regression? A Review of the Empirical Literature. *Psychological Bulletin* 102, no. 1, 42–52.

Nash, Michael R. (1992). Hypnosis, Psychopathology, and Psychological Regression. In Erika Fromm and Michael R. Nash eds. *Contemporary Hypnosis Research*. New York: Guilford Press, 149–169.

Nash, Michael R., Stephen Drake, Stephen Wileh, Sahib Khals, and Steven J. Lynn. (1986). Accuracy of Recall by Hypnotically Age-Regressed Subjects. *Journal of Abnormal Psychology* 95, no. 3, 298–300.

Nobel Lectures, Physiology or Medicine 1901–1921. Charles Richet: The Nobel Prize in Physiology or Medicine 1913. Amsterdam: Elsevier Publishing, 1967.

Noebel, David A. (1965). *Communism, Hypnotism and the Beatles: An Analysis of the Communist Use of Music – the Communist Master Music Plan*. Tulsa, OK: Christian Crusade Publications.

Nogrady, Heather, Kevin M. McConkey, Jean-Roch Laurence, and Campbell Perry. (1983). Dissociation, Duality, and Demand Characteristics in Hypnosis. *Journal of Abnormal Psychology* 92, no. 2, 223–235.

Noizet, François Joseph. (1854). *Mémoire sur le somnambulisme et le magnétisme animal adressé en 1820 à l'Académie royale de Berlin*. Paris: Plon Frére.

North, Carol S., Jo-Ellyn M. Ryall, Richard D. Wetzel, and Daniel A. Ricci. (1993). Multiple Personalities, Multiple Disorders: Psychiatric Classification and Media Influence. *Oxford Monographs on Psychiatry* 1. New York: Oxford University Press.

Nygren, Edward John. (1970). Ruben Peale's Experiments with Mesmerism. *Proceedings of the American Philosophical Society* 114, no. 2, 100–108.

Ochorowicz, Julian. (1891). *Mental Suggestion*. New York: Humboldt.

Orne, Martin T. (1959). The Nature of Hypnosis: Artifact and Essence. *Journal of Abnormal Psychology* 58, 277–299.

Orne, Martin T. (1979). On the Simulating Subject as a Quasi-Control Group in Hypnosis Research: What, Why, and How. In Erika Fromm and Ronald E. Shor eds. *Hypnosis: Developments in Research and New Perspectives*. 2d ed. New York: Aldine, 519–601.

Orne, Martin T., D. F. Dinges, and P. B. Bloom. (1995). Hypnosis. In H. I. Kaplan and B. J. Sadock eds. *Comprehensive Textbook of Psychiatry VI*. 6th ed. Baltimore: Williams and Wilkins, 1807–1821.

Orne, Martin T., David F. Dinges, and Emily C. Orne. (1984). On the Differential Diagnosis of Multiple Personality in the Forensic Context. *International Journal of Clinical and Experimental Hypnosis* 32, 118–169.

Palsson, Olafur, Marsha Turner, and William Whitehead. (2006). Hypnosis Home Treatment for Irritable Bowel Syndrome: A Pilot Study. *International Journal of Clinical and Experimental Hypnosis* 54, no 1, 85–99.

Patterson, David R., John J. Everett, G. Leonard Burns, and Janet A. Marvin. (1992). Hypnosis for the Treatment of Burn Pain. *Journal of Consulting and Clinical Psychology* 60, no. 5, 713-717.

Patterson, David R., and Mark P. Jensen. (2003). Hypnosis and Clinical Pain. *Psychological Bulletin* 129, no. 4, 495–521.

Patterson, David R., Kent A. Questad, and Barbara J. de Lateur. (1989). Hypnotherapy as an Adjunct to Narcotic Analgesia for the Treatment of Pain for Burn Debridement. *American Journal of Clinical Hypnosis* 31, no. 3, 156–163.

Pattie, Frank A. (1937). The Genuineness of Hypnotically Produced Anesthesia of the Skin. *American Journal of Psychology* 49, no. 3, 435–443.

Pattie, Frank A. (1939). William McDougall, 1871–1938. *American Journal of Psychology* 52, no. 2, 303–307.

Pattie, Frank A. (1956). Mesmer's Medical Dissertation and its Debt to Mead's De Imperio Solis ac Lunae. *Journey of the History of Medicine and Allied Sciences* 11, 275–287.

Pattie, Frank A. (1979). A Mesmer–Paradis Myth Dispelled. *American Journal of Clinical Hypnosis* 22, 29–31.

Pattie, Frank. A. (1994). *Mesmer and Animal Magnetism*. Hamilton, NY: Edmonston Publishing.

Peel, Robert. (1971). *Mary Baker Eddy: The Years of Trial*. New York: Holt, Rinehart and Winston.

Perry, Campbell. (1992). Theorizing about Hypnosis in Either/Or Terms. *International Journal of Clinical and Experimental Hypnosis* 50, 240.

Perry, Campbell (2001). Hypnosis in Australia Forty Years Ago: Recollections of Gordon Hammer, Martin Orne, and Philip Sutcliffe. *Australian Journal of Clinical and Experimental Hypnosis* 29, no. 2, 83–92.

Pettinati, Helen M. ed. (1988). *Hypnosis and Memory*. New York: Guilford Press.

Pick, Daniel. (2000). *Svengali's Web: The Alien Enchanter in Modern Culture*. New Haven, CT: Yale University Press.

Pinnell, Cornelia M., and Nicholas A. Covino. (2000). Empirical Findings on the Use of Hypnosis in Medicine: A Critical Review. *International Journal of Clinical and Experimental Hypnosis* 48, no. 2, 170–194.

Piper, August Jr. (1997). What Science Says—and Doesn't Say—About Repressed Memories: A Critique of Scheflin and Brown. *Journal of Psychiatry and Law* 25, no. 4, 614–639.

Podmore, Frank (1909). *From Mesmerism and Christian Science*. London: Methuen.

Poe, Edgar Allen. (1902). *The Complete Works of Edgar Allan Poe*. Edited by James A. Harrison. New York: Crowell.

Porter, Stephen, John C. Yuille, and Darrin R. Lehman. (1999). The Nature of Real, Implanted, and Fabricated Childhood Emotional

Events: Implications for the Recovered Memory Debate. *Law and Human Behavior* 23, 517–537.

Postlethwaite, Diana. (1989). Mothering and Mesmerism in the Life of Harriet Martineau. *Signs* 14, no. 3, 583–609.

Powell, Russell A., and Douglas P. Boer. (1994). Did Freud Mislead Patients to Confabulate Memories of Abuse? *Psychological Reports* 74, no. 3, 1283–1298.

Powell, Russell A., and Travis L. Gee. (1999). The Effects of Hypnosis on Dissociative Identity Disorder: A Reexamination of the Evidence. *The Canadian Journal of Psychiatry* 44, no. 9, 914–916.

Poyen, Charles. (1837). *Progress of Animal Magnetism in New England*. Boston: Weeks, Jordan, and Co.

Prince, Morton. (1906). *Dissociation of a Personality*. New York: Longmans, Green & Co.

Purcell, Edward L. (1906). Trilby and Trilby-Mania, the Beginning of the Bestseller System. *Journal of Popular Culture* 11 (1977), 62–76.

Quin, Jianjian, Gail S. Goodman, Bette L. Bottoms, and Phillip R. Shaver. (1998). Repressed Memories of Ritualistic and Religion-Related Child Abuse. In S. J. Lynn and K. M. McConkey eds. *Truth in Memory*. New York: Guilford Press, 260–283.

Rainville, Pierre, Gary H. Duncan, Donald D. Price, Benoit Carrier, M. Catherine Bushnell. (1997). Pain Affect Encoded in Human Anterior Cingulated but not Somatosensory Cortex. *Science* 277, no. 5328, 968–971.

Ray, William J., and Desmond Oathies. (2003). Brain Imaging Techniques. *International Journal of Clinical and Experimental Hypnosis* 51, no. 2, 97–104.

Richet, Charles. (1875). Du somnambulisme provoqué. *Journal d'anatomie et physiologie* II, 348–378.

Richet, Charles. (1923). *Thirty Years of Psychical Research*. Translated by Stanley de Brath. New York: McMillan.

Rieker, Patricia P., and Elaine Carmen. (1986). The Victim to Patient Process: The Disconfirmation and Transformation of Abuse. *American Journal of Orthopsychiatry* 56, no. 3, 360–370.

Rivers, William H. R. (1918). The Repression of War Experience. *The Lancet*, February 2.

Rosen, Gerald M., Marc Sageman, and Elizabeth Loftus. (2003). A Historical Note on False Traumatic Memories. *Journal of Clinical Psychology* 60, no. 1, 137–139.

Ross, Colin A. (1997). *Dissociative Identity Disorder: Diagnosis, Clinical Features, and Treatment of Multiple Personality*. 2d ed. Hoboken: John Wiley & Sons Inc.

Ross, Colin A., and G. Ron Norton. (1989). Effects of Hypnosis on the Features of Multiple Personality Disorder. *American Journal of Clinical Hypnosis* 32, no. 2, 99–106.

Ross, Colin A., G. Ron Norton, and Kay Wozney. (1989). Multiple Personality Disorder: An Analysis of 236 Cases. *The Canadian Journal of Psychiatry* 34, no. 5, 413–418.

Salter, Andrew. (1941). Three Techniques of Autohypnosis. *Journal of General Psychology* 24, 423–438.

Sarbin, Theodore R. (1950). Contributions to Role-Taking Theory: I. Hypnotic Behavior. *Psychological Review* 57, 225–270.

Sarbin, Theodore R., and William C. Coe. (1972). *Hypnosis: A Social Psychological Analysis of Influence Communication*. New York: Holt, Rinehart & Winston.

Sarbin, Theodore R., and Robert W. Slagle. (1979). Hypnosis and Psychophysiology Outcomes. In Erika Fromm and Ronald E. Shor eds. *Developments in Research and New Perspectives*. New York: Aldine, 273–303.

Sarton, George. (1944). Vindication of Father Hell. *Isis* 35 no. 100, 97–105.

Schacter, Daniel L., and John F. Kihlstrom. (1989). Functional Amnesia. *Handbook of Neuropsychology* 3, 209–231.

Scheflin, Alan W., and Daniel Brown. (1996). Repressed Memory or Dissociative Amnesia: What the Science Says. *Journal of Psychiatry and Law* 24, no. 2, 143–188.

Schoenberger, Nancy E., Irving Kirsch, Paul Gearan, Guy Montgomery, and Steven L. Pastrynak. (1997). Hypnotic Enhancement of a Cognitive Behavioral Treatment for Public Speaking Anxiety. *Behavior Therapy* 28, no. 1, 127–140.

Schreiber, Flora R. (1973). *Sybil*. Chicago: Henry Regency Company.

Schuker, Eleanor. (1979). Psychodynamics and Treatment of Sexual Assault Victims. *Journal of the American Academy of Psychoanalysis and Dynamic Psychiatry* 7, no. 4, 553–573.

Scoboria, Alan, Giuliana Mazzoni, Irving Kirsch, and Leonard S. Milling. (2002). Immediate and Persisting Effects of Misleading Questions and Hypnosis on Memory Reports. *Journal of Experimental Psychology: Applied* 8, no. 1, 26–32.

Sears, Robert R. (1932). Experimental Study of Hypnotic Anesthesia. *Journal of Experimental Psychology* 15, 1–22.

Shamdasani, Sonu. (1994). *Encountering Hélène: Théodore Flournoy and the Genesis of Subliminal Psychology*. London: Routledge.

Sheehan, Peter W. (1991). Hypnosis, Context, and Commitment. In S. J. Lynn and J. W. Rhue eds. *Theories of Hypnosis: Current Models and Perspectives*. New York: Guilford Press, 520–541.

Shermer, Michael. (1997). *Why People Believe Weird Things: Pseudoscience, Superstition, and Other Confusions of Our Time*. New York: W. H. Freeman.

Shobe, Katherine K., and John F. Kihlstrom. (1997). Is Traumatic Memory Special? *Current Directions in Psychological Science* 6, no. 3, 70–74.

Shor, Ronald E. (1962). Physiological Effects of Painful Stimulation during Hypnotic Analgesia under Conditions Designed to Minimize Anxiety. *International Journal of Clinical and Experimental Hypnosis* 10, no. 3, 183–202.

Showalter, Elaine. (1997). *Hystories: Hysterical Epidemics and Modern Culture*. New York: Columbia University Press.

Sidis, Boris. (1911). *The Psychology of Suggestion: A Research into the Subconscious Nature of Man and Society*. New York: D. Appleton.

Simon, Michael J., and Herman C. Salzberg. (1985). The Effect of Manipulated Expectancies on Posthypnotic Amnesia. *International Journal of Clinical and Experimental Hypnosis* 33, no. 1, 40–51.

Sivec, Harry J., Steven J. Lynn, and Peter T. Malinoski. (1997). *Hypnosis in the Cabbage Patch: Age Regression with Verifiable Events*. Unpublished Manuscript, State University of New York at Binghamton.

Slobodin, Richard. (1997). *W. H. R Rivers: Pioneer Anthropologist, Psychiatrist of the Ghost Road*. New York: Sutton.

Sno, Herman N., and Henk F. A. Schalken. (1999). Dissociative Identity Disorder: Diagnosis and Treatment in the Netherlands. *European Psychiatry* 14, no. 5, 270–277.

Spanos, Nicholas P. (1982). Hypnotic Behavior: A Cognitive, Social Psychological Perspective. *Research Communication in Psychology, Psychiatry, & Behavior* 7, no. 2, 199–213.

Spanos, Nicholas P. (1986). Hypnotic Behavior: A Social-Psychological Interpretation of Amnesia, Analgesia, and "Trance Logic." *The Behavioral and Brain Sciences* 9, 449–467.

Spanos, Nicholas P. (1991). A Sociocognitive Approach to Hypnosis. In Steven J. Lynn and Judith W. Rhue eds. *Theories of Hypnosis: Current Models and Perspectives*. New York: Guilford Press, 324–361.

Spanos, Nicholas P., and Theodore X. Barber. (1974). Toward a Convergence in Hypnosis Research. *American Psychologist* 29, 500–511.

Spanos, Nicholas P., Cheryl A. Burgess, and Melissa F. Burgess. (1994). Past-life Identities, UFO Abductions, and Satanic Ritual Abuse: The Social Construction of Memories. *International Journal of Clinical and Experimental Hypnosis* 42, no. 4, 433–446.

Spanos, Nicholas P., and John F. Chaves. (1989). *Hypnosis: The Cognitive-Behavioral Perspective*. Amherst, NY: Prometheus Books.

Spanos, Nicholas P., Maxwell I. Gwynn, and Henderikus J. Stam. (1983). Instructional Demands and Ratings of Overt and Hidden Pain during Hypnotic Analgesia. *Journal of Abnormal Psychology* 92, no. 4, 479–488.

Spanos, Nicholas P., and Erin C. Hewitt. (1980). The Hidden Observer in Hypnotic Analgesia: Discovery or Experimental Creation? *Journal of Personality and Social Psychology* 39, 1201–1214.

Spanos, Nicholas P., and Joanne McLean. (1986). Hypnotically Created False Reports Do Not Demonstrate Pseudomemories. *British Journal of Experimental & Clinical Hypnosis* 3, no. 3, 161–171.

Spanos, Nicholas P., Evelyn Menary, Natalie J. Gabora, Susan C. DuBreuil, and Bridget Dewhirst. (1991). Secondary Identity Enactments during Hypnotic Past-life Regression: A Sociocognitive Perspective. *Journal of Personality and Social Psychology* 61, no. 2, 308–320.

Spanos, Nicholas P., H. Lorraine Radtke, and Lorne D. Bertrand. (1984). Hypnotic Amnesia as a Strategic Enactment: Breaching Amnesia in Highly Susceptible Subjects. *Journal of Personality and Social Psychology* 47, no. 5, 1155–1169.

Spence, Kenneth W. (1952). Clark Leonard Hull, 1884–1952. *The American Journal of Psychology* 65, no. 4, 639–646.

Spiegel, David, and Joan R. Bloom. (1983). Group Therapy and Hypnosis Reduce Metastatic Breast Carcinoma Pain. *Psychosomatic Medicine* 45, no. 4, 333–339.

Spiegel, David, Thurman Hunt, and Harvey E. Dondershine. (1988). Dissociation and Hypnotizability in Posttraumatic Stress Disorder. *American Journal of Psychiatry* 145, no. 3, 301–305.

Spiegel, Herbert, and David Spiegel. (1978). *Trance and Treatment: Clinical Uses of Hypnosis*. New York: Basic Books.

Spinhoven, Phillip, Corry G. Linnsen, Richard van Dyck, and Frans G. Zitman. (1992). Autogenic Training and Self-Hypnosis in the Control of Tension Headache. *General Hospital Psychiatry* 14, no. 6, 408–415.

Spurling, Hilary. (2001). *The Unknown Matisse: A life of Henri Matisse: The Early Years, 1869–1908*. Berkeley: University of California Press.

Steblay, Nancy M., and Robert K. Bothwell. (1994). Evidence for Hypnotically Refreshed Testimony: The View from the Laboratory. *Law and Human Behavior* 18, 635–651.

Stone, William (1837). *Letter to Dr. A. Brigham on Animal Magnetism*. New York: George Dearborn.

Stutman, Randall K., and Eugene L. Bliss. (1985). Posttraumatic Stress Disorder, Hypnotizability, and Imagery. *American Journal of Psychiatry* 142, no. 6, 741–743.

Sunderland, La Roy. (1868). *The Trance and Correlative Phenomena*. Chicago: James Walker.

Sutcliffe, John Phillip. (1961). "Credulous" and "Skeptical" Views of Hypnotic Phenomena: Experiments on Esthesia, Hallucination, and Delusion. *Journal of Abnormal and Social Psychology* 62, no. 2, 189–200.

Syrjala, Karen, Claudette Cummings, and Gary W. Donaldson. (1992). Hypnosis or Cognitive Behavioral Training for the Reduction of Pain and Nausea during Cancer Treatment. *Pain* 48, 137–146.

Szechtman, Henry, Erik K. Woody, Kenneth S. Bowers, and Claude Nahmias. (1998). Where the Imaginal Appears Real: A Positron Emission Tomography Study of Auditory Hallucinations. *Proceedings of the National Academy of Sciences* 95, 1956–1960.

Tart, Charles T. (1983). Altered States of Consciousness. In R. Harris and R. Lamb eds. *The Encyclopedic Dictionary of Psychology*. Cambridge, MA: MIT Press, 19–20.

Tatar, Maria M. (1978). *Spellbound: Studies on Mesmerism and Literature*. Princeton, NJ: Princeton University Press.

Taves, Ann. (1999). *Fits, Trances, and Visions: Experiencing Religion and Explaining Experience from Wesley to James*. Princeton, NJ: Princeton University Press.

Tellegen, Auke, and Gilbert Atkinson. (1974). Openness to Absorbing and Self-Altering Experiences ("Absorption"), A Trait Related to Hypnotic Susceptibility. *Journal of Abnormal Psychology* 83, no. 3, 268–277.

Thigpen, Corbett H., and Hervey M. Cleckley. (1957). *The Three Faces of Eve*. New York: McGraw-Hill.

Townshend, Chauncy Hare. (1844). *Facts in Mesmerism, or Animal Magnetism. With Reasons for a Dispassionate Inquiry into it*. London: Baillerie Press.

Triplet, Rodney G. (1982). The Relationship of Clark L. Hull's Hypnosis Research to his Later Learning Theory: The Continuity of his Life's Work. *Journal of History of the Behavioral Sciences* 18, no. 1, 22–31.

Triplet, Rodney G. (1992). Henry A. Murray. The Making of a Psychologist? *American Psychologist* 47 no. 2, 299–307.

van der Hart, Onno. (1993). Multiple Personality Disorder in Europe: Impressions. *Dissociation: Progress in the Dissociative Disorders* 6, no. 2–3, 102–118.

van der Kolk, Bessel A., Onno van der Hart, and Charles R. Marmar. (1996). Dissociation and Information Processing in Posttraumatic Stress Disorder. In B. A. van der Kolk, A. C. McFarlane, and L. Weisaeth eds. *Traumatic Stress: The Effects of Overwhelming Experience on Mind, Body, and Society*. New York: Guilford Press, 303–327.

Vijselaar, Joost and Onno Van der Hart. (1992). The First Report of Hypnotic Treatment of Traumatic Grief: A Brief Communication. *International Journal of Clinical and Experimental Hypnosis* 40, no. 1, 1–6.

Viswesvaran, Chockalingam, and Frank. L. Schmidt. (1992). A Meta-analytic Comparison of the Effectiveness of Smoking Cessation Methods. *Journal of Applied Psychology* 77, no. 4, 554–561.

Wade, Kimberley A., Maryanne Garry, J. Don Read, and Stephen Lindsay. (2002). A Picture is worth a Thousand Lies: Using False Photographs to Create False Childhood Memories. *Psychonomic Bulletin and Review* 9, no. 3, 597–603.

Wagstaff, Graham F. (1998). The Semantics and Physiology of Hypnosis as an Altered State: Towards a Definition of Hypnosis. *Contemporary Hypnosis* 15, no. 3, 149–165.

Wagstaff, Graham F. (1998). The Hypnotic State: Semantics and Pragmatics. *Contemporary Hypnosis* 15, no. 3, 182–188.

Wagstaff, Graham F. (2001). Different Approaches to Hypnosis. *Psychology Review* 7, 2–5.

Wakeman, John R., and Jerold Z. Kaplan. (1978). An Experimental Study of Hypnosis in Painful Burns. *American Journal of Clinical Hypnosis* 21, no. 1, 3–12.

Watkins, John G. (1995). Organization and functioning of ISCEH, the International Society for Clinical and Experimental Hypnosis. *International Journal of Clinical and Experimental Hypnosis* 43, no. 3, 332–341.

Weaver, Karol. (2006). *Medical Revolutionaries: The Enslaved Healers of Eighteenth-Century Saint-Domingue.* Urbana: University of Illinois Press.

West, Louis J., Karleen C. Niell, and James D. Hardy. (1952). Effects of Hypnotic Suggestion on Pain Perception and Galvanic Skin Response. *Archives of Neurology and Psychiatry* 68, 549–560.

White, Robert W. (1941). A Preface to a Theory of Hypnotism. *Journal of Abnormal and Social Psychology* 36, 477–505.

White, Robert W. (1975). *Lives in Progress: A Study of the Natural Growth of Personality*. 3d ed. New York: Holt, Rinehart and Winston.

Whitehouse, Wayne G., David F. Dinges, Emily C. Orne, and Martin T. Orne. (1988). Hypnotic Hypermnesia: Enhanced Memory Accessibility or Report Bias? *Journal of Abnormal Psychology* 97, no. 3, 289–295.

Wickless, Cynthia, and Irving Kirsch. (1989). Effects of Verbal and Experiential Expectancy Manipulations on Hypnotic Susceptibility. *Journal of Personality and Social Psychology* 57, no. 5, 762–768.

Wilson, Sheryl C., and Theodore X. Barber. (1981). Vivid Fantasy and Hallucinatory Abilities in the Life Histories of Excellent Hypnotic Subjects ('Somnabules'): Preliminary Report with Female Subjects. In E. Klinger ed. *Imagery*. Vol. 2, *Concepts, Results, and Applications*. New York: Plenum Press, 133–152.

Wilson, Sheryl C., and Theodore X. Barber. (1983). The Fantasy-Prone Personality: Implications for Understanding Imagery, Hypnosis, and Parapsychological Phenomena. In Anees A. Sheikh ed. *Imagery: Current Theory, Research, and Application*. New York: Wiley, 340–387.

Winter, Alison. (1995). Harriet Martineau and the Reform of the Invalid in Victorian England. *The Historical Journal* 38, no. 3, 597–616.

Winter, Alison. (1998). *Mesmerized: Powers of Mind in Victorian Britain.* Chicago: University of Chicago Press.

Woody Erik Z, and Kenneth S. Bowers. (1994). A Frontal Assault on Dissociated Control. In Steven J. Lynn and Judith W. Rhue eds. *Dissociation: Clinical, Theoretical and Research Perspectives.* New York: Guilford Press, 52–79.

Wright, Bernadette R., and Peter D. Drummond. (2000). Rapid Induction Analgesia for the Alleviation of Procedural Pain during Burn Care. *Burns* 26, no. 3, 275–282.

Yapko, Michael D. (1993). Hypnosis and Depression. In J. W. Rhue, S. J. Lynn, and I. Kirsch eds. *Handbook of Clinical Hypnosis*. Washington, DC: American Psychological Association, 339–355.

Yapko, Michael D. (2001). *Treating Depression with Hypnosis: Integrating Cognitive-Behavioral and Strategic Approaches*. Philadelphia: Brunner-Routledge.

Yapko, Michael D. (1989). *Brief Therapy Approaches to Treating Anxiety and Depression*. New York: Brunner/Mazel.

Young, Allan. (1999). W. H. R. Rivers and the War Neuroses. *Journal of the History of the Behavioral Sciences* 35, no. 4, 359–378.

Young, Jon, and Leslie M. Cooper. (1972). Hypnotic Recall Amnesia as a Function of Manipulated Expectancy. *Proceedings of the Annual Convention of the American Psychological Association* 7, 857–858.

Young, Paul C. (1925). An Experimental Study of Mental and Physical Functions in the Normal and Hypnotic States. *American Journal of Psychology* 36, no. 2, 214–232.

Zeig, Jeffery K., and Peter J. Rennick. (1991). Ericksonian Hypnotherapy: A Communications Approach to Hypnosis. In S. J. Lynn and J. W. Rhue eds. *Theories of Hypnosis: Current Models and Perspectives*. New York: Guilford Press, 275–300.

Zeltzer, Lonnie K., Michael J. Dolgin, Samuel LeBaron, and Christine LeBaron. (1991). A Randomized, Controlled Study of Behavioral Intervention for Chemotherapy Distress in Children with Cancer. *Pediatrics* 88, no. 1, 34–42.

Index